PRIVATEERS OF THE AMERICAS

Early American Places is a collaborative project of the University of Georgia Press, New York University Press, Northern Illinois University Press, and the University of Nebraska Press. The series is supported by the Andrew W. Mellon Foundation. For more information, please visit www.earlyamericanplaces.org.

ADVISORY BOARD
Vincent Brown, *Duke University*
Andrew Cayton, *Miami University*
Cornelia Hughes Dayton, *University of Connecticut*
Nicole Eustace, *New York University*
Amy S. Greenberg, *Pennsylvania State University*
Ramón A. Gutiérrez, *University of Chicago*
Peter Charles Hoffer, *University of Georgia*
Karen Ordahl Kupperman, *New York University*
Joshua Piker, *University of Oklahoma*
Mark M. Smith, *University of South Carolina*
Rosemarie Zagarri, *George Mason University*

Privateers of the Americas

Spanish American Privateering from the
United States in the Early Republic

DAVID HEAD

The University of Georgia Press
ATHENS AND LONDON

© 2015 by the University of Georgia Press
Athens, Georgia 30602
www.ugapress.org

All rights reserved

Portions of this book originally appeared in the following publications: Parts of the introduction appeared as "New Nations, New Connections: Spanish American Privateering from the United States and the Development of Atlantic Relations," *Early American Studies* 11 (2013): 161–75. Copyright © 2013 The McNeil Center for Early American Studies. Parts of chapter 2 appeared as "Slave Smuggling by Foreign Privateers: Geopolitical Influences on the Illegal Slave Trade," in *Journal of the Early Republic* 33 (2013): 433–62. Copyright © 2013 Society for Historians of the Early American Republic. Parts of chapter 3 appeared as "Baltimore Seafarers, Privateering, and the South American Revolutions, 1816–1820," in *Maryland Historical Magazine* 105 (2008): 269–93. Parts of chapter 5 appeared as "Independence on the Quarterdeck: Three Baltimore Seafarers, Spanish America, and the Lives of Captains in the Early American Republic," in *Northern Mariner* 23 (2013): 1–20.

The paper in this book meets the guidelines for permanence and durability of the Committee on Production Guidelines for Book Longevity of the Council on Library Resources.

Most University of Georgia Press titles are
available from popular e-book vendors.

Printed digitally.

ISBN: 978-0-8203-4400-3 (hardcover: alk. paper)
ISBN: 978-0-8203-4864-3 (paperback: alk. paper)
ISBN: 978-0-8203-4865-0 (e-book)
Library of Congress Control Number: 2015939360

British Library Cataloging-in-Publication Data available

For my mom

Contents

	List of Illustrations, Tables, and Maps	xi
	Acknowledgments	xiii
	Introduction: Captain Chaytor's Dilemma	1
1	Diplomacy with Spain and Spanish America	13
2	New Orleans and Barataria	38
3	Baltimore	63
4	Galveston and Amelia Island	92
5	Service and Toil in Spanish America	122
	Conclusion: Captain Chaytor Comes Home	149
	Notes	153
	Index	197

Illustrations, Tables, and Maps

Illustrations

1. Captain James Chaytor — 3
2. Jean Laffite, an artist's imagining of the notorious smuggler — 40
3. The American privateer *Dolphin* battling during the War of 1812 — 65
4. Commission of the privateer *Esperancia* — 96
5. General Gregor MacGregor — 103
6. Commission issued by Aury at Amelia Island — 113
7. Commodore John Daniel Danels — 130
8. Children of Commodore John Daniel Danels — 131

Tables

1. Slave landings by privateers operating from Louisiana, 1810–1815 — 47
2. Investors, armadores, and agents of Baltimore privateers — 69
3. Slave landings at Amelia Island, 1817–1820 — 110

Maps

1. Spanish America in the Age of Revolution, 1808–1824 — 17
2. The Laffites' Louisiana — 45

Acknowledgments

The backbone of this book's research comes from the case files of the U.S. federal courts, now held by the National Archives, and I would like to thank the staffs of the NARA branches I visited in Waltham, Philadelphia, College Park, Atlanta, and Fort Worth. I was first alerted to the promise of these sources by Donald Petrie, author of *The Prize Game: Lawful Looting on the High Seas in the Days of Fighting Sail*, who wrote that they were an untapped "treasure trove." He was right. I also visited or received materials from many other archives and libraries, and I would like to thank the staffs of the following institutions: American Philosophical Society; Bostonian Society; Delaware Historical Society; Enoch Pratt Free Library of Baltimore; George Peabody Library; Gilder Lehrman Institute of American History; Historic New Orleans Collection; Historical Society of Pennsylvania; Library Company of Philadelphia; Library of Congress; Maryland Historical Society; Maryland State Archives; Massachusetts Historical Society; Morgan Library; New York Public Library; New-York Historical Society; Peabody Essex Museum; P. K. Yonge Library of Florida History/Special Collections Library of the University of Florida; Princeton University Library; and Yale University Library.

Generous assistance from Spring Hill College's Mitchell Family Scholarship supported final research trips to Louisiana and Florida, while earlier assistance from an Andrew W. Mellon Foundation Fellowship allowed me to work at the Library Company of Philadelphia and the Historical Society of Pennsylvania, a Gilder Lehrman Fellowship aided research at the New-York Historical Society, and a Lord Baltimore Fellowship provided access to the Maryland Historical Society. While completing my dissertation at the State University of New York at Buffalo, I received support from a Dean's Fellowship and a Dissertation Writing Fellowship from the College of Arts and Sciences, a Milton Plesur Dissertation Research Grant from the History Department, a Professional Development Grant from the New York State Graduate Student Employees Union, and a Mark Diamond Research Grant from the Graduate Student Association.

Portions of the book previously appeared, in different forms, as articles in the *Maryland Historical Magazine*, *Early American Studies*, the *Northern Mariner/Le marin du nord*, and the *Journal of the Early Republic*. I thank Patricia Dockman Anderson, Elaine Foreman Crane, Roger Sarty, and Susan Klepp for their help publishing the articles and granting permission for them to be used here.

I have accumulated many personal debts to friends and colleagues in writing this book. I am grateful to Rafe Blaufarb, John Belohlavek, and the anonymous press readers for providing feedback on the full manuscript. At the University of Georgia Press, Derek Krissoff signed the project, and Walter Biggins and his team saw it through to completion. Kirk LeCompte shared material on James Chaytor and found a picture of the sea captain, which Chaytor Chandler has graciously permitted to be used in the book. Tom Chambers, Sean Perrone, Samuel Watson, and my colleagues at the University of Central Florida in Orlando and Spring Hill College in Mobile provided encouragement on many occasions. You can't make it through grad school without friends, and I'm lucky to have many good ones: Danielle Battisti, Perry Beardsley, Jonathan Bergman, Mike Halliday, April Kiser, Chuck Lipp, Craig Miller, Ilaria Scaglia, Katrina Sinclair, and Frankie Weaver. Finally, I am grateful to my professors Tamara Thornton and Erik Seeman, who taught me to be a historian.

I am blessed to come from a large family that is sustained by my grandparents, Paul and Deloris Meosky. My brothers, Matthew and Thomas; sisters, Maribeth, Sally, and Susan; aunts, uncles, and cousins, the Meoskys and the Freemans; and my in-laws, Bethsy Harsin, Ray Harsin, and Xavier Bastidas, have all contributed in their own way. The book I've been working on for so long is finally here. In all the time I spent researching Spanish America I never thought I'd end up with a Spanish American family, but that's what happened when I met a nice

Ecuadoran girl named Andrea. We married in 2012. Now Andrea and I have our Dolly Carolina, our little girl who makes us so happy.

This book is dedicated to my mom, Kathleen Head, who passed away too soon to see it finished. A woman of strong faith, she found her greatest joy in serving her children. She encouraged me to write, and she proofread everything for me—articles, chapters, countless job applications. She was my ideal reader, smart and interested in history and eager to laugh at my jokes. I'm delighted to have written something she would love.

Privateers of the Americas

Introduction: Captain Chaytor's Dilemma

In January 1816, the brig *Mammoth*, James Chaytor master, rode at anchor near Cape Henry, Virginia, waiting for a wind. The vessel was bound from Baltimore to Buenos Aires, with munitions for the independent armies battling Spain, and with French dry goods for the civilians. Chaytor was an experienced sea captain. Born in Virginia, he had settled in Baltimore in the mid-1790s and since then sailed from the city to destinations as near as the Caribbean and as far as the Indian Ocean. Soon a breeze picked up, the *Mammoth* rounded the cape, and Captain James Chaytor was off, sailing for Spanish America.[1]

Chaytor sighted his destination in April. Home to a government at war, Buenos Aires was the capital of what would soon be called the United Provinces of the Río de la Plata, a union of states that had defected from Spanish rule (and roughly corresponding to the modern nations of Argentina, Bolivia, and Paraguay). Like the rest of the Spanish Empire, Buenos Aires had been mired in crisis since 1808, when Napoleon seized Spain, overthrew the Bourbon monarchy, and installed his brother as king. Spanish Americans had formed local governing bodies called *juntas* to rule in the king's name until the French interlopers were banished. Some *juntas* were loyal to a resistance government organized in Spain; others sought local control. Across the Americas, a battle for supremacy ensued.[2]

At the moment, the geopolitics of war and revolution mattered to Chaytor only as much as they affected the Buenos Aires market. The *Mammoth*'s arms easily found buyers, but not so the cargo of dry goods.

Even the captain's own venture—"2 Cases of fancy goods"—went unsold. Chaytor was disconsolate. "I make a most miserable business," he wrote.[3]

Chaytor's situation, however, was not as bleak as he imagined. The Buenos Aires government was implementing a new naval strategy that, in addition to defending the Rió de la Plata, called for vessels to attack Spanish shipping wherever it sailed. To achieve such a goal, Buenos Aires called for privateers.[4]

Privateers were privately owned warships that sailed in times of war to capture enemy vessels and their goods. A privateer's captures, called prizes, would be brought before an admiralty court of the privateer's nation. If the capture were made lawfully, the court would declare it a good prize and order the property "condemned"—that is, have its title transferred to the captors for sale. The privateer's officers, owners, and crew enjoyed the proceeds. Governments authorized their privateers' depredations by granting them a license, once known as a letter of marque, but in the nineteenth century more often called a commission.[5]

A foreign sea captain such as Chaytor was a prime candidate to become a Buenos Aires privateer. The emerging republic possessed a small merchant marine of its own, and Chaytor, though most often a peaceful trader, had commanded armed vessels in the past. Yet, it was illegal for him to enlist in the Buenos Aires service. The neutrality laws of the United States prohibited Americans from commanding a foreign armed vessel that intended to attack a nation at peace with the United States.[6]

Chaytor faced a dilemma. He could make up for the months lost voyaging to an unprofitable market by accepting a Buenos Aires commission, converting the *Mammoth* to a vessel of war, and embarking on a cruise against Spain, bringing home, if he were lucky, the rich rewards of a captured Spanish prize. But his wife and children lived in Baltimore, where he would eventually return and subject himself to the penalties of American law.

Chaytor made his decision. He joined the Buenos Aires service. To guard against violating United States law, Chaytor renounced his American citizenship and then presented himself to Buenos Aires officials for naturalization. He swore a new oath of allegiance to his new nation, and he became a citizen. Chaytor also changed the *Mammoth*'s nationality by transferring nominal ownership to the government of Buenos Aires while he retained the vessel for himself and two others. With its new nationality and new purpose came a new name. The *Mammoth* would henceforth be known as the *Independencia del Sud*, the *Independence of the South*.[7]

FIGURE 1. Captain James Chaytor. (Courtesy of Chaytor B. Chandler)

In mid-May 1816, the brig *Independencia del Sud* rode at anchor off Buenos Aires, bound for the coast of Spain. A breeze picked up, and after traveling the Río de la Plata, the *Independencia* rounded Cape St. Mary's at the river's mouth. Once more, Captain James Chaytor was off, sailing for Spanish America.[8]

Across the United States—from Boston to Baltimore, from New York to New Orleans—men like Chaytor sailed aboard Spanish American privateers in the second decade of the nineteenth century. More than one hundred Spanish American armed vessels sailed U.S. waters. They bore commissions from the United Provinces of the Río de la Plata, Cartagena de Índias (a city in what is now Colombia), the Oriental Provinces of the Río de la Plata (what would become Uruguay), Mexico, and Venezuela. Spanish American privateering conducted from the United States involved more than three thousand men directly as captains, officers, sailors, investors, and agents. Hundreds more participated indirectly as the carpenters, caulkers, riggers, armorers, laborers, and grocers who prepared and repaired vessels for sea. Untold thousands of ordinary people bought, often illegally, the goods and slaves captured by privateers and brought to market in the United States.[9]

At sea, Spanish American privateers sailed from North America to the Spanish Main and from Buenos Aires to the Spanish coast, cutting a swath of destruction through the Gulf of Mexico, the Caribbean, and the Atlantic. They captured hundreds of Spanish vessels and more than a few Portuguese ships as well. They hauled in millions of dollars in gold, silver, dry goods, produce, and enslaved human persons—millions in early-nineteenth-century dollars, now worth ten times as much. They outraged Spanish diplomats. They flooded the U.S. federal courts with cases both criminal and civil. They worried presidents and frustrated secretaries of state, who had to devise a response that would keep the United States safe, secure, and neutral in a dangerous world.[10]

In the pages that follow I reconstruct Spanish American privateering from the United States as the far-reaching enterprise that it was in the early nineteenth century. I attempt to discover how Spanish American privateering worked and who engaged in it; how the United States government responded; how privateers and their supporters evaded the law and maneuvered international relations to their advantage; why these men chose this line of work; and, ultimately, what it meant to become privateers of the Americas, sailing from the United States for the new republics of Spanish America.

I have tracked Spanish American privateers anywhere I could find them in the historical record: from the shipping news sections of newspapers to diplomatic correspondence; from government reports to personal papers, pamphlets, and even portraits. Above all, I have examined nearly 350 federal court cases involving privateers that are now held by the National Archive. In these case files, collected from jurisdictions in Boston, New York, Baltimore, Norfolk, Savannah, and New Orleans, Spanish American privateering comes alive. Manifests, customs clearances, and commissions document the comings and goings of vessels from port. Libels, claims, pleas, answers, and petitions detail the identity and actions of owners, commanders, and crews. And depositions and testimony from sailors and captains, privateers and their victims, reveal what happened once a privateer was at sea.

Re-creating the world of Spanish American privateering sharpens our picture of how the United States encountered the world in the early nineteenth century. This encounter took place in the diplomatic activities of the nation, its officials and citizens, as well as through a network of Atlantic relationships, recently tested by a generation of warfare and revolution. It was also worked out in the personal identities of individuals, such as Captain Chaytor, trying to make sense of their lives as they lived in the United States and abroad. Studying Spanish American privateering from the United States, then, contributes to our understanding of the diplomatic and Atlantic history of the early republic in addition to the experience of being an American in a wider world.

The basic story of foreign relations in the first decades of the nineteenth century is well-established as a drama of two parts. In the first act, the United States battles Great Britain and France to maintain its neutrality and its lucrative neutral trade. U.S. policy makers respond to French provocations and British-inflicted humiliations with various degrees of success until tensions boil over in the War of 1812. In the second act, the United States, puffed up with national pride, asserts itself in the world by pushing against its Spanish neighbors. Led by John Quincy Adams, President James Monroe's secretary of state, the nation concludes an agreement with Spain, known as the Transcontinental Treaty, which grabs Florida, settles the disputed border of Texas, and opens a route to Oregon and the Pacific, and it then proclaims the Monroe Doctrine, which asserts U.S. leadership over the Western Hemisphere. By the time the curtain falls, it is clear that the march to superpower status, catalyzed by the Napoleonic Wars and made more muscular by expansion, is already under way.[11]

Spanish American privateering from the United States, however, fits uneasily into this narrative. The privateers knew nothing of Manifest Destiny or Pacific imperialism, much less something called a Cold War. They occasionally crossed paths with private military forces, called filibusters, which gathered in the United States to attack Mexico and Florida. But as we will see, these men had goals of their own and were not agents of U.S. expansion. For actors on the ground (or on the water), it was the immediate geopolitical context of four interlocking developments that mattered most: the Napoleonic Wars, the Spanish American Wars of Independence, the War of 1812, and the United States' pursuit of neutrality between France and Britain and between Spain and its colonies. I employ the term "geopolitics" as a shorthand for these developments to draw attention not only to the ways in which the United States was embedded in larger international events but also to highlight the ways that rivalries between nations, especially the powers of Europe, were experienced in particular places, such as the United States and Spanish America.[12]

A study of Spanish American privateering also provides a way to unite Atlantic scholarship on the Age of Revolutions with histories of the early American republic. Attempts to write an Atlantic history of the early republic encounter two problems. Among Americanists, a dominant theme of this period has been the expansion of the United States as an internal matter. Thus, the most successful Atlantic histories of the early republic focus on the borderlands of Florida and the Gulf Coast, where national power was weakest and where the relationship between regions and the world was most direct. Among Atlanticists, the early nineteenth century is often cited as an appropriate end point for the Atlantic world paradigm. Although many factors are cited, chief among them is the unraveling of imperial relationships. With the encounters experienced by Europeans, Indians, and Africans transformed, an Atlantic approach to the new world of independent states and redefined European priorities lacks coherence, in this view.[13]

Spanish American privateering from the United States, however, suggests that nationhood created something new: new connections between people around the Atlantic world because of the power of nations. In the United States, the nation arose as a new mediator between the local and the world by virtue of federal law. Federal neutrality, piracy, slave trade, and revenue laws exerted a powerful influence on Spanish American privateers. As lawbreakers, they always had to be on guard against authorities. But the influence of these federal laws was far broader and more complex. Sometimes the law encouraged illegal privateering. For example, the embargo and nonimportation laws as well as the slave trade acts unintentionally created incentives for men to become privateers, capture goods and slaves, and sell them to an artificially constrained market. Other times, the demands of America's neutrality policy opened loopholes—such as the right to enter port extended to vessels said to be "in distress"—that privateers used to confound the law's restrictions. Such vessels could make repairs, add fresh food, or replenish their water supplies, but once in port, privateers regularly took advantage of this hospitality and engaged in illegal conduct such as augmenting their crews, adding guns, or landing untaxed goods for sale. Privateers knew these weaknesses in the law and went to great lengths to exploit them.[14]

Thus, the United States did not need to be a strong state for its laws to exert strong influence. Indeed, the simple existence of these laws was often enough to change the privateers' behavior. Without restrictive importation laws, smuggling would have been trade, dominated by mainstream merchants rather than by men whose easy consciences were a valuable asset. Without the policy of neutrality, privateers could have been kept out of U.S. waters completely. The law affected privateers in complex, often unintended ways, demonstrating that we can better understand what was new and Atlantic about the early republic when the nation is placed between the local and the international.[15]

Finally, why people found Spanish American privateering attractive demands an explanation. What kind of person fights in a foreign war, anyway? One popular answer has been "a bad person": the privateers are labeled pirates, marauders, or mercenaries. Another explanation imagines these men as pawns, stressing that foreigners who joined the fight against Spain were furthering the U.S. government's goal of weakening Spanish claims to territories the United States coveted. Whether they knew it or not, these men actually fit into the larger pattern of national expansion. More recently, the global turn in American historiography has led historians to see foreign participants in the Spanish American Wars of Independence not as rogues or pawns but as high-minded cosmopolitans who displayed a forward-thinking rejection of the nation-state. In this view, men fought for Spanish America because they were committed to international values of colonial liberation.[16]

None of these explanations will do. The men who operated privateers in the Spanish American service defy easy classification. They were Americans as well as foreigners: Frenchmen, Englishmen, Spaniards, Mexicans, and citizens of the emerging Spanish American republics.

Some foreigners resided in the United States permanently, others, temporarily. Those involved in privateering were sailors, sea captains, and merchants. Some had strong ties to their communities. Some were most comfortable at sea far from shore. A few were bound to their families while also faring the sea a thousand miles from home. Some men were international fighters for freedom. They went privateering to advance the ideology of independence. Others were opportunists. They sailed to make money. Others did both at the same time. As a group, then, they were good and evil, noble and depraved, selfish and self-sacrificing, cosmopolitan and attached to one place. As individuals, they exhibited any number of these traits. A few men, over the course of a career, exhibited them all.

Dealing fairly with these men, therefore, means coming to grips with their individuality as well as their common circumstances, their character as well as their context. What appears to have mattered most was the experience of sailing in a foreign war. Whatever first brought them to privateering, and whether or not they were committed to anything larger than themselves, Spanish American privateers who operated from the United States formed crucial new links throughout the Atlantic world. Attempting to understand why these men sailed foreign warships, then, makes them appear less like marauders, mercenaries, pirates, pawns, or even stateless cosmopolitans and more like what they were: early-nineteenth-century men.

The following chapters take us from place to place through the world of Spanish American privateering. Chapter 1 sets the stage by outlining the geopolitical conditions within which Spanish American privateering would arise and U.S. officials would respond. Rather than stressing a long-term fixation on expansion in the borderlands, the chapter examines U.S. relations with Spain and Spanish America while also unfolding the story of how privateering began, how Spanish American independence was achieved, and how Americans responded.

The next three chapters focus on the four locations from which Spanish American privateers most frequently operated: New Orleans and Barataria, a region of the Louisiana coast; Baltimore, Maryland; Galveston, a Texas island situated in a zone contested between the United States, Spain, and Mexico; and Amelia Island, in Spanish East Florida, a mile from the Georgia border. Although privateers landed across the country, they operated out of Louisiana, Baltimore, Galveston, and Amelia far more often than any other place.

Chapter 2 examines how the peculiar geographic, logistical, and legal conditions of Louisiana—intensified by the geopolitical conditions of the period immediately before and during the War of 1812—animated Spanish American privateering. We will see how the opportunity for privateering arose, how privateers operated, how privateering was connected to smuggling and slave dealing, and how law enforcement responded.

Chapter 3 moves to Baltimore. Like the previous chapter, this one looks at how local conditions combined with legal and geopolitical developments to encourage Spanish American privateering. Unlike in Louisiana, however, privateers from Baltimore sailed farther from home, employed larger vessels, required greater capital investments, and drew on the resources of the upper levels of the city's merchant community. Baltimore privateers also captured richer prizes, calling forth a more vehement response from foreign diplomats.

Chapter 4 explores how privateering worked at Galveston and Amelia Island, places outside U.S. control. Some practices were the same as at the other locations. The goal was still to capture Spanish vessels and sell their cargoes to American buyers. Yet, the geopolitics and legal situation were different. Groups at each location claimed to represent legitimate Spanish American republics, while their often illegal conduct complicated U.S. relations with Spain at a crucial point in negotiations between the two over the possession of Florida and the U.S. border with Spain in North America.

Chapter 5 takes a different tack. Rather than examining a physical place, it examines the place of privateering in the lives of its participants. The question in this chapter is simple: Why did they do it?

Finally, a word on sources and terminology. Illegal trades present special methodological challenges. The following account is drawn principally from the case file of the U.S. federal courts, now held by the National Archives. Although criminal indictments were common, the bulk of information on Spanish American privateering comes from civil suits that were heard by the federal district courts by virtue of their admiralty jurisdiction. The way these civil suits came to be heard reveals their utility. Some cases originated when the navy or customs service seized a vessel or cargo. The district attorney would then file a suit, called a libel in admiralty parlance, asking that vessel or cargo be condemned and title transferred to the United States for auction. Other cases arose when the original owner of a captured vessel or cargo, such as a Spanish merchant, tracked down his property in the United States, usually with the help of an agent or the local consul, and filed a suit seeking restoration. Information on captures abounded, since privateers, with only a few exceptions, released the captain and crew of their prizes. *Lloyd's List*, the newspaper of the London maritime insurer, regularly detailed captures, and Spanish consuls maintained an active network of information sharing to help merchants win back their property in court. Finally, when privateers attempted to smuggle slaves, the law provided an incentive for witnesses to come forward. Slave trade laws promised informers a portion of the proceeds generated by an auction of illegal slaves. In addition, private citizens could file a suit by a process known as *qui tam*, in which legal action is commenced on behalf of the government and a private person, who is entitled to a reward if the suit succeeds. Although some details of privateering activities necessarily escaped notice in court, the financial incentive for unearthing the activities of privateers was so strong that the overall picture emerges from the case files.[17]

Given the multiple loyalties of participants and the complex geopolitics involved, any system for identifying the national and regional groups to which privateers belonged is bound to have its difficulties. What to call Spain's former colonies is especially challenging. "Latin America," the current term of choice for the nations of Mexico, Central America, South America, and the Caribbean, is anachronistic since it was created in the mid-nineteenth century by French intellectuals hoping to define a distinct Latin race. Furthermore, Latin America includes areas such as Haiti and Brazil that, while part of the story of colonial liberation in the early nineteenth century, were not part of the privateering conducted from the United States. "Spanish America" was often used in the early nineteenth century, and it is more directly related to the privateering carried on against Spain. However, it also includes territories that did not seek independence, such as Cuba and Puerto Rico, and it excludes areas, such as Brazil, that were involved in the geopolitics of revolution. "South America" was also frequently used, although it does not include Spanish territories elsewhere in the hemisphere. Finally, while citizens of the United States think of their country as "America," people south of the border are more likely to think of the entire hemisphere as "America."[18]

I have used each of these terms when needed for clarity or precision. When discussing the larger process of independence among the colonies of Spain and Portugal, I use "Latin America." When discussing privateering and developments in the emerging nations that sponsored privateering, I use "Spanish America." Less frequently, when discussing events that took place on the continent of South America but not elsewhere, I use "South America." When discussing national affiliations, I use the term "Americans" to refer to citizens of the United States, since they would have identified themselves as such. I use "Spanish American" to denote the people of the Spanish colonies and the newly emerging nations, a usage employed both in the nineteenth century and today.[19]

The sea has a logic of its own, and so this scheme requires some modification when applied to privateers. "Privateer" can refer to both vessels and the men who sailed them. This latter group was sometimes denoted as "privateersmen," a usage I employ when necessary for clarity. I use "Spanish American privateer" to indicate the nationality of the vessels involved, as drawn from the commissions they bore (or claimed to bear). When referring to people, "Spanish American privateer" refers to the character of the activity, not to the nationality or citizenship of individuals. Thus, a U.S. citizen such as Chaytor would be a Spanish American privateersman. Similarly, the nationality of any vessel I mention denotes the nationality of its registry, rather than the nationality or citizenship of its sailors, captain, or owners.

In addition, it is often necessary to differentiate between U.S. national privateers, such as those commissioned in the War of 1812, and foreign-commissioned privateers manned by sailors not native to the commissioning nation, which I call "foreign privateers." Privateering of this sort is an understudied phenomenon that does not fit the national scheme of much maritime history. Finally, some Spanish American privateers claimed that they sailed aboard government-owned naval vessels and were in fact naval officers and crew. The Spanish American republics did field navies. Yet, in many cases, such as with Captain Chaytor and the *Independencia*, the vessels remained privately owned. For this reason, I have chosen to call these vessels privateers, while noting that nominal naval status could be a strategy to claim greater legitimacy. As I said, the sea has a logic of its own, and penetrating that logic to understand how privateers thought is one purpose of this book.

1 / Diplomacy with Spain and Spanish America

In the spring of 1819, Secretary of State John Quincy Adams was angry with the Supreme Court. In a case involving piracy committed against a British ship by the crew of a Buenos Aires privateer that had ended up in the United States, the Court had ruled that U.S. piracy law applied only to U.S. citizens. When the British minister complained, Adams could only deflect—and fume. "Their reasoning is a sample of judicial logic," Adams wrote in his diary, "disingenuous, false, and hollow—a logic so abhorrent to my nature that it gave me an early disgust to the practice of the law, and led me to the unalterable determination never to accept a judicial office." Adams detested Spanish American privateers. He called them "piratical privateers," or just plain "pirates." Adams had good reason to feel prickly. He often fielded complaints from Spanish, British, and French victims of privateers as he negotiated with Luis de Onís, the Spanish minister to the United States, over their nations' boundaries, and assured everyone that, despite the popularity of privateering in the United States, the country really was neutral. Given to self-pity, Adams felt everyone was against him. Privateering "brought the whole body of the European allies upon us in the form of remonstrances," he told his diary. "I must take the brunt of the battle upon myself, and rely upon the justice of the cause."[1]

Diplomatic historians today best remember Adams for his role concluding an agreement with Spain, known as the Transcontinental Treaty or Adams-Onís Treaty, that acquired the Floridas for the United States, settled a border between the two nations in the West, and won access to the Pacific. Much less remembered is the contemporaneous issue of Spanish American privateering and the frustration Adams felt from the diplomacy of Spanish American vessels operating from the United States. This chapter recaptures the geopolitical context of U.S. relations with Spain and its rebelling colonies that made possible not only the Transcontinental Treaty but also Spanish American privateering. In doing so it pushes against a tendency in diplomatic histories to diminish the context in which the treaty was originally negotiated. Since the treaty was rich with significance for the country's future growth, it is tempting to focus on its role promoting expansion to the exclusion of the other pertinent issues. But the treaty was achieved not as the next step along a predetermined path to power but rather within the particular circumstances of the early nineteenth century as the United States worked out its relations with the rest of the world. It was the geopolitical present that determined the course charted by U.S. policy makers, and it was the geopolitical present that made possible, in time, the expansionist future.[2]

The chapter follows several major statesmen of the day: Napoleon imprisoning Spanish King Fernando VII and touching off a revolution; President James Madison affirming United States neutrality; John Quincy Adams negotiating with Luis de Onís; and Speaker of the House Henry Clay pushing the United States to become the first to recognize the independence of the Spanish American republics. Examining how these men navigated their world reveals the larger picture of the wars in Europe and the Americas that privateers would exploit and that U.S. policy makers needed to navigate as they responded to foreign privateering. Geopolitical context thus emerges as the crucial factor shaping the decisions made by both the policy makers and the privateers.

War in Spanish America

In April 1808, Napoleon laid a trap for the Spanish king, Fernando VII, calling him to a meeting across the Pyrenees in Bayonne. Spain and its royal family were already in turmoil. Fernando had ascended to the throne only the previous month when rioting, brought about by Spain's disastrous cooperation with France in the conquest of Portugal, had forced the abdication of his father, Charles IV. With one hundred thousand French soldiers occupying Spain, Fernando should have known better, but he believed Napoleon's intentions peaceable—to build a buffer zone along the border or support his claim to the throne or even to cement their bonds by providing a French princess for him to marry.

Instead Napoleon made Fernando a prisoner. He was taking Spain for his family. Fernando was deposed. Napoleon's brother Joseph was installed as king.³

Napoleon taking the Spanish throne unleashed a crisis of authority in the Spanish world that would ultimately result in more than a decade of war, death, and destruction, and the dissolution of the Spanish Empire and the birth of new independent republics in the Americas. Throughout the eighteenth and early nineteenth centuries, a war breaking out led immediately to the commissioning of privateers, and the first private armed vessels sailed with the first favorable tide. In the Spanish Wars of Independence, however, privateering arose over time according to local conditions. Among the five emerging republics whose vessels sailed from the United States, the movement toward independence, war, and privateering unfolded according to their own rhythm within the larger drama of Spain's contest with its colonies.

The Spanish people, in Spain and the Americas, immediately rejected Joseph Bonaparte, the usurper. They formed local governing bodies, called juntas, to organize resistance and govern in Fernando's name according to the Spanish tradition that in the king's absence sovereignty devolved to the people. The juntas in Spain came together to form a national governing body, the Junta Central, although in time it gave way to an executive body, the Regency, and a legislature, the Cortes. However constituted, this Spanish resistance government faced constant pressure from Napoleon's troops, which forced the government to take up residence in Cadiz, a fortified port city protected by the British navy. Across the Atlantic, Spanish American juntas disputed the leadership of the Cadiz government. Some Spanish Americans juntas recognized the Cadiz government's gesture toward power sharing. Spanish Americans served in the Junta Central, for example. But others balked. The Spanish kingdom rested equally on two pillars, Spain and America, they argued. Spanish Americans had the responsibility to exercise their own sovereignty, governing in the king's name as well. ⁴

At the same time, tensions between Spanish America and the mother country had simmered for some time, and the crisis brought to the fore an element interested in independence. Some of these leaders, such as Simón Bolívar and Father Miguel Hidalgo, contrived to "wear the mask of Fernando," as the saying went: resisting the claims of Cadiz by pretending loyalty to the king while preparing for the opportune moment in which to assert independence. Tensions also existed between Spanish American regions, and it was not uncommon for neighboring cities to form their own juntas, sometimes cooperating with each other, sometimes working at cross purposes, and, in the worst of times, engaging in open warfare.[5]

The Spanish American wars thus combined a foreign war against France with a civil war for power in the Spanish Empire, and the progress of the wars in any given place depended on how local conditions combined with events in the larger Spanish world. In Mexico, Father Hidalgo ignited the drive to independence with the *grito de Dolores*, his cry for rebellion voiced on September 16, 1810. A priest from a creole family, Hidalgo had given up an academic career to minister to the rural parish of Dolores and practice liberal politics. He built a peasant army of some eighty thousand men, inspiring their loyalty by consecrating the movement to the Virgin of Guadeloupe and enacting reforms such as ending slavery, abolishing Indian tribute payments, and redistributing property. Despite their numbers, Hidalgo's forces were still peasants, and in the engagements that followed in late 1810 and early 1811, the defeats were crushing and the victories all too often pyrrhic. In March 1811, he was captured and sent to Mexico City, where he was tried, excommunicated, and, in July, put to death.[6]

Leadership of the Mexican independence movement then fell to Father José María Morelos, a former mule driver turned priest turned general. Morales scored several victories in 1812, and under his guidance a legislature, styled the Congress of Anáhuac in a nod to Mexico's Aztec heritage, convened to declare independence (November 6, 1813) and to write a constitution. Following independence, however, Morales suffered a string of defeats, and the Spanish took charge, forcing Morales and the Congress of Anáhuac to flee across Mexico, one step ahead of their enemies. In late 1815, the Spanish apprehended Morales as he accompanied the Congress to the coast. He was, like Hidalgo, brought to Mexico City, condemned, and, just before Christmas, executed. As 1815 ended, the Mexican independence movement seemed defeated, with the resistance to be carried forward by informal forces, filibusters, and privateers recruited abroad.[7]

Meanwhile, in the Captain-Generalcy of Venezuela, juntas had formed in several regions with Caracas, the capital, asserting its supremacy, a status that some cities recognized but that others did not. A declaration of independence followed on July 5, 1811, with a constitution adopted in December. Venezuela became the first republic to arise in Spanish America. Its first republican period was short-lived, however. Trouble began in March 1812, when an earthquake devastated Caracas. Hitting

MAP 1. Spanish America in the Age of Revolution, 1808–1824

on Holy Thursday, it was interpreted as God's judgment on independence seekers. Military defeats followed in the months ahead, first in Caracas and then Puerto Cabello, where Simón Bolívar was forced to flee, one step ahead of the enemy, to a Caribbean-bound boat. Bolívar regrouped in Cartagena. Once a part of the Viceroyalty of New Grenada, Cartagena formed a junta in June 1810 compromised of members who bowed neither to the resistance government in Spain nor to the junta at Bogotá, the former vice-regal capital. Cartagena declared independence on November 11, 1811, and its privateers plied the Gulf of Mexico and Caribbean by the end of the year, often stopping in New Orleans. Bolívar joined the Cartagenan army, taking a command and leading his men into Venezuela, which he proceeded to conquer. In August 1812, Bolívar entered Caracas as a hero, acclaimed as "el Liberador." Venezuela's second republic lasted no longer than the first. In June 1814, a Spanish force of *llaneros*, rough cowboys from the plains, defeated Bolívar at the Battle of La Puerto and forced him back aboard another Caribbean-bound boat.[8]

Bolívar's situation worsened. The year 1814 brought a major turning point in the Wars of Independence. With Napoleon defeated in the Peninsular War, Fernando returned to Spain and his throne in May. Unhappy about the way his subjects exercised sovereignty in his absence, Fernando revoked the Constitution of 1812 (and its liberal provisions), restored the monarchy to its full powers, and began preparations to send an expedition to reconquer Spanish America. The expedition, ten thousand men strong, the largest ever to leave Spain, sailed the next February under the command of Pablo Morillo and landed in Venezuela in April. Morillo's men made quick work of whatever resistance remained. Bolívar escaped to Jamaica, where he relied on the kindness of a British merchant friend until heading to Haiti in early 1816 to begin planning his next foray to Venezuela.[9]

Cartagena was also in desperate straits by early 1816. After pacifying Venezuela, the Spanish moved west to New Grenada, landing at Santa Marta in July 1815 and then laying siege to Cartagena. The city was heavily fortified, one of the strongest in the Caribbean. But the Spanish forces waited them out. Supplies dwindled. An evacuation was attempted. The city finally fell in early December 1815. When Morillo's troops moved in, they found the streets strewn with bodies. The surviving patriots were soon among them.[10]

In Buenos Aires, a junta formed in 1810 and set about establishing control over the other provinces of the Viceroyalty of the Río de la Plata. The interior provinces were amenable, but along the periphery resistance mounted. An expedition against Asunción (in modern Paraguay), for example, was rebuffed by a fellow local junta, and several expeditions against a Spanish stronghold in Upper Peru were also turned back. A third area of difficulty was the Banda Oriental, located across the Río de la Plata along the eastern shore of the Uruguay River. A small, lightly populated region, the Banda Oriental was nevertheless strategically vital as a buffer between Buenos Aires and Brazil and economically important because of its port at Monte Video and its river links to the interior. The Buenos Aires and the Banda Oriental juntas nursed a mutual resentment, eying each other warily across the river. But leaders could set those feelings aside, as they did in 1811 to attack a Spanish garrison at Monte Video.[11]

José Gervais Artigas led the Banda Oriental forces. In a previous life, Artigas had been a cattle rustler and smuggler before he joined the Spanish army and was assigned to arrest cattle rustlers and smugglers. Artigas had gained some distinction in the province and received a command from the junta at Buenos Aires. In the assault on Monte Video, however, Artigas issued his own call for rebellion, the *grito de Asencio*, a signal that cooperating with Buenos Aires was a means to an end—and that end was not Buenos Aires's hegemony. As the siege progressed, a fourth party entered the fray: Portugal. The Spanish commander in Monte Video joined forces with Princess Carlotta Joaquina, the wife of the Portuguese prince regent and, it so happened, the sister of King Fernando of Spain. Like the rest of the Portuguese royal family, Carlotta Joaquina had fled Napoleon and taken up residence in Brazil. She agreed to send an army to rescue her brother's lands and expand her own influence south. Over the next nine years, warfare along the Río de la Plata would be a mixture of shifting alliances and hostilities among Buenos Aires, the Banda Oriental, Spain, and Portugal.

For Artigas the high point came in February 1815, when he entered Monte Video as a hero and founder of a new nation, the Oriental Republic. (Actually, Buenos Aires had liberated Monte Video but gave it to Artigas as more trouble than it was worth.) Artigas then established an alliance of former Río de la Plata provinces called the Federal League, although despite being esteemed the Protector of Free Peoples, he wielded power only in the Banda Oriental. Artigas's rule in Monte Video would last less than two years. In August 1816, Portugal reentered the Banda Oriental. Attacked anew, Artigas looked outside the country for help, including from privateers, but he was unable to save Monte Video. Artigas surrendered the city in January 1817 and commenced a guerilla war from the countryside and on the water as he continued to commission privateers, an anomaly given his lack of a sea port. Artigas held out until 1820, when he was finally defeated and forced into exile in Paraguay.[12]

Across the Río de la Plata in Buenos Aires, the challenge of controlling the provinces, fending off the Spanish, and building a new government coincided with the launch of privateering. By 1815, Buenos Aires had passed through several forms of government, and rumors swirled that General Morillo would head south following his conquest of Venezuela and Cartagena, augmenting Spain's stronghold in Upper Peru. To address the military danger, Buenos Aires projected its sea power abroad, beyond its previous focus on the Río de la Plata. Naval vessels and privateers took to sea in late 1815. To meet the political fractiousness, a national congress assembled in Tucamán, restoring a measure of unity. The congress declared independence in July 1816 and drafted a constitution for a new nation to be called the United Provinces of the Río de la Plata. Problems remained, especially as wrangling continued in the provinces, but the United Provinces would never again fall under Spain's control.[13]

Neutrality

In September 1815, President Madison officially pledged neutrality in Spain's contest with its rebelling colonies. Receiving word that "sundry persons" were "conspiring together to begin and set on foot, provide, and prepare the means for a military expedition or enterprise against the dominions of Spain," Madison warned all involved to desist, "as they will answer the contrary at their peril," and called on "all good and faithful citizens and others in the United States" to exert themselves in "the discovery, apprehension, and bringing to justice" of the perpetrators. The United States would continue to welcome Spanish American vessels to its ports. So long as they did not increase their arms or crew, the newness of their flags was no barrier to entry. The United States would likewise continue to permit Spanish American agents to visit. So long as they did not recruit men to serve in a foreign war, the uncertain status of their nations was no barrier to engaging in any lawful political or commercial activity. But Madison drew the line at participation and promotion of privateers and filibusters. Madison made the proclamation because privateering and filibustering threatened the nation's ability to achieve its foreign policy goals vis-à-vis Spain and Spanish America. At best, Americans involved in privateering and filibustering could derail negotiations with

Spain, upsetting the relationship with a bordering nation. At worst, the United States might be embroiled in another European war, triggered by Spain's anger with U.S. interference in its colonial affairs. As Madison affirmed, neutrality was the best course for the United States to follow.[14]

By the time of Madison's proclamation, two long-running issues caused friction in U.S. relations with Spain: the proper border between the two and damages that U.S. officials believed Spain owed to Americans. The border dispute stretched back to the American Revolution, when, despite treaty negotiations that set a boundary at the Mississippi River in the west and the 31st parallel in the south, Spain demurred, only acceding to the terms in the 1795 Treaty of San Lorenzo. The 1803 Louisiana Purchase opened the issue anew. Spain objected to Napoleon selling the land (he had promised not to); Spain also believed Louisiana was much smaller than the United States claimed it was. The purchase treaty specified the land in question only by reference to the 1800 Treaty of San Ildefonso, through which France had reacquired the land from Spain, as "the Colony or Province of Louisiana with the Same extent that it now has in the hand of Spain, & that it had when France possessed it; and Such as it Should be after the Treaties subsequently entered into between Spain and other States." U.S. policy makers said that Louisiana included the portion of West Florida between the Mississippi River and the Perdido River (the border between the modern states of Alabama and Florida) and stretched west to the Rio Grande. Spain countered that Louisiana ended at the Mississippi in the east and the midway point between the Mermentau and Calcasieu Rivers in the west (about fifty miles east of the present border between Louisiana and Texas). Anything else was Florida and Texas and therefore Spanish.[15]

Washington also clashed with Madrid over money it believed Spain owed to Americans. The claims originated in two incidents. The first occurred during the U.S. Quasi-War with France. According to the United States, Spain had overstepped the bounds of neutrality. Spanish privateers had captured more than one hundred American vessels, and French privateers had used Spanish courts to condemn their prizes, which were then sold to Spanish buyers. These actions amounted to "spoliations," the United States claimed, and it demanded that the American merchants be made whole. In 1802 it appeared they would receive satisfaction as an agreement was reached to settle the claims through a joint commission. It was never ratified, however. The Senate approved, but the Spanish Cortes failed to consent, leaving the matter unsettled. A second class of damages were sustained in 1802, when Spain revoked the right of deposit in New Orleans, citing abuse by American smugglers, and did not provide another city for deposit as required by treaty. American merchants with goods in the city found themselves bereft, as did merchants and farmers whose produce was already floating down the river to market. In the future, the spoliation claims and deposit damages became linked to the border issue as the United States offered to assume the responsibility of paying its citizens in exchange for Spain ceding the Floridas.[16]

The emerging independence movements added a new dimension to U.S. foreign relations, and U.S. policy toward Spain became bound up with its policy toward Spanish America. The official U.S. response to Spanish America was friendly, but cautious, eager to advance U.S. goals, hopeful for the expansion of republicanism, but wary of the dangers posed by such tumultuous conditions. President Madison, for example, distinguished between faraway territories, such as Venezuela, Buenos Aires, and Chile, and closer ones, such as Cuba, Mexico, and the Floridas. In the former, the ramifications of independence—or Spanish reconquest—were far enough away to be of little consequence to the United States. Madison's chief concern was that these Spanish American nations might give favorable trade status to British merchants. Cuba, Mexico, and the Floridas were more important to U.S. interests, and Madison took a cautious approach to encouraging any regime change in them. A revolution in Cuba, for example, might become a Haitian-style slave rebellion that, in addition to setting a bad example for American slaves, would invite intervention by Britain to the detriment of U.S. trade in the Gulf of Mexico. In Mexico, the patriots were already receiving men, money, guns, and supplies from Americans along the border. Any official support, even verbal, could pull the United States into a war with Spain. In the Floridas, one false move might bring disaster, given West Florida's proximity to New Orleans and the importance of the rivers of East Florida to commerce in the Southeast. Moreover, Madison, like other U.S. policy makers in the period, wanted Spain to keep the Floridas so they could be traded to the United States. He went so far as to secure a secret law, enacted by Congress in 1811, authorizing U.S. occupation of any Florida lands east of the Perdido River in danger of falling under the control of a power other than Spain.[17]

U.S. policy makers emphasized neutrality between Spain and its rebelling colonies, but neutrality did not mean quarantining the United States from the combatants. Spain ran a delegation, headed by Minister Luis de Onís, from Philadelphia, although between 1809 and 1815 it was unofficial as the United States avoided taking sides on which Spanish government, Napoleon's or the resistance's, was legitimate. Spanish American agents likewise visited the United States (also using Philadelphia as a base). They were not received officially, which would have been tantamount to U.S. recognition, and Madison did not meet them personally. But otherwise the agents were free to do as they pleased, and several hundred representatives came to the United States in the 1810s seeking to influence U.S. policy, buy weapons, commission privateers, and organize filibusters. The munitions trade was perfectly legal. According to the law of nations, neutrals were free to permit the trade as long as the trade was open to all belligerents and if a munitions shipment were captured by a belligerent, the neutral nation could not protest. The legality of privateering and filibustering was a bit murkier. U.S. neutrality law, enacted in 1794 and 1797 and expanded and refined in 1817 and 1818, forbid U.S. citizens and any foreigners in the United States from attacking nations at peace with United States by accepting a commission, owning a privateer vessel, equipping a privateer vessel, joining a crew or expedition, or recruiting men to join a crew or expedition (unless the men joining or recruited were foreigners transiently in the country). But Americans could equip a privateer and gather weapons to sell outside the United States to groups who then used them for privateering and filibustering, as those actions were considered a munitions trade. Spanish American agents would become adept at skirting the prohibitions.[18]

Overall, the official response of the United States government to the events of 1808 and the subsequent crisis of authority in the Spanish Empire emphasized amicable, neutral relations. The United States wished the patriots well, and the law of nations permitted neutrals wide latitude to maintain contacts with belligerents, including contacts that might seem warlike. Nevertheless, the United States would not actually participate in the conflict. Whatever the psychological benefits of advancing the cause of independence and republican government, the reality of the geopolitics dictated that the United States stay on the sidelines. Interests in the gulf, along the Louisiana border, and, especially, in the Floridas surpassed all other considerations.

Americans at large followed the events in Spain and Spanish America avidly, and their reactions displayed a range of emotions, from anger at Napoleon's audacity to skepticism of the Spanish Americans' capacity for self-government to cautious optimism that independence might be possible to affection for a people engaged, like Americans, in a battle for liberty. Like the official responses, ordinary Americans tended to view

Spain and Spanish American affairs through the lens of their own concerns, giving priority to how events affected the United States.[19]

The initial newspaper reactions to Napoleon's usurpation of the Spanish throne expressed dismay. "Napoleon has stretched forth his arm to Spain, and Spain is no more," one paper wrote. "The Spanish monarchy, as if by enchantment, is overwhelmed, and the Spanish people, by a base deed of cession, are transferred to the *Imperial Jacobin*." In addition to sympathizing with the fate of Spain, some editors took time for partisanship, using each new development as a cudgel to bludgeon opponents. The anti-Jefferson *New-York Post*, for example, opined that "circumstances are daily arising to confirm suspicions, which have been long since entertained, that our cabinet are in *secret* league with Bonaparte."[20]

For Spanish America, newspapers offered encouragement. "What a glorious time for the South Americans to make themselves independent," one paper wrote. The actions of Spanish Americans, though, were most admirable for their imitation of the United States. As another paper argued, Venezuela's vote to declare independence "varies no more from the course pursued by the United States of North America, than what differences of circumstances have rendered unavoidable." Alongside the expressions of enthusiasm, however, doubts emerged. Were Spanish people really capable of republicanism? They were Catholics, after all, and the traditional Anglo-American paranoia of priestcraft and popery abounded. Still, some editors expressed hope that a new age was dawning. *Poulson's American Daily Advertiser* found it noteworthy that "wherever independence has been declared, the inquisition immediately falls."[21]

Newspapers were the creations of their editor-printers and the parties that sponsored them, and although they may represent the attitudes of a community, they were also highly selective. What ordinary Americans thought about Spanish America is much harder to determine. One interesting source that provides some insight into the feelings of Americans comes from the practice of publishing the toasts at public gatherings. The toasts celebrating the Fourth of July were regularly reprinted, and, if the reports are to be believed, Spanish American independence was a popular subject. A gathering outside Philadelphia praised "South America—The embers of liberty, may they burst into flame, and establish its independence in a government of the people." The toast elicited "3 cheers," the paper noted. Comparisons to the American Revolution were frequent. The Columbian Society of New York quoted the Marquis de Lafayette in its toast to "The people of South America—'For a nation to be free, it is sufficient that she wills it.'" In Northumberland, Pennsylvania, a group drank to "The lovers of freedom in South America: may their patriotic efforts, procure as glorious an independence, as the heroes of '76 did for their posterity." The toasts were self-flattering: *Hurray, South America!* they seemed to say. *You're just like us!* Still, the toasts were frequent and heartfelt, at least in the moment, and linked the United States with the cause of Spanish America. The Spanish American agents who came north to publicize their cause were no doubt satisfied. They had argued that the causes of independence of the United States and their southern brethren were one and the same, and although they aimed to influence policy makers rather than Fourth of July merrymakers, the association was becoming a commonplace.[22]

U.S. relations with Spain and Spanish America, along with Americans' interest in their hemispheric neighbors, receded as the tensions with Britain boiled over into the War of 1812. The Spanish borderlands were still important to U.S. security, and operations along the gulf coast—such as Andrew Jackson's campaign against Indians believed to be collaborating with the British, the Battle of New Orleans, and the annexation of Mobile—were vital pieces of the war. But relations with Britain came first. After all, it did no good to keep the Floridas in Spanish hands if the British took them by force. At the same time, the popularity of toasting South America also waned during the war. With the United States engaged in its second war of independence against Britain, the Spanish Americans would have to wait.[23]

The Transcontinental Treaty

John Quincy Adams found negotiations with Spain slow going. By the time he had taken up his post at the State Department in 1817, wrangling with Spain had become a tradition of more than twenty years and neither the end of the War of 1812 nor the restoration of King Fernando spurred new action. When, in December 1815, Onís presented himself to President Madison for official reception, the president recoiled. During the war, Onís had advocated Spain teaming up with Britain to attack the Gulf Coast and carve the United States into two or three pieces. Madison condemned Onís's "indecorous & *criminal* conduct toward the U.S." Spain responded by refusing to grant a passport to the U.S. ambassador, George W. Erving. The standoff persisted for fifteen months. With Adams at the helm, talks proceeded no faster. At his first official meeting with the Spanish minister, the two spoke for hours, but Onís offered the same treaty terms that had been previously offered to the American minister in Spain: "I told him [the terms] were so inadmissible that it would be useless to enter upon the discussion of them." Many useless discussions followed. Onís rehearsed the long, tedious history of the Louisiana claims again and again and again; Adams brushed Onís off with perfunctory responses or ignored him altogether. On one occasion, Adams complained about having to see Onís "since I knew he would beat about the bush, and not make any proposition at all."[24]

And yet by February 1819, the two men had concluded a landmark treaty, settling all the outstanding issues between the nations they represented. The deadlock between the United States and Spain and the rapid progress toward a treaty were bound up with the geopolitical conditions of the post-1815 world. Earlier on, both sides wanted delay, as they appraised their goals and calculated that their bargaining position would only improve with time. But time also brought new developments along the U.S.-Spanish borderlands and in Spanish America and Europe. Those developments increasingly favored the United States, leading Onís to stop beating about the bush and come to the bargaining table, where Adams increasingly had the upper hand.

For U.S. leaders, delay was desirable because when they looked out at the world, they saw danger, and when they looked at the United States, they saw vulnerability. The recent European peace was unstable, Americans feared, with war debts weighing down European economies and glory-hungry monarchs restored to power. A collision with Spain over Spanish America and the borderlands was especially fraught with concern for U.S. leaders. One false move could escalate and bring the United States to war with Spain, which would also mean war with its ally, Britain. Indeed, Britain lurked in the background of U.S. relations with Spain and Spanish America, with the potential for British intervention—and the need to stop it—forefront in the minds of policy makers.[25]

Given this analysis of the nation's position in international affairs, U.S. leaders chose a cautious approach. The United States would placate potential adversaries for the time being, reducing the tensions with Europe and smoothing the points of friction in the Americas but without formally resolving any of the major issues existing with other countries. The United States would stall for time, because, as its leaders believed, time was on their side. In time, the United States would grow richer. In time, the United States would grow more populous. In time, the lessons of fighting the War of 1812 would be absorbed and applied to the future. In time, the United States would grow stronger. Simultaneously,

American leaders believed that the nation's enemies would grow weaker. Spain would lose its colonies. Britain would turn its attention to the continent. Indians, smashed by recent U.S. victories, would diminish in power. Peace would be preserved—on American terms.[26]

Hopes for delay aside, the U.S. policy makers developed a clear vision of their priorities for treaty negotiations. The Floridas came first. Over the previous years, the United States had made progress securing its claim to West Florida. Most of the territory had been acquired in 1810, when local residents, many of whom were American immigrants, rose up against the Spanish governor, proclaimed an independent republic, and then requested annexation by the United States. Annexation of Mobile followed in 1813, during the War of 1812. The United States thus occupied all of the West Florida territory it said was part of the Louisiana Purchase. Nevertheless, Spain had never acknowledged U.S. positions in West Florida, and it still held East Florida.[27]

Next in importance was the preservation of U.S. claims in the Pacific Northwest, where the United States asserted ownership of the Columbia River as a site for the fur trade and a possible launching point for a future commerce to China. The last area of concern for the United States was Texas. The western boundary of the Louisiana Purchase was also disputed, but unlike West Florida, U.S. policy makers were willing to make concessions. The Louisiana-Texas border, wherever the proper lines, proved notoriously difficult to police, with a zone of joint administration in the area, known as the Neutral Ground, turning into a refuge for smugglers, slave dealers, privateers, pirates, filibusters, Indian raiders, drifters, and bandits. Better to have a firm border under someone's control, U.S. officials reasoned, than an unstable zone of overlapping jurisdiction. Plus, the United States would have to trade something to get the territories it really wanted. By 1816, the U.S. position became clear. The negotiations should seek to obtain the Floridas, the sine qua non, as well as a border that provided access to the Columbia River in the Pacific in exchange for Texas and the United States assuming responsibility for the spoliation claims and deposit damages.[28]

Spain also counted on delay to preserve the peace, increase its strength, and win a treaty on its terms. The reconquest expedition would do its job. Support from Britain and the European powers would increase as Spanish lobbying efforts took effect. In the meantime, the promise to talk would keep the United States at bay while also preventing U.S. aid to the colonies, which would cut off their best hope for reinforcement. In its negotiations, therefore, Spain concentrated on retaining as much territory as possible while keeping the United States from interfering in Spanish America. Retaining control over Texas was important as well; though sparsely populated, it put distance between New Spain and the Americans. In addition, Onís demanded that the United States close its ports to Spanish American vessels, amend its neutrality laws to punish privateers and filibusters, and promise not to recognize the independence of any Spanish American colony. From the time of his reception, Onís deluged U.S. officials with complaints about "the mischiefs resulting from the toleration of the armament of privateers in the ports of this Union, and of bringing into them, with impunity, the plunder made by these privateers on the Spanish trade"; demands for "the punishment, according to law, of those turbulent and seditious individuals who have taken up arms within the territory of this confederation, and from thence carrying desolation, destruction, and horror into the frontier provinces of the Crown of Spain"; and lectures on U.S. obligations "to adopt energetic measures to restrain these excesses, which so deeply compromit the neutrality of the United States in the eyes of all nations."[29]

As relations with Spain settled into a stalemate, relations with Spanish America, though always linked to Spanish affairs, underwent a subtle shift in 1817 as James Monroe assumed the presidency and convened his administration. Monroe was interested in crafting a new Spanish American policy, even to the point of considering recognition of independence. Developments in Spanish America called for a reevaluation of U.S. policy. By the summer of 1817, the wars of independence seemed to be going somewhat better at least for some of the republics. Buenos Aires had declared independence in 1816, and, as far as could be gleaned in the United States, its independence appeared secure. General José San Martín had then led a daring march across the Andes Mountains to liberate Chile from Spanish control. Simón Bolívar also began to make progress, gaining a foothold in Venezuela at Angostura in July. Ultimately, Monroe acted with characteristic caution, and over a series of cabinet meetings he decided not to push for recognition. The status of the wars in Spanish America was still too uncertain. The likelihood of Spanish opposition leading to war was still too great. Thus, in his first annual message to Congress, delivered in December, Monroe's support was mostly verbal. He expressed, in a general way, the nation's warm sentiments toward the Spanish Americans, and he stated that the government viewed "the contest not in the light of an ordinary insurrection or rebellion, but as a civil war between parties nearly equal," a significant difference in the Law of Nations. Finally Monroe announced his intention to send a three-man team to Buenos Aires on a fact-finding mission. Publicly, that was as far as the president was willing to go.[30]

Spain had calculated correctly. As strong as the popular sentiment was in favor of Spanish America, the United States could not proceed as long as the treaty negotiations were going on. Certainly, Onís was not pleased by American participation in filibustering, privateering, and the munitions trade, and he tended to suspect that the United States government was responsible. Yet, on the whole the status quo was acceptable, even as it proved frustrating to the officials of both sides. In 1818, however, developments in North America and in Europe would combine to break the stalemate, and by February 1819, the long-delayed treaty was signed.

In North America, Andrew Jackson's invasion of Florida ignited a diplomatic and political firestorm that pushed Spain and the United States to make a deal. Ordered to pacify Indians attacking American whites along the Florida-Georgia border, Jackson led an army into Florida in March. Jackson superseded his instructions, attacking not only local Indians but also the Spanish and British he believed were their sponsors. To Jackson, the security of the border depended on solving the problem at its root. Jackson thus captured the Spanish settlements at Fort St. Marks and Pensacola, and when two British subjects fell into his hands, he had them tried and executed for collaborating with the Indians.[31]

News of Jackson's foray into Florida reached Washington in June, and Monroe and his advisers found themselves in a quandary. The administration had to avoid appearing to sanction the general's conduct, for fear of angering Spain (and therefore Britain) or of seeming to condone illegality. But the administration could not appear to condemn Jackson either, for fear of angering his supporters or of seeming weak internationally. In the end, the administration, led by Adams, defended Jackson by blaming Spain for not controlling the Creeks and Seminoles as they had pledged in Pinckney's Treaty. It was their own fault that Jackson had to capture their forts. Onís blasted Jackson's conduct in public, demanding that the president condemn the general's behavior and make reparations for his lawlessness. Nevertheless, negotiations continued. By this point, Onís did not want a rupture any more than the United States did. Breaking off talks might lead the United States to take Florida anyway and then follow it with recognition of Spanish American independence. Onís swallowed hard and kept talking.[32]

The Spanish minister's willingness to persevere in spite of Jackson's attack on Florida derived from Spain's softening position among its

European allies. In 1818, it became apparent that the powers that had restored King Fernando to the throne were not going to take any further steps to protect his American colonies. In one critical development, Spain failed to secure British mediation of its dispute with the United States. Britain, wary of becoming involved, made the offer in a perfunctory way, and the United States rejected it. Later in the year the European powers, gathering at the Congress of Aix-la-Chapelle, again refused to intervene in Spain's American affairs when they turned down King Fernando's request to force a mediation of the Spanish American wars. Rebuffed by its friends, Spain had little choice but to negotiate with the United States. Onís was instructed to get the best deal he could while he could.[33]

Over the ensuing months, Adams and Onís hammered out the details of the agreement. The United States received the Floridas and agreed to pay up to $5 million for the spoliation claims and deposit damages owed to U.S. citizens. A border between the two nations was then established west of the Mississippi starting at the Sabine River, the western boundary of the state of Louisiana, and then moving stepwise north and west, using a combination of rivers and lines of latitude and longitude on the way to the Pacific. The United States gave up its claims in Texas while preserving access to the Columbia River on the Pacific. The Senate assented to the treaty on February 24 and sent across the Atlantic for approval in Spain—where the agreement was imperiled yet again.[34]

The problem stemmed from King Fernando's attempt to keep as much of Florida as possible in Spanish hands by making several large land grants to Spaniards, on the belief that as private property the United States would be bound to respect them. On the surface, the parties had addressed the issue, agreeing that no grants made after January 24, 1818, would be recognized, but due to an error, several grants intended to be excluded were actually recognized. Officials in Spain used the land grant error as an opening to renegotiate for a stronger neutrality law, a promise not to recognize Spanish American independence, and a promise to respect the integrity of Spain's possessions in the future. This stalemate would be broken by events in Spain, as the king found himself mired, yet again, in crisis. In January 1820, a group of army officers revolted in protest against their poor treatment. Emboldened by the officers, Spanish liberals forced the king to resurrect the Constitution of 1812. The Cortes approved the treaty. The king signed it. And after traveling back across the Atlantic, it was again ratified by the Senate. On February 22, 1821, the treaty became official.[35]

New Republican Neighbors

Congressman Henry Clay took it upon himself to advance his own Spanish American policy from his position as Speaker of the House. Throughout the first session of the Fifteenth Congress, as 1817 gave way to 1818, Clay advocated not warm feelings and impartial neutrality but recognition of Spanish American independence. Rising in the House to respond to the president's first Annual Message to Congress, Clay expressed pity for the condition of the Spanish Americans. In their contest with Spain they had no established power to champion their cause as France had once done for the United States. "Their situation was worse than ours," he said, "for we had one great and magnanimous ally to recognize us, but no nation [has] stepped forward to acknowledge any of these provinces." Clay returned to the theme again in March during the debate over the annual appropriations bill. He argued that sending a fact-finding mission to Buenos Aires was not enough and offered a resolution calling for eighteen thousand dollars to fund a minister to the United Provinces, an act that would effectively recognize independence and establish regular diplomatic relations. Spanish America had suffered under "an odious tyranny," he said, and deserved U.S. support. Once independent, Spanish America would become a trusted trading partner, an active market for American agriculture, a staunch ally against the European powers.[36]

Ultimately, Clay's arguments proved unconvincing, and his motion was defeated. The outcome pleased Monroe and Adams, who did not appreciate Clay's attempt to circumvent what they saw as the executive's prerogative on extending recognition. Moreover, Spanish America was still in flux, and as Adams had come to believe, the United States should recognize independence as a fact accomplished not a condition aspired to. But events on the ground were changing. As the United States reached agreement with Spain, Spanish America was advancing toward independence. Interest in Spanish America soared in the United States. Recognition became more viable. It seemed that Clay's vision of economic and strategic cooperation among the republican nations of the Americas—an Americas System, to modify his famous domestic plan—was at hand, especially after the United States seemed to stand with Spanish America against European interference in the Monroe Doctrine. The close connections did not last, however. As the 1820s ended, independence was achieved, but relations cooled.[37]

Clay's call for recognition was made possible by the stunning improvement in Spanish American prospects. In 1816, the revolutions were all but dead. Mexico was firmly under the control of Agustin Iturbide; General Morillo's expedition was triumphant in Venezuela and New Grenada; Upper Peru and Chile were holding out against San Martín's attacks from Buenos Aires; and the Oriental Provinces were threatened by Spain, Buenos Aires, and Portuguese Brazil. Buenos Aires enjoyed independence, but plans were already under way in Spain for a second reconquest expedition, this one aimed at the Río de la Plata. The turnaround began in early 1817. San Martín led an assault on Chile, marching his Army of the Andes over the mountains from the United Provinces and capturing the Chilean capital. San Martín then prepared to move north against Peru.[38]

Also in 1817, Bolívar finally made headway in Venezuela. Following his arrival in Aux Cayes, Haiti, from Jamaica, Bolívar received aid from Haitian president Alexandre Pétion in exchange for his promise to abolish slavery. Bolívar's First Aux Cayes Expedition ended ignominiously, with the Liberator once more retreating to a Caribbean-bound boat (this time chased by one of his disgruntled men running down the docks swinging a sword). The Second Aux Cayes Expedition, however, worked. Bolívar captured Angostura and began consolidating his power. In early 1819, he convened a meeting to forge unity among the juntas of Venezuela and New Grenada, and although most territory was still in Spanish hands, the gathering created a new nation, Gran Colombia, comprising the modern nations of Colombia, Venezuela, Ecuador, Panama, and Peru. Its president would be Simón Bolívar. The new president then returned to the field and began clearing away Spanish resistance. He attacked Bogotá, marching from the coast, slogging across the rain-soaked plains, and ascending the mountains. Reaching his target in August, Bolívar defeated the Spanish at the Battle of Boyacá Bridge. There would be no more retreating.[39]

As San Martín and Bolívar surged, Spain faltered, weakened by turmoil at home. The difficulty of military demobilization and economic recovery following Napoleon's defeat was compounded by the king's hard-line approach to his restoration and his profligate spending on reconquering the colonies, which increasingly appeared a lost cause. A revolt of army officers, preparing to risk their lives in the Americas, led Fernando to accept demands for change. He brought back the liberal Constitution of 1812, reducing his own power. The second reconquest expedition never sailed.[40]

In Spanish America, victories for the insurgents continued. San Martín gained control over Lima by November 1820, although Spanish resistance remained strong in the highlands. Meanwhile, Bolívar gained ground in the wars' northern theater. By the end of the year, only Cartagena and Pasto remained in Spanish hands. Bolívar and Morillo called a truce in November, only to renew their fighting six months later. Bolívar then led his forces to victory at the Battle of Carabobo, liberating Venezuela for good. In July 1822, Bolívar linked up with San Martín at Guayaquil, in modern Ecuador. In another eighteen months, the Spanish American triumph was achieved. Pushing into the Peruvian highlands, Bolívar defeated the Spanish at the Battle of Junín in August. His lieutenant Antonio Sucre won at Ayacucho in December 1824. Some resistance continued into the next year, but Spain's hold over South America was broken.[41]

In Mexico, independence had already been achieved and by a much less violent route. Following the 1820 revolt in Spain Iturbide reassessed his position. He struck a deal with the leader of the patriot movement by promising to uphold the three guarantees: independence from Spain, protection for the Catholic Church, and equality for citizens. Thus, independence was brought to Mexico by a conservative Spanish official who did not want to go along with the liberal reforms at home.[42]

Despite Clay's failure in 1818, the United States did become the first outside nation to recognize the independence of the new Spanish American nations. The president officially received diplomats from Gran Colombia and Mexico in 1822 and the United Provinces of Central America in 1824. A minister from Brazil was also received in 1824. The United States sent its own diplomats to the United Provinces and Chile in 1823 and to Peru in 1826. The change in U.S. policy had been brought about by changes in geopolitics. The wars in Spanish America had turned decisively against Spain, and with independence mostly accomplished, the United States could claim it was not breaking any new ground by acknowledging reality. Moreover, the United States could afford to be more assertive once Spain had ratified the Transcontinental Treaty. With the agreement official, there were no longer any Spanish barriers to commencing formal diplomatic relations. The decision to offer recognition was not easy, however. The governments of the new nations were unstable. The Holy Alliance was still a menace. The domestic politics of the Missouri Crisis, breaking out in 1819, gave a worrisome sectional cast to the potential effects of any administration policy toward Spanish America. Nevertheless, recognition promised to bring Spanish America closer into the U.S. orbit and, critically, out of Europe's. Avoiding European interference was still paramount.[43]

Recognition coincided with a rising tide of American enthusiasm for the patriots of the south. The Fourth of July toasts to Spanish American independence flowed as freely as the whiskey, and Spanish American independence showed up everywhere toasts were drunk. Even the Typographical Society of New York worked South America into its many toasts punning on the printing profession. "Liberty has commenced a second edition of the *work* of Independence, which her favorite sons have *put to press* on a *Columbian* form," they said. (The "*Columbian* form" no doubt refers to the then recently invented Columbian printing press; it was probably funnier once the printers were soused.)[44]

When they were not toasting independence, Americans sang about it, with Bolívar as an especially popular subject for melodious commemoration. Songsters could choose from "General Bolívar's Grand March," "Gen. Bolivar's grand march & quick step," and "General Bolivar's favourite Scotch march." Or, to slow things down, "General Bolivar's waltz." Some Americans both toasted and sang. A Philadelphia group, for example, raised a glass to "South America," hoping "she will soon command Independence and Respect," and then raised their voices to the song "Millions be Free."[45]

Americans also liked to name things after Spanish American people and places, with Bolívar again a popular choice for the founders of new towns, counties, and other institutions, from New York to Georgia, Mississippi to Missouri, Pennsylvania to Tennessee. For a few Americans, naming a town after the great general was not enough. A farmer in Massachusetts named his bull Bolivar, and Andrew Jackson called his stud colt Bolivar, too. (Given his famous *pasión de amor*, Bolívar might have appreciated the comparison.) The most personal gesture of all came from the men and women who chose to name their children after a Spanish American hero. According to Caitlyn Fitz, as many as two hundred little Bolivars (or "Bolivers") could be found in the antebellum United States.[46]

The United States continued to define its relationship with Spanish America in the 1820s as independence was achieved and recognized. At first U.S. policy drew the nation closer to its fellow American republics with the Monroe Doctrine. A parcel of ideas originally set forth in the president's 1823 Annual Message to Congress, the doctrine would come to be seen as a major statement of U.S. diplomacy and an assertion of the nation's presence on the world stage, but at the time it was an immediate response to a particular crisis that had developed between Spanish

America and the European powers as rumors circulated that Russia was developing a plan to help Spain recover its departed colonies. The British discountenanced the idea of intervention in Spanish America, since its shipping had thrived with the restoration of peace and the opening of free trade in Spanish American, and it proposed to the United States that the two nations issue a joint statement condemning Russia's plan. Monroe favored the proposal. By recognizing the independence of Spanish America, the United States had committed itself to favoring the success and survival of its new, ideologically compatible neighbors against the Old World's monarchies. A joint proclamation was a different matter. Adams persuaded Monroe that a joint statement would make the United States appear as the junior partner (which it would have been) and Britain would appear as the primary protector and guarantor of Spanish American security (which it was). In the end, the president decided to act unilaterally. According to the message, North and South America "are henceforth not to be considered as subjects for future colonization by any European powers." Any European intervention in the Americas would be seen as "dangerous to our peace and safety." Finally, in reference to the ongoing Greek War for Independence, the United States pledged to stay out of European affairs. In Spanish America, the president's message was welcomed. But the policy also caused concern, for in closing off the Americas to European domination it seemed possible that the United States might be opening up that role for itself.[47]

With U.S. foreign policy committed to a role in Spanish America, the hemisphere's republics seemed closer than ever. Yet by the end of the decade the relationship had frayed, pulled apart by partisan recriminations and growing doubts that Spanish America ever really had much in common with the United States, after all. The trouble sprung from a noble notion: Simón Bolívar's 1824 call for the creation of an inter-American Congress, a body that could foster cooperation among neighbors, settle disputes, and provide unity against common enemies. It would meet in Panama. John Quincy Adams, now president, received the offer warmly, and in December 1825 he announced his desire to send commissioners to the Panama Conference. Anti-Adams partisans pounced. Sending ministers to Panama would subvert U.S. sovereignty, some charged. "What is the character of the Congress of Panama?" asked Senator Martin Van Buren of New York. Was it "a mere Diplomatic Council," he wondered, or something far worse: "an efficient public body, the permanent organ of a confederation of free States, formed for great national purposes?" Other critics feared for the fate of slavery at the hands of the dangerous emancipators and racial egalitarians of Spanish America. In the Senate, Thomas Hart Benton of Missouri condemned the Spanish American nations that "have already put the black man upon an equality with the white, not only in their constitutions but in real life." Those nations even had "black Generals in their armies and mulatto Senators in their Congresses!" The Spanish American republics had been more aggressive fighting slavery and the slave trade, often forbidding the traffic in humans as they declared independence, facts had been largely overlooked during the previous decade, ignored in the fervor for fellow republicans battling an Old World foe. Now opposition to slavery was the new nations' salient feature. If the ministers were approved, senators such as Benton argued, the United States would see a bunch of black and mulatto agitators take away American slaves. When the debate settled, Adams won approval for the commissioners, but the meeting in Panama came to nothing. As the Americans wrangled, the Panama Congress, afflicted by the feverous climate on the isthmus, dispersed. By the time a U.S. commissioner arrived, the meeting had already broken up. There would be no inter-American Congress.[48]

It was a sad end for a project that had begun in a spirit of cooperation. The partisanship that greeted the president's request for commissioners set the stage for the battles that lay ahead as Adams's enemies coalesced around Jackson and the emerging Democratic Party, a party that would come to define itself in its racial identity. The republics of Spanish America were no longer neighbors but potential enemies, a source of disquiet and disunity. The Clay-Adams vision for an expansion of the American system—one that included all of the Americas—also faded. The United States would trade with Spanish America, and the Monroe Doctrine would remain a statement of U.S. foreign policy principle, but there would be no integrated hemispheric economy. The public praise for Spanish America also vanished. No longer would Americans celebrate their Fourth of July with a whiskey glass for Spanish America. The little Bolivars who grew up in the 1820s would only provide a curious reminder that relations had once been different.

Conclusion

John Quincy Adams produced a laudable achievement in the Transcontinental Treaty, and U.S. expansion followed. Years of bickering with Spain over the limits of the Louisiana Purchase were resolved, the United States could claim Florida as its own, and a path to the Pacific was opened in the West. In the coming years, the United States, through war and strong diplomacy, extended its control over Texas and vast swaths of Mexican land in the Southwest. In the more distant future lay the acquisitions of Alaska and Hawaii and the Philippines and Puerto Rico and the kind of global influence that made the United States a superpower. It is tempting to trace these developments back to the early nineteenth century, linking one event to another. Yet, looking too far ahead risks missing the context in which U.S. foreign relations developed. Secretary Adams was not so much making a policy for the ages but solving a particular, if long-standing and vital, problem in the 1810s. In this way, a focus on the international context of the period recaptures the flow of decisions as they were made. Napoleon, Spanish American juntas, King Fernando, and U.S. policy makers all played a role, creating new challenges, responding to old threats, and creating the geopolitical backdrop against which Spanish American privateers would sail from the United States.

2 / New Orleans and Barataria

On September 3, 1814, the Royal Navy sloop *Sophie* dropped anchor off Louisiana and Captain Nicholas Lockyer set out in the ship's boat with a packet of letters addressed to "Monsieur Lafite—or the Commandant at Barataria." In preparing to assault America's Gulf Coast, Britain's naval brass hoped to undermine U.S. defenses by forging alliances with anyone thought restive under American rule, such as Indians, runaway slaves, and Spanish and French nationals. "The whole country," argued one officer, "is ripe for a change and longing anxiously to rid themselves of the Americans." Jean Laffite, his half brother Pierre, and their associates were just the kind of men Britain hoped to enlist. From their headquarters in Barataria, a region below New Orleans along the Louisiana coast, the Laffites had built a robust smuggling and privateering business that brought them work with French and South American privateers, outfitting their vessels and smuggling the goods and slaves they captured into the city or onto plantations nearby. British intelligence officers believed they "would cheerfully assist in any operation against the Americans if afterwards protected by Great Britain."[1]

Approaching the shore, Lockyer was met by Jean Laffite, coming out in a boat of his own. In his early to mid-thirties, Jean was tall, over six feet according to some, and had dark-brown hair, brown eyes, and sideburns that came down to his chin. Jean had grown up in Pauillac, France, a small town near Bordeaux. Pierre, older by about twelve years, stood about five foot ten, with light-brown hair, dark eyes, and a fair complexion. A stroke suffered in 1810 impaired his health and left him, according to one description, "some what cross eyed." The brothers typically split their business duties with Jean operating in the field at Barataria and Pierre managing their affairs in New Orleans.[2]

After landing, Lockyer was handled roughly, "receiving much personal insult and my life threatened," as he later wrote. Nevertheless, Lockyer delivered the letters and asked for the Baratarians' assistance. Much confusion has arisen over what happened next. Just what the British offered has been obscured both by legend—a thirty-thousand-dollar bribe Jean is said to have ignored is suspiciously high—and by the fact that Jean received multiple letters, each vaguely worded and containing different promises. However, this much is certain: the British offered grants of lands in America following their victory; a commission for Jean as a captain in the British service (most likely in the Colonial Marines); and protection from the Americans. The next day, Jean responded positively (not that he had much choice: the letters also threatened to destroy the Baratarians if he refused). Jean wrote Captain Lockyer, now back aboard the *Sophie*, agreeing to his terms and claiming to look forward to "the reward of the services which I may render you." Then Jean betrayed his new allies to their enemy, the United States.[3]

Captain Lockyer's appearance promised to help Jean solve a problem. Pierre was in jail, arrested for failing to appear in court on a bail warrant related to smuggling violations. A grand jury had also begun handing down indictments against Pierre on piracy charges. The information about British plans could be traded to secure his freedom. That same day, September 4, Jean wrote Jean Blanque, a New Orleans merchant, state legislator, sometime slave dealer, and recipient of smuggled prize goods, asking him to take the British letters to the Americans and begin working on Pierre's release. As it turned out, Pierre had plans of his own. Unbeknownst to Jean, someone entered the jail that very night and let Pierre out, and he then made his way through the bayous and swamps of Louisiana's backcountry to join his brother at Barataria. With Pierre already free, Jean attempted to strike a new bargain, and on September 7 he again contacted Blanque. The Baratarians would defend their ground against the British invasion described in the letters. In return, Jean asked authorities to back down and stop "the proscriptions against me and my adherents." He wanted only to be a good citizen again, he said. In a letter to Louisiana governor William C. C. Claiborne, Jean professed contrition: "I am the stray sheep, wishing to return to the sheepfold."[4]

LAFITTE.

FIGURE 2. Jean Laffite. An artist's imagining of the notorious smuggler. (From Henry S. Thrall, *A Pictorial History of Texas from the Earliest Visits of European Adventurers, to A.D. 1883* [1883].)

New Orleans was not heaven, so there was little rejoicing about the penitent's return. Governor Claiborne had long been alarmed by the Laffites' trade in illicit goods. In 1813, he condemned the smugglers in a proclamation and promised a five-hundred-dollar reward for anyone who brought Jean Laffite to justice. However, Jean responded mischievously by posting a one-thousand-dollar reward for Claiborne. The commander of the U.S. Navy's New Orleans station, Daniel Todd Patterson, was no more impressed. Since August he had been planning to raid Barataria, destroy the smugglers, and secure the coast against invasion. The raid went forward in spite of Jean's offer, and on September 16, the navy broke up the smugglers' lair and arrested many Baratarians, although the Laffites eluded capture.[5]

Jean and Pierre were now caught between British and American military ambitions with their base destroyed and many of their associates in jail. Yet, the Laffites had an uncanny ability to maneuver geopolitical tensions to their advantage, and although their latest move had not worked, they kept trying. Deciding that their best bet at the moment lay with America, they renewed their offer to defend Barataria.

By mid-December the British had landed on Louisiana soil, and with their forces expected to outnumber the Americans by thousands, local officials became convinced they would need every last man to defend the city. They now took Jean's offer seriously and tried to make the Baratarians' legal troubles go away. Every level of government soon fell in line. Even General Andrew Jackson, who had once called the Baratarians "hellish banditti," came around when he learned the Laffites had a cache of musket flints, needed to fire the weapons, of which he was then in short supply.[6]

And so it came to pass that the Laffite brothers and the Baratarians fought at the Battle of New Orleans. Numbering between fifty and one hundred of the five thousand men Jackson commanded, they made a small but not unimportant contribution to the American victory. Jean likely served as a messenger and guide. Pierre helped reinforce the American line's left side. Other Baratarians manned artillery positions along the river or served aboard the U.S. sloop *Louisiana*. Following the battle, President James Madison pardoned Jean, Pierre, and their associates. "They have abandoned the prosecution of the worse cause for the support of the best," Madison wrote, and "exhibited in the defense of New Orleans unequivocal traits of courage and fidelity."[7]

This is usually where the Laffites' story ends. They were the pirate-smugglers who set aside their criminal ways, spurned a British bribe, and threw their lot in with America, helping to win the Battle of New Orleans and ending more than two decades of hostility from the new nation's old foe. Yet fighting at New Orleans was only the latest—and not the last—of the Laffites' intrigues. By the time the British came calling, Jean and Pierre were well-versed in exploiting the conflicts of their day. They were also old hands at finding the weakness in U.S. customs, slave trade, and neutrality laws so they could help French and Spanish American privateers violate U.S. neutrality to smuggle goods and slaves. In only a few years, the Laffites had transformed themselves from small-time merchants hustling a living on the margins of commercial society to important players in the geopolitics and law of one of the nation's most important—and most vulnerable—regions.[8]

Smuggling into Louisiana

In the winter of 1805–6, Pierre Laffite left New Orleans to buy slaves in Baton Rouge, located seventy-five miles up the Mississippi in Spanish West Florida, where the foreign slave trade was legal, unlike in Louisiana. Pierre had arrived in New Orleans in 1803, most likely from the Caribbean after growing up in France, and suffered setbacks in his first attempts to build a merchant business in the Crescent City. His latest venture was more successful. Pierre bought eleven slaves on his trip, and once back in New Orleans he sold them for five thousand dollars. The next year, he was at it again, buying slaves in Pensacola and also in Spanish West Florida. Its slave market was brisk—so brisk, in fact, that Pierre sold a slave he had rented in New Orleans for the trip in the hope that the slave's owner would approve of his initiative. The owner did not approve, however, and a lawsuit ensued. Nevertheless, Pierre had discovered his talent for smuggling, the work that suited him best.[9]

Smuggling thrived in early-nineteenth-century Louisiana. Like any business, it required a market, and Louisiana had a vibrant economy fueled by cotton planting in the arid upcountry, sugar cultivation in the wetlands of the low country, and river trade through New Orleans, where farm produce from as far away as Pennsylvania was sent out to the world. The region's population surged to more than seventeen thousand in the first decade of the nineteenth century. The Louisiana Purchase lured Americans westward, and the revolution in Haiti drove thousands northward to Louisiana's shores. In the 1810 federal census, New Orleans was the seventh-largest city in America.[10]

Smuggling, however, is a special kind of business that does not exist without laws that restrict buyers' access to the goods (and in the case of Louisiana, slaves) they want at prices they are willing to pay. The international conditions of the early-nineteenth-century Atlantic world ensured numerous commercial restrictions as the United States, Britain, and France passed laws targeting each other's trade, such as Britain's Orders in Council, France's Berlin and Milan Decrees, and the United States' embargo and nonimportation laws. Meanwhile, U.S. slave trade policy, culminating in the abolition of the foreign slave trade in 1808, forced the supply of slave labor far below what planters in the region wanted. As one planter wrote in protest of an 1804 law restricting the trade into Louisiana, without slavery the territory would become "a vast swamp unfit for any creatures outside of fishes, reptiles, and insects."[11]

Louisiana's geography, both political and natural, made smuggling easy. Sandwiched between Spanish territory to the east and west, New Orleans and its environs were a smugglers' paradise. Anyone who wanted access to a foreign nation's laws could have it without much trouble, as Pierre had discovered. Lower Louisiana was a vast network of marshes, swamps, little lakes, tiny bays, and bayous that flowed between the Mississippi River and the Gulf of Mexico. It was easy to get lost among all the twists and turns, but with a boat and local know-how, smugglers never had a problem getting where they wanted to go.[12]

Jean joined his brother in New Orleans sometime in 1809. Though conditions inside Louisiana were ripe for smuggling, supply problems remained. By 1810, the Laffites had found a regular source of goods and slaves: the French privateers rendered homeless in the Caribbean when Britain conquered France's last West Indian possession, the island of Guadeloupe. Once their business was up and running, the Laffites easily transitioned from servicing French privateers to servicing privateers from Cartagena, which began turning up in Louisiana once the city declared its independence. As time went on, privateers from Mexico and Venezuela followed.[13]

Practical considerations and the progress of the wars led foreign privateers to sell their cargoes in Louisiana rather than in their own countries' ports. For the French privateers, sailing to France was out of the question. On the trip home they might run out of food and water or run into storms, the British navy, or even pirates. Distance was less of an issue for Spanish American vessels, and some privateers sailed to their own ports to have prizes condemned and sold. Yet with war raging all around them, these ports were often unstable and offered poor markets (the threat of military conquest tending to sour the demand for European luxury goods). Furthermore, Louisiana was a more profitable destination for slave traders. Warfare in Spanish America disrupted the local economies, and revolutionary governments had outlawed the slave trade, including Mexico in 1810, Venezuela in 1811, and Cartagena in 1812. The laws were flouted, and effective abolition of the slave trade often arrived only once independence was secure, but if privateers were smuggling slaves anyway, then they might as well visit Louisiana, where an expanding planter class hungered for slave labor.[14]

One nation at war whose privateers should have streamed in and out of Louisiana rarely did: the United States commissioned just six vessels there during the War of 1812. It is not clear why since U.S. privateers would have received legal title to their prizes. Perhaps the fees and duties assessed on prizes were too expensive. Perhaps regulation of privateers, such as the requirement that captains be U.S. citizens, was too burdensome. Perhaps smuggling was too attractive. In one instance, a U.S. privateer smuggled a legally captured prize through Barataria, subjecting the cargo to seizure, much to the dismay of the vessel's owner.[15]

With suppliers found and buyers waiting, the Laffites' prospects looked bright, and as for any business, location was vital to their success. What Barataria lacked in ambience it made up in smuggling convenience. Most often, the Laffites worked from four locations inside the region. (To contemporaries, Barataria was the entire area south of the Mississippi River and west to the Bayou Lafourche or even farther to Terrebonne Bay.) The most important was Grand Terre, which was also sometimes called Barataria Island. An oversized sand dune with a mangrove swamp on its north end, Grand Terre lay close to the water, with no point more than five feet above sea level. Aside from a few groves of oak trees, there was no shelter. Even so, smugglers apparently lived there for long stretches. The Laffites' second-favorite locale, Grand Isle, lay nearby across a narrow pass from Grand Terre. Though providing no better living conditions, Grand Isle combined with Grand Terre to form a barrier between the gulf and Bayou Barataria, the gateway to New Orleans and points nearby. Ships might approach either island, but the pass was narrow and shallow and kept the smugglers safe from assault by sea.[16]

The Laffites also favored a chênière—a mass of sand, shells, and decaying trees common in the bayous—called the Temple and located north of Grand Terre and Grand Isle at the confluence of Bayou Perot, Bayou Rigolets, and Little Lake Barataria. Closer to New Orleans, it offered buyers greater convenience. Finally, the Laffites and their fellow

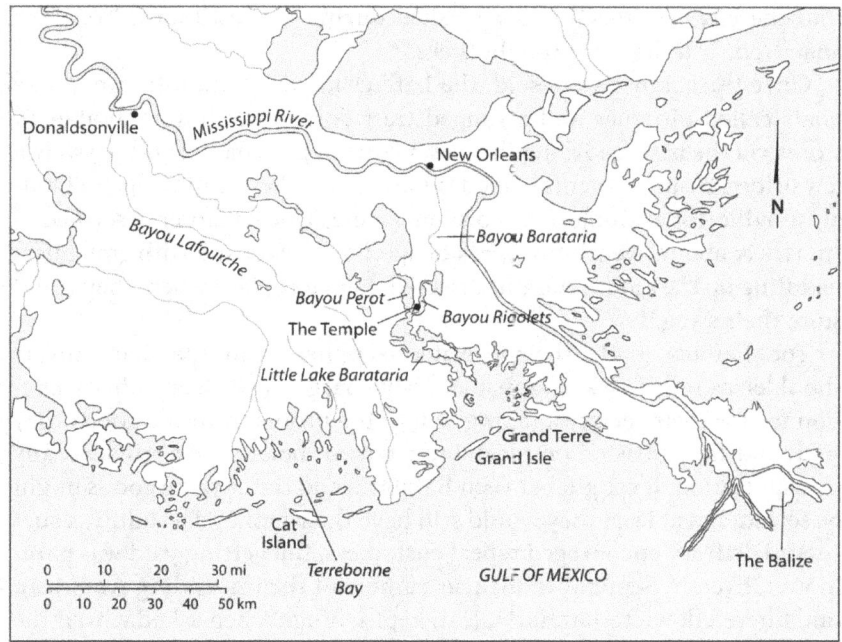

MAP 2. The Laffites' Louisiana

smugglers resorted to Cat Island, a location farther west down the coast and situated near the Bayou Lafourche, which provided access deep into the Louisiana backcountry and a connection to the Mississippi at Donaldsonville, sixty miles above New Orleans and an easy float past numerous sugar plantations.[17]

Setting up in Barataria, Jean and Pierre dealt openly in prize goods and slaves and established a business model that depended on quick transactions. When a prize hove in sight, the Laffites summoned buyers to their depots and the selling commenced. John Oliver, a sailor aboard the Cartagenan privateer *La Misere*, observed a flourishing prize goods trade at Barataria. "Privateers frequently arrived there from Carthagena with vessels they had captured," he later testified, "the cargoes of which were landed & sold." Sometimes, the Laffites did not wait to unload a cargo before selling it. A sailor from a captured Spanish vessel recounted that "they made a vendue of [the vessel's] cargo, which was bought by persons coming from N. Orleans, the goods being sold bale by bale on the Deck." No one had any illusions about where the goods came from. "Were not the goods landed there with the view of smuggling them into the city?" John Oliver was asked during his testimony. "Yes!" he answered. "All that are brought there."[18]

Once the cargoes were sold, the Laffites loaded them into canoe-like boats called pirogues and arranged transport to the buyers' homes or stores via the bayous. Along the way, planters, merchants, and possibly a few bribed customs agents helped them conceal their shipments. In Donaldsonville, for example, Francois Mayronne, a local planter described as "portly & about twenty-five years of age," rendezvoused with smugglers paddling up the Lafourche and directed them to a place where they could store their swag.[19]

The Laffites made their privateer-suppliers and merchant-buyers shoulder as much risk as possible. They charged privateers a hefty auction fee for their services, taking half of the profits from the goods they sold, and they insisted on receiving payment before they provided any transportation. If caught between Barataria and the city, the goods might be seized, but at least they would still have their money. Certainly, a successful delivery encouraged repeat customers. But getting paid was paramount. Even in September 1814, as rumors of the impending American raid filtered down to Barataria, Jean kept selling. When asked why, if the privateers and smugglers knew trouble was coming, they did not simply pack up their goods and sail away, John Oliver swore that Jean wanted to sell everything while he could. According to Oliver, Jean "expected to have been able to sell them [the goods] off there, leaving people there buying." As soon as he had the money, Jean planned to make a quick escape. The buyers were on their own.[20]

Privateers hoping to sell slaves in Louisiana followed the same basic strategy as those selling goods. They landed at Barataria, sold the slaves on the spot, and received help from others—most often the Laffites—to transport the bondsmen to their new owners' homes. In one instance, a group of French privateers landed 113 slaves on Cat Island. The slaves had been taken from the Spanish brig *Bolador* off the Florida Keys while the vessel was bound to Pensacola from Africa. In another instance, a different group of French privateers brought four prizes into Barataria with ninety-one slaves and sold them for an estimated five thousand doallars. Similarly, the Cartagenan privateer *Le Legislateur* brought 570 slaves into Louisiana from the slave ship *Santa Rosalia*.[21]

For the Laffites, a quick transaction was again essential. When a privateer arrived with the Spanish slaver *Dorada*, they immediately sold the vessel's seventy-seven slaves to Joseph Sauvinet, a New Orleans merchant and privateer owner, for $170 each, or thirteen thousand dollars

TABLE 1. Slave landings by privateers operating from Louisiana, 1810–1815

Year	Vessel	Number of slaves	Outcome
1810	*Alerta*	170	14–17 sold at sea, 153 seized by U.S.
1810	*Bolador*	113	Landed in Louisiana
1810	*Massavito*	105	Landed in Louisiana
1810	*Duc de Montebello*	3	Seized by U.S.
1811	Four prizes to French privateer	91	Landed in Louisiana
1811	*La Sirena*	—	Seized by U.S.
1813	*Santa Rosalia*	570	Landed in Louisiana
1813	*Dorada*	77	Landed in U.S.
1813	Captured by *Felix*	7–8	—

SOURCES: *U.S.* v. *The Ship* Alerta, LA Fed. Ct., case no. 379; *Blas Moran* v. *The Schooner* Alerta, LA Fed. Ct., case no. 380; *William Allen* v. *The Ship* Alerta *and Cargo of Slaves*, LA Fed. Ct., case no. 381. *Voyages Database* no. 41572; *Vincent Dorgoigoite* v. *Michel Bruard*, LA Fed. Ct., case no. 390; *P. N. Paillet* v. *Caudole*, LA Fed. Ct., case no. 392; *P.N. Paillet* v. *Cadet Bayonne*, LA Fed. Ct., case no. 393; *P. N. Paillet* v. *Bonal*, LA Fed. Ct., case no. 394; *P. N. Paillet* v. *Coulon*, LA Fed. Ct., case no. 395; *William Carter* (qui tam) v. *Louis Aury*, LA Fed. Ct., case no. 376; *U.S.* v. *The* Guillaume, LA Fed. Ct., case no. 377; *U.S.* v. *The Duc de Montebello*, LA Fed. Ct., case no. 363; *Pedro de Reano and Others* v. *Pierre Liquet and Certain Negro Slaves*, LA Fed. Ct., case no. 949; *Diego Francisco Unzaga* .v *The Schooner* Dorada, LA Fed. Ct., case no. 763; *Francisco Graw* v. *The Spanish Polacre* San Francisco de Paula *and Robert de Bray, Commander of the Schooner* Felix, LA Fed. Ct., case no. 505; Davis, *Pirates Laffite*, 75.

altogether. By selling all the slaves for one price, the Laffites took no account of differences in age, sex, and health that could significantly alter a slave's value. Still, it allowed them to maximize volume and make money quickly. From the end of 1809 through the first half of 1812, the Laffites sold an estimated 142 slaves for a sum close to fifty thousand dollars. And their business was growing. In January 1814, the Laffites sold 415 slaves at once, their largest single auction.[22]

New Orleans grew as the great depot of the West, the place that received produce from faraway farms and sent it out to the world. Thanks to the privateers and smugglers, Barataria was becoming the reverse: the place that received goods and slaves from as far away as Africa and sent them into Louisiana. "Smuggling is carried on to a great degree," one

Louisiana lawyer observed. "Fortunes have been made in a few months, and European goods are frequently cheaper than before the Embargo." In February 1814, Customs Inspector Walker Gilbert reported that smugglers had "secured far more than a million of dollars with this last six months." Smuggling reached that volume because, as John Oliver testified, privateers "were in the daily habit of selling" their wares at Barataria. When the Laffites held an auction, the otherwise deserted region saw its population swell to some three hundred to four hundred men with the sailors, smugglers, and buyers gathered there. Gilbert had it on good authority that "eighty to one hundred persons of New Orleans attend them regularly." The sale of prize cargoes produced a stream of pirogues heading north for New Orleans or Donaldsonville. John Foley, a planter on the Lafourche, found the traffic unsettling. "The quantity of goods which passed by my House during the High Water is incredible," he wrote. "Day and night continually passed Pirogues."[23]

The smuggling conducted through Barataria was surprisingly open for an illegal activity. According to military engineer and author Arsène Latour, people from all over lower Louisiana "resorted to Barataria, without being at all solicitous to conceal the object of their journey." Contraband buyers were no more secretive about their business while in the city, Latour contended, for "in the streets of New Orleans, it was usual for traders to give and receive orders for purchasing goods at Barataria, with as little secrecy as similar orders are given for Philadelphia or New York." Latour indulged his poetic license. The trade in prize goods was still illegal, and if a shipment were intercepted, it would have been seized, unlike a lawful shipment arriving from Philadelphia or New York.[24]

Nevertheless, officials were scandalized by the public's enthusiasm for contraband. Even their peers, the state's leading citizens, were involved. "What depravity!" exclaimed Customs Inspector Gilbert, "citizens hitherto of undoubted integrity and first respectability, uniting with a piratical band and sharing with them in their ill gotten booty." The market for illegal goods had grown so out of hand that in 1813 Governor Claiborne issued an official proclamation urging Louisianans to shun the "ill begotten treasure [of which] no Man can partake, without being forever dishonored, and exposing himself to the severest punishments."[25]

Defying the law to deliver goods and slaves to Louisiana's coast worked well for some privateers. It was quick, efficient, and profitable thanks in no small part to the Laffites. Other privateers took a different approach and attempted to enter New Orleans itself, not so much by avoiding the law as by using the law's weaknesses to their advantage. The biggest loophole available to privateers was an exemption to port-entry regulations granted to vessels in distress. U.S. law permitted neutral foreign vessels to enter port to receive shelter from storms, to replenish low food or water, to make repairs, and to escape enemies. Thus, even privateers and slavers had a legitimate reason to enter Louisiana waters, though, of course, that legitimacy could be stretched to cover illegal conduct, too.[26]

The French privateer *Petite-Chance*, for example, caused a stir in New Orleans when it arrived in the spring of 1810. The vessel looked suspicious from the start. According to one rumor, a hole in the vessel's hull appeared a little too new and little too neat to have come from the natural wear and tear of a cruise. More officially, the port warden who inspected the vessel did not like the look of its sails, reporting that they "had suffered greatly by having been shut up in the hold" rather than being out in the wind. As a result, he said, they were "in danger of perishing by mildew."[27]

Standard practice allowed captains of distressed vessels to pay for repairs or fresh provisions by selling part of their ship's cargo. To make sure they did not sell more goods than authorized, customs agents required an inventory of the ship's cargo on entering port, which they would match against the ship's cargo on leaving. Despite these measures, privateers still found loopholes. In one incident, Dominique Youx, captain of the French privateer *Pandoure*, short-circuited the process by arriving in port but never leaving. Entering New Orleans in August 1812, Youx asked for refuge since his vessel had lost a mast. Youx presented customs with the required paperwork, detailing the seven prizes he had taken, the cargoes captured from each, and the arms his vessel carried. Then Youx sold it all—vessel and cargo together—and walked away with the proceeds. Since he never departed port, there was no outgoing inventory with which to catch him.[28]

Claiming distress also appealed to privateers with slaves. In an 1810 case, a Portuguese slave ship captured by the French privateer Louis-Michel Aury entered Louisiana by claiming distress. The prize vessel, called the *Massavito*, entered the Mississippi in need of provisions but stayed in the lower river near the Balize, an outpost on the river's mouth where pilots waited to guide ships to the city. Once resupplied, the *Massavito* left the river and hopped west to Barataria, where the vessel's master landed 105 slaves and sold them to a slave dealer for seventeen thousand dollars. The slaves were then moved up the Lafourche to Donaldsonville, from where it was an easy passage down the Mississippi.[29]

Another French privateersman, Marcelin Battigne, ordered a prize slaver all the way up to New Orleans while claiming distress, apparently unconcerned that its slaves would be seized. In June 1810, Battigne's *L' Epine* captured the Spanish slave ship *Alerta* off Cuba with 170 slaves. According to one Spanish sailor, Battigne took off "fifteen of the finest looking negro boys," whom he later sold at sea to an American captain. The rest were sent aboard the *Alerta* for Louisiana, most likely with orders to enter the river claiming to need repairs. Since testimony is contradictory, the vessel's condition is uncertain. At one point, the pilot who guided the *Alerta* into the Mississippi swore he found the vessel "in a situation the most wretched and deplorable, liable to be wrecked with the first breath of wind," with the crew and slaves "all endeavouring to pick up a miserable and precarious subsistence by catching pelicans for their food." At another time, he indicated the crew were killing birds and salting them, perhaps for amusement more than anything else. Whatever the case, Battigne sent instructions for the *Alerta* to send the slaves to a Mr. Michel in the city for safekeeping until he could arrive to claim them as his property and transport them out of the city, almost certainly to smuggle them somewhere else. Battigne underestimated the vigilance of authorities, however, and U.S. agents seized the slaves before he could leave.[30]

Jean and Pierre rarely went through the trouble of finding loopholes. Firmly established at Barataria, they could avoid the law altogether—except when they wanted to use the law for their own purposes. In the summer of 1810, Pierre went to work for the sheriff of Ascension Parish tracking down the *Bolador* slaves, who had been smuggled into Donaldsonville. Working with local authorities as well as the *Bolador*'s captain, Pierre recovered at least four slaves and served a writ from the court on one of the buyers. Why did Pierre work for the sheriff? He may have hoped to receive a portion of the fines assessed for violating the slave trade act, which the government split with whomever helped seize illegal slaves (the *Bolador*'s captain sued for his share of nearly ninety thousand dollars). Yet, turning customers over to authorities would not be good for future business. It seems more likely that the move was payback. The *Bolador*'s captors bypassed the Laffites' operation and smuggled the slaves up the Lafourche on their own. By volunteering to use their knowledge of slave smuggling to punish a rival, Jean and Pierre sent a message to other privateers: deal with us or you will regret it.[31]

Fitting Out for a Gulf Coast Cruise

In 1812, Jean and Pierre expanded their business and became ship owners as well as smugglers. They bought a schooner, whose name is not known, and the French privateer *Diligent*. In January 1813, they put another privateer into service when they converted the Spanish slave ship *Dorada*, the vessel from which they took the seventy-seven slaves they sold to Joseph Sauvinet, into a vessel of war. At sixty-nine tons and mounting eight guns, the *Dorada* was small but productive. Under three captains hired by the Laffites—Pierre Cadet, Louis Fougard, and a man named Gianni—the *Dorada* completed at least three cruises in the first half of the year, sailing around Cuba and off the Spanish-held ports of Vera Cruz, Campeche, and Tampico. A stream of prizes arrived in Barataria, and the Laffites continued adding vessels to their fleet. The Spanish schooner *Louis Antonio* became the *Petit Milan*, commanded by Italian sea captain Vincent Gambi. Later, another Spanish schooner, name unknown, became the *Sarpi*, commanded by Laurent Maire, also an Italian. (New Orleans had a sizable Italian population of seafarers and laborers; in fact, some of the original European settlers were Italians.)[32]

Since fitting out vessels for others was already part of their business, Jean and Pierre easily moved into owning privateers as well. All ships entered port periodically not only to sell their captured cargoes but also to prepare their ship for its next cruise: caulking gaps between planks, mending sails, replacing frayed ropes, and shipping new hands to replace sailors lost at sea as well as sailors who preferred to retire from the sea and spend their prize money ashore. The same routes that led into the city also led out of it, of course, and so the same pirogues the Laffites sent up to New Orleans with contraband returned with fresh provisions, new sailors, and more arms.

But there was a catch to fitting out in Louisiana, especially if privateers hoped to take on new arms and munitions or to recruit new sailors. Though foreign privateers were allowed to repair damages and replenish provisions, U.S. neutrality law prohibited foreign armed vessels from increasing their "warlike equipments"—that is, their firepower or manpower—while in U.S. territory. No one was permitted to equip a foreign armed vessel in America with the intent to attack a nation at peace with the United States. There was one exception: a foreign privateer could sign aboard sailors from its own nation who happened to be in port between jobs, as long as they did not reside in the United States; the reasoning apparently was that sailors should be allowed to return home rather than accrue debts in a foreign port. Nevertheless, enterprising men devised ways around the law.[33]

The simplest method to evade the law was to fit out at Barataria. Equipping in a swamp often worked because most Gulf Coast privateers were relatively small and lightly armed: fore-and-aft rigged vessels, such as schooners, of less than one hundred tons. Mounting a single gun, they carried between thirty and seventy men. Occasionally, a privateer might be nothing more than an open boat with five or six tough-looking men brandishing guns and swords.

Details of equipping are murky, but several sailors testified that they were hired in the city and transported down the bayous to join a vessel at the coast. For example, sailor Andrew Whiteman was in New Orleans when, he said, he was approached by "an Italian to go in a French privateer." The Italian, Captain Gianni, commanded a vessel for the Laffites. Meeting at Gianni's home, Whiteman received a ten-dollar advance, and before long he boarded a boat with other men recruited in the city, traveled up the Mississippi to Donaldsonville, and then down the Lafourche to Grand Isle, where his vessel was waiting. Similarly, John Connel swore that he was hired in the city by "Lafite, the larger of the two brothers of that name"—meaning Jean. The big Laffite then accompanied his new employee in a pirogue to the coast. In another case, the Laffites hired a baker to come down from the city to help victual the *Diligent*. Recruiting in the city was not always necessary. Some sailors and vendors were evidently drawn to Barataria by word of mouth alone. William Hoey, a "seaman by profession," headed down the coast looking for a ship. On the way, he ran into some men from Kentucky hoping to sell provisions to the privateers. Hoey found a berth, and the Kentuckians, having sold all their wares, decided to sign up for a cruise, too.[34]

Barataria did not work for everyone, however. It was the Laffites' domain, and although they could be helpful, anyone who did not want to do things their way would not be welcomed. The captors of the *Bolador* learned this lesson the hard way. Moreover, some privateers needed services Jean and Pierre could not provide. Vessels in need of extensive repairs—and the services of a real shipwright, an experienced carpenter, or a skilled rigger—forced captains to run the extra risk and enter New Orleans. Still, the law and local geography were on their side.

The distress exemption—the privateer's old friend—allowed some captains to use their legal conduct of arranging repairs to conceal their shadier dealings. For example, Marcelin Battigne, captain of *L' Epine*, received permission to sell part of his prize goods to pay for repairs. He also received permission to use the money to help defray his legal bills since he faced a piracy charge as a result of his harassment of an American vessel on a previous cruise. Acquitted, Battigne did not learn much from the experience. He shipped additional hands in the city before leaving port and then captured the slave ship *Alerta* with his augmented crew.[35]

NEW ORLEANS AND BARATARIA / 53

Privateers found another ally in the river itself. Departing vessels were inspected in the city, where customs agents issued clearance papers and marked a vessel as having officially left port. New Orleans was 120 miles upriver from the gulf, and the route was mostly deserted. As a traveler ascending the river remarked, between the city and the gulf there was only swampland cluttered with rotting trees and "enormous, shifty-eyed alligators."[36]

With only the alligators watching, privateers did as they pleased. As Customs Collector Beverly Chew testified, privateers "sometimes lay several days in Port after they are cleared out & during which time they have an opportunity of increasing their number of hands." Furthermore, he admitted, "it is easy to send men down the river to the vessels when going out." The customs service did operate another checkpoint on the river's mouth at the Balize. Yet, agents there inspected only incoming vessels. Since the customs service was tasked chiefly with collecting duties on imports, it did not have the manpower to check outgoing vessels a second time. Requiring a second inspection would not have done much good, anyway. At its very end, the river splits into four passes. The customs house was located on the south pass, the most popular route into and out of the river. But any of the other passes worked just as well. Captains with something to hide could reach the gulf without sailing past any authorities. Between the city's location, the river's deserted course, and its multiple exits, privateers held the upper hand once they cleared port. "In defiance of every vigilance," Chew complained, "they violate the law, not whilst they remain in port, but before they leave our waters."[37]

This approach worked especially well when combined with a claim of distress. For example, the Venezuelan privateer *La Guerriere* entered New Orleans in June 1817, underwent repairs without incident, and then cleared customs in September. However, the *Guerriere* stayed in the Lower Mississippi for another six weeks and did not actually reach the gulf until November. The vessel spent more than one-third of its time in Louisiana unsupervised in the lower river.[38]

The Laffites preferred to fit their vessels out at Barataria, since they liked to stay as far from authorities as possible. But when they did use the city, their efforts were unmatched for their sophistication. In one incident in February 1813, Jean sailed the *Diligent* to the Balize with a cargo of prize goods, but rather than trying to get past the agents on his own, he enlisted the help of the French consul in New Orleans. Writing the consul from the coast, Jean represented himself as the unfortunate captain of a

French privateer suffering from the prejudice that U.S. officials harbored toward French vessels. Jean said he needed help entering New Orleans for repairs and paying his crew, who were supposedly growing restless after a long cruise. Jean also wanted an extension for the commission he had obtained from the vessel's previous owner. The consul was Jean Baptiste Laporte, a New Orleans merchant temporarily occupying the post, and considering his later role as agent for several Spanish American privateers, he was predictably accommodating. Laporte leaned on U.S. officials to allow the *Diligent* to enter port, he secured a line of credit for Jean to pay the crew, and he extended Jean's commission for another month. With entry approved, Jean left the vessel and returned to Barataria. Pierre, who was already in the city, took Laporte's agent aboard the vessel, and as one sailor remembered, the agent "encouraged those on board." Though U.S. officials were wary, the French consul's collaboration gave the Laffites cover. The *Diligent* left port safely with the Laffites' man, Captain Gianni, at the helm.[39]

Enforcing the Law

The Laffites inevitably lost a cargo from time to time, and when they did, Jean and Pierre did not yield without a fight. In October 1813, customs agents intercepted one of the Laffites' shipments near Donaldsonville, sending the Laffites' men splashing through the river in flight. The next day, the smugglers met Jean, who was staying with an associate, and reported what happened. Later a man rode up from Donaldsonville with a message: a customs boat with the seized goods would be descending the river that night. According to one of the smugglers, Jean then "proposed that they should join and take her," since "but one man on board her was to be feared." Jean rushed to prepare a trap of his own.[40]

As it turned out, he need not have hurried, since the anticipated boat did not pass by until two days later. When the customs boat approached, Jean was ready. Three of Jean's men rowed into the river. They boarded the customs boat and "demanded the goods as Mr. Laffites." Then the shooting started. A man on each side was wounded. During the confusion, the boat drifted close to shore, allowing Jean and some others to leap aboard, seize control, and reclaim the goods. After landing the boat, Jean left to find a doctor (he hardly needed the murder of a federal agent on his hands), while the goods were unloaded. By the next day Jean had returned and another auction had begun. The smugglers won again, after all.

Stopping the smugglers and privateers of Barataria was much more difficult than investigating crime and prosecuting the offenders. It was sometimes armed warfare, and most of the time, the United States was on the losing side. The legend of the Laffites has it that no one could stop them because just about everyone in Louisiana supported them. They were lovable rogues who served the easygoing people of New Orleans and were sheltered from the law in return. There is a grain of truth to this—but only a grain. Although Louisiana consumers and planters were happy to buy goods and slaves at favorable prices, a combination of logistic, political, and geopolitical factors favored privateers and smugglers and thwarted the authorities who tried to crack down on them.[41]

The customs service and the navy had the chief responsibility for enforcing the law, although both were periodically reinforced by the army, which also posted a force in New Orleans. Most of the time, customs agents either worked in the city, where they inspected outgoing vessels, or at the Balize, where they examined incoming ones. As smuggling escalated, agents were dispatched into the bayous and along the river, especially to Donaldsonville to intercept shipments from the Lafourche. The customs service also operated a revenue cutter, a small craft that policed the river and the coast just outside it. Meanwhile, the navy maintained several hundred men at its station in the city. Most of its vessels were gunboats, shallow-draft vessels with one or two masts (though they could also be rowed), one or two long guns, and a crew of up to forty. Designated by number rather than name—*Gunboat No. 156*, for example—the vessels were designed for the coastal defense role favored by Republican politicians anxious to keep defense spending down rather than the blue-water cruising favored by naval strategists. Together, customs and the navy scored a number of important victories, and the dozens of criminal and civil cases heard in the Louisiana federal court often arose from the success of these services. Such victories, however, were the exception rather than the rule. Privateers and smugglers thrived despite the occasional seizure or arrest.[42]

Sympathy for smugglers and privateers was one factor, and the Laffite legend is not wrong in pointing out the widespread support they enjoyed. Public officials complained about it all the time. "A Sympathy for these offenders is certainly more or less felt by *many of the Louisianans*," Governor Claiborne moaned. "I have been at great pains to convince the people of this state that Smuggling was a moral offense; but in this I have only partially succeeded." Treasury Secretary William Jones was dubious about the customs service's prospects for success. "Whilst the inhabitants of Louisiana continue to countenance this illegal commerce and the courts of justice forbear to enforce the laws against the offenders," he wrote, "little or no benefit can be expected to result from the best concerted efforts." Secretary of the Navy Paul Hamilton likewise doubted the law could be enforced in Louisiana. In 1810, he advised naval commanders to send captured vessels to Savannah or Charleston, where the navy was more likely to obtain a condemnation—and prize money—than in New Orleans.[43]

No one was more infuriated by the public's sympathy for smugglers than Master Commandant David Porter, commander of the navy's New Orleans station from 1808 to 1810. According to Porter, pressure from the French population made authorities turn a blind eye to the misdeeds of their countrymen. When the federal court's marshal stepped down in 1810, Porter wrote President Madison demanding that he appoint "an American in principle," because, he said, "while the marshall is a Frenchman there will be allways a large majority of Frenchmen on the Juries and a Frenchman can never be convicted however heinous his crimes."[44]

Jones, Hamilton, and Porter made a serious charge: that sympathy for smugglers and privateers had spread so far as to corrupt the judicial system. It is true that criminal prosecutions did not produce convictions. Sixty-six men were indicted for smuggling, slave trading, neutrality violations, or piracy as a result of their involvement with French, Cartagenan, Venezuelan, and Mexican privateers before 1815. Records are not complete, but there is no evidence that a single man was convicted. Of any charge. At any time.[45]

Still, the lack of convictions alone does not prove that sympathy for privateers and smugglers motivated juries. Intent was an essential component of the crimes for which these men were tried. A prosecutor needed to show that defendants knew that what they were doing was wrong. But because privateers observed at least part of the law, they created the appearance that they wanted to follow the law and that their failure to do so was accidental. In only one case was a jury's thinking recorded: the trial of Marcelin Battigne for slave smuggling. (Battigne was captain of the French privateer *L'Epine*, captor of the slave ship *Alerta*.) The jury voted for acquittal because they believed Battigne had violated the law unintentionally when the *Alerta* entered port in distress. The trial of the *Alerta*'s prize master, Francis Brosquet, suggests that something similar was on the minds of the twelve men who judged him, since they at first deadlocked on the verdict. (At a second trial Brosquet was acquitted.) Nevertheless, some Louisiana jurors were willing to convict a Frenchman.[46]

In addition, criminal prosecutions were not the only way the justice system challenged smuggling and privateering. The court also heard dozens of civil actions brought by Spanish merchants seeking to recover their property and by the United States government attempting to seize property used in smuggling or foreign privateering. Unlike criminal cases, civil suits were heard under the court's admiralty jurisdiction according to admiralty rules of procedure. Thus, they were decided not by a jury but by the judge, Dominick Hall.

Twenty-eight civil cases came before Judge Hall's court. Outcomes can be found in twenty-six, and Hall did not take the privateers' or smugglers' side very often. Privateers were able to keep their property— either prizes or armed vessels—five times. Spanish merchants received their property back ten times, either when the court ordered restoration or when the United States gave up its claim to a prize. The United States received five privateer vessels condemned to be sold for the government's benefit.[47]

Several cases produced more complicated decisions. In three cases, the U.S. government and Spanish merchants divided the property in question, with the United States receiving the privateer vessel and the Spanish receiving the prize. In one case, the property was divided among three parties: the prize vessel was restored to the Spanish, the cargo of sugar was divided between the Spanish and the privateers, and salvage (an award due for meritorious service in the preservation of a cargo) was given to the U.S. Navy for rescuing the prize vessel from privateers. Finally, two cases involved Cartagenan captains who harmed other Cartagenans. In the one, the captain ran away with a ship; in the other, the captain robbed his passengers. In both instances, the court ordered a restoration to the privateers' Cartagenan owners. The final results, then, look like this: five privateer victories; twenty losses (including the two Cartagenan versus Cartagenan cases); and one split decision. Privateers, then, won less than 25 percent of the time.

Sympathy for smuggling and privateering existed. It may explain the reluctance of juries to hand down convictions that would have led to a death sentence. But charges that this sympathy made it impossible to obtain justice do not hold up to evidence. Spanish merchants and the U.S. government were likely to come out ahead if they could get to court.

If they could get to court. That was no certainty due to a host of forces beyond officials' control. The logistical challenge of patrolling an area so favorable to smuggling was daunting. The navy and customs service both demanded enormous resources, but neither felt they had even the bare minimum. When Porter arrived in New Orleans, he expected to find a thriving station of four hundred men and fifteen gunboats. He found eight vessels worthy for sea. The navy had ordered many of them from a boatbuilder in Ohio, and either through fraud or the shoddy workmanship of government contracts awarded to the lowest bidder, the vessels were so poorly constructed that they quickly rotted in the steamy southern sun. It was just as well that Porter had so few vessels at his disposal. He could not have manned them all, anyway. Desertion, disease, and death—the Louisiana heat and humidity were an excellent breeding ground for malaria and yellow fever—so depleted the station's ranks that there were only enough men to send four boats on patrol. Over time the number of men and vessels stationed at New Orleans increased, but neither Porter nor his successors were satisfied.[48]

The customs service was no happier with Washington. Collectors regularly pleaded with the Treasury Department to appoint new inspectors, but New Orleans labored under a suspicion of corruption that made it a tough sale. "The appointment even of Inspectors, unless they are proof to the temptation of bribes, so far from operating as a check upon smuggling, will only contribute to diminish the chances of detection," Treasury Secretary William N. Jones believed. Secretary Jones did hire an additional six men in 1813, but he should have listened to his doubts. One of the men appointed, a local judge named Hubbard, actively supported smugglers by loaning them his slaves to help move their goods. Inspector Walker Gilbert denounced Hubbard for having a "friendship to those villains."[49]

Without sufficient resources to combat the lawbreakers, U.S. forces found themselves outgunned. At virtually the same time that Jean was retaking his goods by force on the Mississippi, Pierre was defending another shipment on the Bayou St. Denis. Leading a party of men in pirogues, Pierre came across an army unit out on antismuggling patrol. The sides exchanged gunfire, three soldiers were wounded, and Pierre made his delivery as scheduled. The Laffites were not the only ones to play rough. In January 1814, Customs Inspector John B. Stout was killed by smugglers. Stout had taken a dozen men to occupy the Temple. When he spotted some smugglers and attempted to stop them, a firefight broke out. Stout died, and the rest of his men—including two who were wounded—were taken prisoner by the smugglers.[50]

Such violence weighed heavily on customs agents. Unlike the navy and army, customs was not a fighting service. As historian Herbert Heaton points out, a customs officer's "normal tasks" included "collecting duties, paying drawbacks, punishing men who unloaded cargoes 'between sunset and sunrise,' detecting false entries or untrue invoices, [and] seizing porter which came in casks of less than forty gallons or in crates of less than six dozen bottles." Customs officers were more comfortable handling an invoice than handling a gun; shootouts were not part of their job.[51]

Navy officers and crews were ready to fight, but their morale suffered nonetheless. No one liked gunboats. Considered "dull sailors," the boats maneuvered better when rowed than when under sail, and they would capsize if taken too far out to sea—a humiliation for sailors with salt water in their veins. The gunboats' size made them unusually cramped, and men spent most of their time on deck, where it was more comfortable than the stifling heat and dripping humidity below. On top of it all, gunboat sailors received little financial reward for their efforts. In addition to wages, naval officers and crews hoped to receive prize money won by capturing enemy vessels. Similar to privateers, naval vessels brought captured goods and ships before an admiralty court, and if judged a good prize, everybody aboard split the proceeds. Coastal patrols in small boats offered poor odds for catching a fat merchantman, and as it turned out, intercepting privateers and smugglers, whose business depended on carrying valuables, also offered scant rewards. The navy occasionally received a few thousand dollars in salvage when it recovered Spanish property for its owners, but its more lucrative prize claims were dismissed.[52]

Officers found their duty at New Orleans even more demoralizing. Not only did they suffer the same hardships as their men, but they labored under the unnerving possibility that their efforts would not advance their careers. Officers in the early republic's navy—and indeed in all Age of Sail navies—rose in the ranks by displaying leadership abilities, sailing skills, and the character proper to a gentleman. At New Orleans, officers could not demonstrate any of these qualities. The Department of the Navy looked down on gunboat commanders as inferior seamen, and although arresting pirates, chasing smugglers, and policing privateers may have been necessary, it had no honor in it. They were all the scum of the sea as far as the higher-ups were concerned. Daniel Todd Patterson, station commander from 1812 to 1824, spoke for his brothers-in-arms when he complained that "Officers Serving [here] are exposed to hazard[s] far beyond those of battle without having the evil compensated by any chance of exerting or signalizing themselves in the service of their country." It was, he said, an "inactive, forlorn station."[53]

Sympathy for lawbreakers, insufficient resources, and low morale threw large obstacles in the way of law enforcement. Yet, they were not the only ones. Political factionalism was also important, particularly when it came to suppressing French privateers. The main cleavage in Louisiana politics was between the French and American populations, and at a time not long after the Louisiana Purchase, the loyalty of the French population was still doubted by federal officials. The hostility between the two groups can be exaggerated, especially in light of the mythology of Creole-American antagonism that developed in Louisiana over the nineteenth century in which Creoles were imagined to be the white descendents of the land's original French and Spanish settlers, courtly in their manners, Catholic in their religion, and disdainful of the dirty work of politics and business, wholly unlike the Protestant American interlopers—those rustic Kentucky backwoodsmen and sharp-dealing Yankees—who invaded after the Purchase. In reality, Frenchmen were often divided among themselves. Creoles did not always have the same interests as recent immigrants from France or Haiti. Even Haitian refugees clashed with each other, depending on when they had migrated. At the same time, white Louisianans could put their ethnic differences aside if they became afraid that the free black population was growing too large or the slave population too dangerous. Still, as a generalization it was true that Louisiana politics was divided into French and American factions.[54]

Tensions between the two flared over privateering when the navy, suspecting violations of U.S. neutrality were taking place, started seizing French armed vessels. In one incident in 1810, the privateer *Duc de Montebello* was found landing some stockings, handkerchiefs, and suspenders while in port, violating the U.S. interdiction of French goods. David Porter wasted no time ordering it seized. The *Duc*'s owner, Ange-Michel Brouard, denounced the seizure to Claiborne as "an act of arbitrary violence." Claiborne was in a difficult position politically. He was a federal official (territorial governors reported to the secretary of state), charged with upholding federal law, and Claiborne personally favored scrutinizing French privateers, lest they use Louisiana to commit some outrage against Britain or Spain and embroil the United States in a diplomatic crisis. However, Claiborne had to consider his position in Louisiana amid the large French population, whose loyalties to the United States were uncertain. By backing Porter, an American with little patience for anything Gallic, Claiborne risked offending the French.[55]

Thus the governor chose encouraging the French population's loyalty over the demands of neutrality. Writing the city's French consul,

Claiborne offered only minor criticism of the privateer while distancing himself from Porter. "The transaction at the Balize will I assure you be disapproved by my government," Claiborne wrote. "It is alike opposed to the American Character, and to that correct Deportment which the President requires of all his officers." Porter felt betrayed. "The *Massavito* & *L'Epine* stick in my gizzard," he later groused.[56]

Authorities had more than enough to worry about with the sympathy felt for smugglers, the logistical challenges of law enforcement, and the constraints placed on them by local politics. And yet one more factor kept opponents of privateering and smuggling from making headway: the geopolitics of war and diplomacy.

The War of 1812 increased the incentives for smuggling, and it was no coincidence that the Laffites expanded their business during the war. To increase the pressure on Britain, President Madison escalated the Restrictive System by signing into law five additional acts that curtailed foreign trade. Meanwhile, Britain declared New Orleans under blockade in March 1813 and choked off the flow of goods into the city. Smugglers and privateers picked up the slack. The war also weakened the vigilance of law enforcement. Whatever the nation might lose in customs revenue or friendly relations with Spain paled in comparison to losing New Orleans. What's more, naval officers preferred fighting the British. Defeating an enemy naval commander required superior seamanship, and, because enemy commanders were fellow gentlemen, it brought honor to the victor. It might be an American officer's ticket out of New Orleans. Lieutenant Thomas ap Catesby Jones, a veteran of gunboat duty against smugglers, remembered fondly the day he saw a British man-of-war off Pensacola. He set out in chase planning to "be a dead man before sunset or a post captain in thirty days."[57]

The diplomacy of U.S. neutral relations with France and South America likewise militated against vigorous punishment. Customs collectors knew to be suspicious of foreign privateers claiming distress. Yet, they never received instructions from Washington to take any precautions other than the normal vigilance their position required. Abuse of the distress exemption could have been prevented by barring all French and Spanish American vessels from New Orleans. But doing so would have been neither just nor wise. Not all foreign privateers used distress to conceal illegal conduct. Dominque Youx's *Pandoure* really was damaged in a storm, with Youx said to have "been nearly killed" and requiring medical attention. Likewise, the Cartagenan privateer *Carimasi* received repairs—but not arms or men—in New Orleans, and the federal court refused to stop it from sailing. Moreover, closing New Orleans to all French and Spanish American privateers would have shown favoritism toward their opponents, Britain and Spain, by extending a favor to one belligerent that was denied to the other. The law of nations required neutrals to treat each side equally. Besides, barring French and Spanish American vessels from U.S. ports would likely have caused the governments of those nations to bar U.S. ships and sailors from their ports. What would a shipwrecked sailor off Cartagena or Bayonne do then? Given the geopolitical circumstances, vigilance and tolerating some abuse of the distress provision were the best customs could do.[58]

Conclusion

Jean and Pierre Laffite were skilled opportunists who turned the geopolitical and legal circumstances of their place in Louisiana to their advantage. Wars in Europe and North and South America flooded the seas with privateers and encouraged restrictions on trade. Privateering became profitable; smuggling became attractive. Jean and Pierre brought buyers and sellers together to consummate their illegal transactions. The geopolitical and legal world of Louisiana—caught between the United States, France, and Britain as well as Spain and its rebellious colonies—allowed the Laffites to thrive and prevented law enforcement from making inroads against them. The Laffites thrived in part because they did not pick sides unless they had to. They were running a business, and making money was their goal. Once the battle was over and their crimes forgiven by President Madison's proclamation of pardon, Jean and Pierre needed to take stock. There was peace in Europe and North America. Their world was changing. They would have to change with it.

3 / Baltimore

In September 1816, a group of Baltimore businessmen organized a Spanish American privateering venture under the leadership of a sea captain lately arrived from Buenos Aires named Thomas Taylor. A native of Delaware, Taylor had gone to sea in his youth and ended up in South America, smuggling along the Río de la Plata. When Buenos Aires broke from Spain, Taylor was inspired. He took the oath of citizenship, swore fidelity to the cause of independence, and joined the Buenos Aires navy. He was captured in battle and briefly imprisoned, and then he became one of the first to receive a privateering commission, cruising the South Atlantic in the *Zephir*. In the fall of 1815, Taylor received a new assignment from the government of Buenos Aires: go north to Baltimore and recruit privateers.[1]

Entering the city in January 1816, Taylor purchased a schooner, the *Romp*, converted it to the privateer *Santefecino*, and hired a captain and crew. Though at first the venture was a success, netting twenty thousand dollars' worth of prizes off the coast of Spain that spring, it deteriorated when the *Santefecino*'s men, growing exasperated with their commander, mutinied and sailed home, only to find themselves and their employer arrested for piracy. Taylor was released when the prosecutor dropped the charges for lack of evidence. Undaunted, he assembled a new group of investors, who began meeting at the Fell's Point home of Taylor's landlord, John Sands, a merchant-tailor who had recently purchased a brand-new brig, the *Fourth of July*. Taylor spied an opportunity. "She would in a certain business," he said, "make a fortune for any concern who would fit her out ... and that in a few months."[2]

In its broad strokes, Spanish American privateering from Baltimore resembled Spanish American privateering from New Orleans and the Louisiana coast. Residents of both places fit out foreign vessels, snuck them by the customs house, captured Spanish merchantmen, and returned to shore, where they landed their booty, sold it, and refit for another cruise. As in Louisiana, geopolitics played a crucial role in bringing foreign privateering to Baltimore. The differences between Baltimore and Louisiana privateering, however, are telling. Baltimore privateers sailed much farther than their Gulf Coast counterparts, crossing the Atlantic longitudinally, to Buenos Aires, and latitudinally, to Spain. As a result, Baltimore privateers employed larger vessels, which carried more men and went on longer cruises and involved logistics that were correspondingly complex.

Most telling of all was the way in which Baltimore privateers manipulated the law. Whereas the Laffites preferred to ignore the law outright, Baltimore privateers, particularly the merchant-investors and sea captains, used their knowledge of international business, its rules and procedures, to get their vessels to sea and to gain ownership of prizes. In this way, U.S. law was a key mediator of Baltimore privateers' interactions with the Atlantic world. U.S. neutrality law aimed to limit contact with Spanish America, but loopholes encouraged men on two continents to work together. The law was both an obstacle to be overcome and a facilitator of new relationships—the kind of new relationships that Taylor was forming with his new friends of Buenos Aires in Baltimore.

Geopolitical Changes and Baltimore's New Business

Taylor succeeded in his recruiting mission, and within a few years, the city was famous—or notorious—for its embrace of Spanish American privateering. Why did Taylor come to Baltimore rather than, say, Philadelphia or New York? Ideology may have been a factor. Baltimore was a stronghold of Republican politics, and the city had gained a reputation during the late war with Britain for patriotism and hostility to European tyranny. Whatever the case, Spanish American privateering commenced in Baltimore at a key moment of transition, driven by the geopolitical realignments of the post-1815 world. Baltimore merchants, captains, and sailors became interested in foreign privateering at the same time that Spanish American governments of the United Provinces, the Oriental Provinces, and Venezuela sought to employ foreigners as privateers.[3]

FIGURE 3. The American privateer *Dolphin* of Baltimore (center) battles two British vessels during the War of 1812. Its commander, William Joseph Stafford, will later sail Spanish American privateers under the name Jose Guillermo Estifano. (From George Coggeshall, *History of the American Privateers, and Letters-of-Marque, During Our War with England in the Years 1812, '13, and '14* [1856].)

Baltimore had grown up during a generation of conflict in the Atlantic. Between 1776 and 1810, the city's population swelled from 6,000 to 46,000 souls. The marine sector, whose members learned how to succeed during war, was an important part of the rapid growth. In the American Revolution, Baltimore was the only major port never blockaded or occupied by the British, and the trade that would have gone through New York or Philadelphia (or even Annapolis or Norfolk) flowed through Baltimore instead. In the 1790s and 1800s, when the European wars raged, Baltimore shippers excelled at the neutral-trade game. Americans, because of the nation's neutrality, profited by carrying British cargoes in defiance of French laws and French cargoes in defiance of British ones. The city's shipbuilders gave their merchants a unique advantage: the Baltimore clipper. With a schooner rig (typically two masts with sails parallel to the vessel's sides), sleek lines, and raking masts, Baltimore clippers sailed faster and closer to the wind than other vessels. They eluded the swiftest enemies.[4]

The War of 1812 brought hardships to the city, most dangerously when the British entered the Chesapeake and attacked Fort McHenry. Yet overall, Baltimore's merchants and mariners adapted. They ran blockades and fit out privateers and letter-of-marque traders (vessels seeking to trade but also commissioned to capture enemies). More private armed vessels sailed from Baltimore during the war than from any other port, and according to one estimate, nearly one-fifth of the city's population—from sailors to merchants, shipbuilders to armorers, laborers to lumbermen, draymen, and teamsters—owed part of their livelihoods to armed vessels. Baltimoreans expected a bright future when the war ended, and migrants flocked to the city, hoping its fortunes would continue ever upward. But the long-term consequences of peace soon became clear as European carriers reentered the Atlantic and Caribbean trades, encroaching on the routes Baltimore shippers had dominated. Quick clippers, once such assets, became liabilities compared to the slow, high-capacity brigs and ships that now traversed the ocean unmolested.[5]

The years 1814 and 1815 marked a moment of transition in the Atlantic world as Napoleon was defeated, the War of 1812 ended, and the Spanish king, restored to power, sought to assert control over his American colonies. In Baltimore, these effects were felt in the need to adapt business practices learned over nearly thirty years of war. Some merchants, sailors, and captains found themselves enticed by the chance to continue working in a familiar field—albeit with a new Spanish accent.[6]

Financing and Preparing for Sea

During the fall of 1816, the *Fourth of July* group finalized their membership and structure. Joseph Karrick, an insurance company director and merchant with dealings throughout Europe and the Caribbean, took charge as business manager. Joseph Snyder, a grocery store owner and chandler, became his assistant. Sands took on the day-to-day work of hiring, supervising, and paying the carpenters, caulkers, riggers, and grocers. Other investors included Joseph W. Patterson, youngest son of Baltimore merchant prince William Patterson; Matthew Murray, former sheriff of Baltimore County; and John S. Skinner, the postmaster of Baltimore as well as a lawyer, agricultural journalist, editor of a newspaper that promoted Spanish American independence, and friend of Thomas Jefferson and James Madison. As costs rose, Karrick brought in new investors: John G. Johnston, a sea captain who had recently sailed a Spanish American privateer; B. K. Harrison, a merchant; and two others,

James Holmes and James Williams of Annapolis, about whom no information can be found. Karrick kept a low profile. He asked that his shares be concealed under the name "Slaymaker and Morrison," since he was director of an insurance company and his customers might not approve of this particular side venture. Postmaster Skinner also wanted anonymity; he used the alias "William Wright." Preparations proceeded steadily, but as the *Fourth of July* investors witnessed, fitting out a Spanish American privateer was complex, time-consuming, secretive, and expensive. To make it all work, businessmen on two continents—some of whom were prominent in their communities and many of whom sought to attract as little attention as possible—had to cooperate.[7]

Like most Baltimore privateers, Captain Taylor intended to sail his new vessel far out into the Atlantic, cruising for the big prizes of Spain's long-distance trade, and to do so he needed the right vessel, one similar to the privateers that had cruised against Britain. Such vessels were costly. In his study of War of 1812 privateering from Baltimore, Jerome Garitee estimates that the typical privateer cost $40,000 when fully equipped, armed, and provisioned. Given that the *Fourth of July* and the *New Republicana*, the only ventures for which numbers are available, were capitalized at $38,500 and $35,000 respectively, Garitee's figure is a reasonable benchmark. Few Baltimoreans, then, could afford privateering. Garitee further estimates that in 1810, 3,500 of Baltimore's 46,000 inhabitants held assets worth at least $4,000 and that only 400 people possessed assets of $15,000 or more. Privateering, therefore, was not for those who lacked resources: laborers, sailors, mechanics, small farmers, or any of the thousands of others who made up the ranks of the working poor.[8]

Table 2 lists fifty-one men financially interested in Baltimore's Spanish American privateering business. It most likely underestimates the full scope of their participation, given the illegal nature of the enterprise. Law enforcement and foreign consuls unearthed the names of twenty-four Baltimoreans who owned a share in one or more privateers, but they failed to discover the involvement of Henry Didier, John N. D'Arcy, David De Forest, William P. Ford, and Juan Pedro Aguirre. With jail time and fines facing anyone who owned a privateer, investors were discreet, and even among themselves they were tight-lipped. For example, David De Forest, a U.S. citizen by birth but a longtime resident of Buenos Aires, openly advocated separation from Spain when he traveled to the United States in 1817 as a minister of the United Provinces. Yet he was reserved when writing to his privateering associates. De Forest rarely spoke of owners or investors, and he seldom employed such phrases as "my" vessel, "your" vessel, or "his" vessel. Rather, De Forest spoke of agents—agents for the owners, agents for the officers and crew, agents for other merchants—thereby separating himself and his correspondents from potential trouble. U.S. neutrality laws spoke of punishing anyone "knowingly concerned" in owning, fitting out, or arming a vessel with the intent that it would attack a nation at peace with the United States. If De Forest and his associates acted only as agents, doing favors for fellow men of business, then it would be difficult to prove they were "knowingly concerned" in a foreign privateer or that they intended to harm a neutral nation.[9]

Baltimore investors were very much from the mainstream of the city's merchant community. They were respected businessmen, occupying positions of trust as directors, presidents, and managers of banks and insurance companies, and they were pillars of the community, leading fire companies, charities, and civil defense organizations. David Burke, for example, invested in a privateering venture but also traded as proprietor of the David Burke and Sons merchant house, operated a wharf and warehousing business, and directed the Franklin Bank of Baltimore. Burke oversaw poor relief for his ward, promoted the construction of a poorhouse, and served as president of the Deptford Fire Company. In the 1820s, he returned to his Irish roots, managing the local Hibernian immigrant assistance society and serving on the admissions committee of the Hibernian Free School for Children of Irish Immigrants.[10]

Similarly, Nicholas Stansbury's investment in the *Irresistable* was only one of many activities. A ship chandler, grocer, merchant, and ship owner, Stansbury was also director of the Marine Bank of Baltimore (in which some of the *Irresistable*'s captured specie was deposited). Stansbury had served in the Maryland militia during the War of 1812, directed the Columbian Fire Company, and stood as candidate for presidential elector. Running lotteries for charity seems to have been one of his specialties: he managed one lottery to build a new Masonic hall and another to raise funds for "a House of Industry for the honest and deserving poor."[11]

Investors were an economically mixed group. Despite all possessing greater than average wealth, there were gradations between them. Some were great merchants, the mercantile elite. Dr. William T. Graham, Dr. Lyde Goodwin, and Thomas Sheppard all operated extensive houses and commanded substantial resources. Graham had moved up from ship's surgeon to marry into the powerful banking family of Alexander Brown and Sons. A merchant and ship owner on his own account, Graham

TABLE 2. Investors, armadores, and agents of Baltimore privateers

Name	Role	Select activities
Juan Pedro Aguirre	*Armadore*, investor	Merchant; De Forest associate; Buenos Aires arms buyer in the U.S.; president, United Provinces legislature; banker and rancher
Joseph Almeida	Captain, investor	Sea captain
James Barnes	Captain, investor	Sea captain
John Barron, Jr.	Investor	Wharfinger, merchant, rope seller; partner of John Craig
Samuel Brown	Investor	
David Burke	Investor	Merchant, proprietor, David Burke and Sons, wharfinger; director, Franklin Bank of Baltimore; trustee, "house of Industry and Asylum"; president, Deptford Fire Co.; ward manager for poor relief; manager, Hibernian Society; admissions committee, Oliver's Hibernian Free School for Children of Irish Immigrants
Mr. Castello	Investor	Tailor
Clement Cathell	Captain, investor	Sea captain
Obadiah Chase	Captain, investor	Sea captain
James Chaytor	Captain, investor	Sea captain
John Craig	Investor	Grocer, owner of scows, vessel charterer, merchant; partner of John Barron Jr.; bucket man, Columbia Fire Co.
John D. Danels	Captain, investor	Sea captain; trustee, St. Vincent de Paul Roman Catholic Church
John N. D'Arcy	Agent, investor	Merchant, partner, D'Arcy and Didier; partner, D'Arcy, Dodge, and Co. (Haiti)

continued on next page

TABLE 2. Investors, armadores, and agents of Baltimore privateers (continued)

Name	Role	Select activities
David De Forest	Armadore, agent, investor	American merchant at Buenos Aires; United Provinces consul to the U.S. (unrecognized); benefactor, Yale University
Col. Richard Dennis	Investor	Savannah merchant?
Henry Didier	Agent, investor	Merchant, partner, D'Arcy and Didier; partner, D'Arcy, Dodge, and Co. (Haiti); director, City Bank of Baltimore
Dorsey	Investor	
Pierre Dupont	Investor	Savannah merchant?
William P. Ford	*Armadore*, investor	Merchant at Buenos Aires; from Philadelphia
John Gooding	Investor, agent	Merchant, ship owner, proprietor, John Gooding and Co.
Dr. Lyde Goodwin	Investor, agent	Doctor, merchant, ship owner; former supercargo and agent in Calcutta; occasional partner of Hollins and McBlair, merchants and ship owners; officer, Savage Manufacturing Company; director, Universal Insurance Co.; First Lt., 6th Cavalry, Maryland Militia
Robert M. Goodwin	Marine, investor, agent	Merchant; relative of Ridgely family
Dr. William T. Graham	Investor	Merchant, ship owner; former ship's surgeon; president, Farmers and Merchants Bank; director, Universal Insurance Co.
Adam Guy	*Armadore*, agent	British merchant at Buenos Aires
Thomas Lloyd Halsey	Agent	U.S. consul at Buenos Aires; member, American Antiquarian Society

TABLE 2. Investors, armadores, and agents of Baltimore privateers (*continued*)

Name	Role	Select activities
B. K. Harrison	Investor	Merchant; partner, Harrison and Thompson
John Higginbotham	*Armadore*, investor?	American merchant at Buenos Aires
James Holmes	Investor	
John G. Johnston	Captain, investor	Captain, merchant in Haitian trade
Joseph Karrick	Investor	Merchant; director, Patapsco Insurance Co.; Committee of Vigilance and Safety at defense of Baltimore (War of 1812)
John La Borde	Investor	Merchant
Nathan Levy	Agent, investor?	U.S. consul at St. Thomas
William Lowell	Investor	Biscuit baker
Patricio Lynch	*Armadore*, investor, agent	Merchant at Buenos Aires; De Forest associate; partner, Lynch, Zimmerman and Co.
John R. Mifflin	Investor	American merchant at Buenos Aires; from Philadelphia
Jero Miner	Investor	Merchant at Savannah
Edward Morgan	Investor, agent	Merchant
Matthew Murray	Investor	Sheriff of Baltimore County
Robert Oliver	Agent	Merchant, ship owner
Joseph W. Patterson	Investor	Merchant, son of William Patterson; founding member, B&O Railroad
Adam Pond	Investor, agent, captain	Sea captain
John Sands	Investor	Merchant tailor, dry goods seller; member, Ancient and Honorable Mechanical Company of Baltimore
Thomas Sheppard	Agent, investor	Flour miller, merchant, ship owner; director, Mechanic's Bank; manager, Baltimore–Havre de Grace Turnpike Road Co.; proprietor, Athenian Society (insurance); president, Columbian Fire Co.

continued on next page

TABLE 2. Investors, armadores, and agents of Baltimore privateers *(continued)*

Name	Role	Select activities
John S. Skinner	Investor	Lawyer, Baltimore postmaster, journalist; publisher, *Maryland Censor, American Farmer, American Turf Register and Sporting Magazine, The Plough, The Loom and The Anvil*; son-in-law of Judge Theodorick Bland; investor, Gregor McGregor expedition?
John Snyder	Investor	Former sea captain; ship chandler, grocer, merchant, ship owner; manager, Charitable Marine Society of Baltimore; lane man, Deptford Fire Co.; member, committee to inspect penitentiary
William J. Stafford	Investor	Sea captain
Nicholas Stansbury	Investor	Ship chandler, grocer, merchant, ship owner; director, Marine Bank of Baltimore; director, Columbian Fire Co. private, Maryland militia; Republican candidate for presidential elector; lottery manager
Thomas Taylor	Investor	Sea captain
Thomas Tenant	Agent, investor(?)	Merchant, ship owner, wharf owner, ropewalk owner; director, Bank of Baltimore; director, Baltimore Insurance Co.; vice president, Charitable Marine Society; member, Relief Committee for Easton, Maryland; major, Maryland Militia
James Williams	Investor	Merchant at Annapolis
John Zimmerman	*Armadore*, investor	Merchant at Buenos Aires; De Forest associate; born in Berlin

SOURCES: David Head, "Baltimore Seafarers, Privateering, and the South American Revolutions, 1816–1820," *Maryland Historical Magazine*, 105 (2008), 286–87. All individuals are from Baltimore unless otherwise noted.

speculated in government securities and served as president of the Farmers and Merchants Bank and director of the Universal Insurance Company. Another doctor, Lyde Goodwin, was born into the prestigious Ridgely family and in his youth served as a supercargo on voyages to Calcutta, India. By the 1810s, he owned ships and traded extensively, sometimes on his own and sometimes as partner of the prosperous Hollins-McBlair merchant house. He made more than two hundred thousand dollars in privateering during the War of 1812. Thomas Sheppard was a flour miller, merchant, ship owner, bank director, proprietor of an insurance company, president of a fire company, manager of a turnpike road firm, candidate for presidential elector, and captain in the state militia. He, too, made more than two hundred thousand dollars privateering against Britain.[12]

Perhaps the wealthiest of all Spanish American privateering investors was also one of the most active: John Gooding, who owned a share of at least three vessels. During the War of 1812, Gooding and a partner invested in eleven privateers, from which they made more than a half million dollars. Gooding traded, with success, throughout the Caribbean and South America. He owned a large home in the city, a 300-acre farm in the country, and the Timonium Estate, a hotel in the Maryland countryside with an icehouse, mineral springs, stables, jockey club, and race track.[13]

Alongside these wealthy investors were men of more modest means. John Craig, John Barron Jr., and John Lowell, for example, each owned part of the *Paz/Patriota*. Craig and Barron operated a wharf together. Craig also owned scows, chartered vessels, and sold groceries. Barron sold rope. Each dabbled in trade. Lovell, meanwhile, was simply a biscuit baker. Sea captains, too, became investors. Clement Cathell, Obadiah Chase, James Chaytor, John D. Danels, and Thomas Taylor all owned a piece of the vessels they commanded. Joseph Almeida, moreover, owned a portion of two vessels at the same time: the *Wilson* and the *Almeida*. Though necessary to raise the required capital, these smaller-scale investors stood apart from their wealthier associates.[14]

Once the requisite capital was raised, privateering groups needed commissions. Throughout the age of sail, many privateers employed an agent, known variously as a ship's husband, an *armateur*, or, in Spanish-speaking countries, an *armadore*. He secured commissions, posted bond to guarantee the good behavior of privateers, looked after the interests of investors, and provided various financial services such as redeeming bank notes and holding prize shares. Ordinarily, agents and privateers were citizens of the country issuing the commission, and agents simply smoothed the financial and regulatory path for the privateers. But because Spanish American governments sought to recruit foreigners, *armadores* also linked men on two continents.[15]

In some instances, Spanish American governments sent *armadores* north to recruit, as was the case with Thomas Taylor. Other privateering concerns fitted out their vessels in the United States before sailing south to obtain a commission. As a result, merchants living in Spanish America proved vital. For example, U.S.-based privateers who carried Buenos Aires's commissions received help from foreigners who resided in Buenos Aires such as Americans William P. Ford, John Higginbotham, and David De Forest; British merchants Adam Guy and George MacFarlane; and John C. Zimmerman, a German who had also lived in New York City and Baltimore before moving to Buenos Aires. South Americans such as Patricio Lynch, part of an Irish merchant family in Buenos Aires, and the Aguirre brothers, Manuel and Juan Pedro, also played an important role.[16]

North Americans in the Buenos Aires merchant community were also vital to the privateering conducted by the Oriental Provinces, since the Oriental Provinces had lost its major seaport, Montevideo, to the Portuguese in 1817. Commissions were distributed by agents meeting along the coast or through government contacts in Buenos Aires. In exchange for a piece of the prize money, Thomas Lloyd Halsey, the U.S consul to the United Provinces; John R. Mifflin, an American merchant; and Adam Pond, a sea captain and agent, obtained commissions signed by General Artigas and handed them out to privateers. Though this was potentially lucrative for Halsey, he overstepped his diplomatic powers, and when his dealings came to light, both the United States and the United Provinces objected. He was quickly recalled to Washington.[17]

Although some privateers eschewed using a formal *armadore*, acquiring a commission still took cooperation. An especially sophisticated approach used a legal loophole that allowed a U.S. citizen and a foreigner to do together what neither was allowed to do on his own. The strategy involved clearing a U.S. port as an American vessel, sailing to a foreign port, and selling the vessel to a foreign owner, who would then prepare it as a privateer. David De Forest and Captain James Barnes used this approach to turn the schooner *Swift* into the privateer *Mangoré*. Barnes sailed the vessel to Port-au-Prince, Haiti, and then acted as agent to purchase the vessel for De Forest, who was a naturalized citizen of Buenos Aires. With the vessel sold, Barnes put into effect a commission previously obtained by De Forest. The two men thus used one aspect of the law to maneuver around another aspect of the law. It was illegal for a U.S.

citizen to fit out a foreign privateer. Likewise, it was illegal for a foreigner to fit out a privateer in the United States. But it was not illegal for a U.S. citizen to arm a vessel, sail it beyond U.S. waters, and sell it to a foreigner who then used it as a privateer. The law regarded such a transaction as a form of the munitions trade, in which neutrals had a right to engage and which the United States had no obligation to prevent.[18]

In a similar way, William Saunders, captain of the *Felix*, left Savannah, Georgia, with a cargo of munitions, officially clearing port as bound to the West Indies. Saunders sailed to Aux Cayes, apparently hoping to meet with one of the vessel's investors before shaping his course for Margarita, off the coast of Venezuela. There he sold the vessel to Ignacio Arismendi, received a Venezuelan commission, renamed the vessel *Coranee*, and embarked on a cruise. Again, the munitions trade was legal, and it was legal for a citizen to sell an armed vessel to a foreigner. The one potential problem arose when a U.S. citizen accepted a foreign commission. But a simultaneous expatriation, changing one's citizenship to match the vessel's country of origin, could take care of that problem.[19]

Despite the need for cooperation, rivalries developed between some investors. De Forest and Halsey, for example, looked askance at each other. De Forest coveted Halsey's position as U.S. consul, while Halsey blamed De Forest for poisoning his relationship with the Buenos Aires leadership and for tattling on him to the State Department. De Forest once invited Halsey to a soirée and promised to "bury our animosities," but the consul refused. De Forest then called him "a most contemptible coxcomb," ridiculed his character ("I know you to be a bankrupt as to property; and believe you to be nearly so as to reputation"), and heaped abuse on his standing in the community ("Thos. Wilson not only despises but abhors you").[20]

More often, though, investors formed a close-knit group, at least initially. Those associated with De Forest were especially tight. Ford, Higginbotham, and Juan Pedro Aguirre all had ongoing business relationships with each other and with De Forest that went beyond their privateering interests. De Forest paid special attention to the Lynch family. He made Patricio his partner and employed his brothers Benito, Manuel, and Felix as clerks. De Forest set up a fifth Lynch brother, Estanislao, as a merchant in Chile. When De Forest left for the United States, he turned his affairs over to Patricio, who had formed a new firm with John Zimmerman. De Forest cherished his young protégés, saying he felt bound to them "as a Father is to a child."[21]

Spanish American privateering was, in many ways, just another business. A major investment with a potentially lucrative return attracted the attention of businessmen great and small. Yet because of Baltimore's legal status and international character, its investors worked closely with merchants abroad to provide extra capital as well as to acquire the commissions that made privateering possible at all. As the wars for independence progressed, businessmen in North and South America forged new links.

Getting to Sea, Capturing Prizes, and Making Them Pay

At last the *Fourth of July* was ready to sail. In December 1816, Sands, still the owner of record, went to the customs house and filed paperwork declaring the vessel a merchantman bound to the West Indies. Captain Taylor came aboard as the brig descended the bay. He raised the blue and white flag of Buenos Aires, read the republic's articles of war, and rechristened the brig *El Patriota*. Once out of U.S. waters, Taylor and Sands's agent, James Watkins, changed the vessel's registry by executing a sale and putting it in the name of the Buenos Aires government. Theoretically, *El Patriota* was property of the United Provinces, commanded by a citizen, and authorized to raid Spanish shipping.[22]

Over the next six months, Taylor cruised aggressively. He took prizes near Puerto Rico, off the Virgin Islands, around Cuba and Haiti. At one point acting like a naval commander, he created a squadron of Spanish American vessels and declared Cuba under blockade. Taylor took anything of value from the ships he overhauled. A few of his victims: a Spanish brig with wine, brandy, raisins, salt, and $20,000 to $30,000 of dry goods; a coastal felucca with tobacco, "segars," and dry goods worth $30,000; and a Spanish schooner with $16,000 in specie. Taylor started cashing in before he returned to Baltimore. When meeting a U.S. vessel at sea, Taylor put a portion of his goods aboard and arranged transport to the United States. When visiting Caribbean ports, he put prize goods up for sale. Eventually, Taylor returned to the Chesapeake, dropping anchor and unloading his cargo before reaching the city and reporting to its customs officers.[23]

As in New Orleans, the customs house was the privateers' chief obstacle to getting to sea, and Baltimore privateers similarly fooled officials with false papers. Also like New Orleans privateering, Baltimore vessels would clear port in the city but stay in U.S. waters for days to add arms and men. Unlike New Orleans, however, Baltimore privateers often used the paperwork of ships' registries and the laws of citizenship to outmaneuver the neutrality laws, as Taylor and Watkins had done. Once at sea,

Baltimore privateers cruised far and wide, much farther from home than gulf privateers ventured. They also overhauled richer prizes, found off the coasts of Spain and Portugal. When ready to call it a cruise and turn prizes into profit, Baltimore privateers smuggled, as Louisiana privateers did. But more often, Baltimore privateers used the procedures of international commerce to make their prizes pay. Baltimore privateers understood that some aspects of U.S. law and foreign policy might be used to defeat other aspects, which brought Americans and Spanish Americans together.

At the customs house, privateers usually swore they were American merchant seamen bound on a voyage to some foreign port. The vessels were initially manned by a small crew appropriate to such a venture. On at least two occasions, privateers cleared for a sealing voyage to the Pacific, which may have helped explain why they carried extra men. Appearances were important. When it came time to sign the clearance papers, the privateer captain rarely did so himself. Instead, an officer would present himself as master and sail the vessel from port. This gave the captain an extra layer of insulation from the law. Privateers left port with little of the necessary manpower or equipment, but sailing down the Chesapeake to the Atlantic afforded privateer captains many opportunities to bring their ships up to full strength.[24]

To rendezvous with supply boats required planning and execution. The *Republicana*'s trip down the bay was especially intricate. Led by Obadiah Chase and Robert M. Goodwin, the *Republicana* left Baltimore in company with the *Athenian*. As a foreign warship, the *Republicana* was allowed to enter Baltimore to refit, repair, or resupply so long as it left with the same complement of men and arms with which it entered. The owners of the *Republicana*, however, wanted to replace the vessel with the faster-sailing *Athenian*. The two cleared port separately, the *Republicana* as a privateer under Chase and the *Athenian* as a merchant vessel bound for St. Bart's with Goodwin as passenger, John Smith as master, and thirteen men as crew (a crew extraordinarily well-supplied with food and water, one sailor observed). Next, the *Athenian* headed for New Point Comfort while the *Republicana* stopped near Annapolis to meet a schooner owned by James Hooper, the innkeeper and shipping agent who had recruited the privateer's crew. This vessel brought a shipment of powder, ball, ammunition, grapeshot, rammers, sponges, worms, ladles, and stink pots. The *Republicana* then met the *Athenian*, and Cathell transferred the men and arms from one vessel to the other.

Finally, the *Athenian* was renamed *Republicana*, in order to fully assume the other vessel's identity, and the two sailed for St. Bart's.[25]

Once cruising, Baltimore privateers followed a predictable pattern. They searched for Spanish targets off Cuba, or they crossed the Atlantic, sailed through the Canary Islands, and hovered off Spain. Oriental Provinces privateers, meanwhile, also cruised for Portuguese vessels, prowling along the coast of Brazil, around the Cape Verde Islands and the Azores, and near Portugal. As much time as they spent at sea, privateers needed ports at which they could refit, repair, and resupply. Baltimore was the northernmost port of call; Buenos Aires the southernmost. In between, privateers favored Caribbean destinations at Margarita, which provided an admiralty court, and the so-called Five Islands, near Swedish St. Bartholomew's, which, despite its name was actually one island with five mountain peaks that looked like separate islands from a distance. Known today as Île Fourchue, the island, according to one sailor, was "barren and disolate." It was, he said, "inhabited by only one man, who is an old Swede named Girard, who has retired from the world to the solitude." On the Five Islands, the privateers, like Girard, were left alone.[26]

Privateers were not concerned about what a prize carried, so long as it was valuable. Specie was probably their favorite find, and privateers carried off gold and silver bullion worth millions of dollars. Other cargoes were less shiny but no less desirable. Ships bound to Europe transported colonial produce such as indigo, tobacco, sugar, coffee, cotton, and a brilliant-red dye called cochineal. Meanwhile, ships bound to the colonies conveyed dry goods and European merchandise. Prizes also carried extra sails, spars, and rope, as well as other items sailors wanted to keep themselves going, such as wine, brandy, and rum. The value of some prizes was staggering. The *Republicana* captured almost $4 million in sugar, coffee, rice, rum, ox hides, and ivory—from only three ships. John Danels hauled in $4.5 million in specie, including $400,000 of gold and silver from the *Asia Grande*. Marcena Monson seized the richest single prize: the Spanish Royal Philippine Company's *Triton* worth $1.5 million (more than $26 million in present-day dollars).[27]

Baltimore privateers also captured slaves, but not with the avidity of their Gulf Coast counterparts. Most of the slaves were captured by one man, a Captain Metcalf. In October 1817, Metcalf, commanding the *Successor*, overhauled the Spanish ship *Isabelita* with 112 slaves. A year later, Metcalf commanded a new privateer, the *Constantia*, and he captured vessels with 640, 250, and 240 slaves. On a subsequent cruise, again aboard a new vessel, the *Colombia*, Metcalf sailed the coast of Africa and took at least 280 slaves. All told, Metcalf captured more than 1,500 people. Yet, none of them were landed in Baltimore, Maryland, or the Chesapeake region. Metcalf took the *Isabelita*'s slaves to Amelia Island, East Florida, from where they were smuggled into Georgia. The Venezuelan navy seized the men and women captured by the *Constantia* in the Caribbean, while the United States Navy apprehended the *Colombia* slaves off the coast of Georgia. Captain Joseph Almeida was also active taking slaves. On one cruise he captured two Spanish Guineamen with a combined human cargo of 500. Reports of smaller incidents of slave trafficking emerged from time to time. Taylor took "5 little negroes" from one vessel and sent them to the Chesapeake. Samuel Franklin, commander of the Oriental privateer *Tigre*, captured fifteen slaves from a Portuguese brig and brought them to Baltimore. But for the most part, Baltimore privateers did not introduce slaves into the United States. It is possible the reason was economic as the demand for new slaves was shifting west, where Louisiana planters bought slaves from their counterparts in the Chesapeake, although slaves were still in demand for urban work in Baltimore. It is also possible the reason was geographic: Baltimore privateers sailed more often off the coast of Spain, where they were less likely to intercept slavers, than did the Louisiana privateers hovering off Cuba.[28]

Unless they captured specie alone, privateers needed to sell their cargoes. In theory, privateers were obligated to bring captured ships and goods to a port of the country that issued their commission and submit to a prize proceeding. Although some Baltimore privateers followed the law and brought their prizes into Spanish American ports, others ignored their obligations. Distance to a legal port and greed were certainly factors. Markets were unpredictable, especially in wartime and especially for the luxury goods some privateers captured. Geopolitics and the law played a role as well. The decree of an admiralty court in a prize proceeding transferred the title to the property in question to the captors, but such a transfer might not be respected abroad if it came from the court of a colony in rebellion, as Spain viewed Spanish America, rather than a widely recognized sovereign state. Privateers who followed the rules were taking a risk that potential buyers, wary of a Spanish merchant's lawsuit if they exported the goods, might stay away. So long as they were taking risks with potential lawsuits, then, privateers might as well take their chances landing in the United States.[29]

As when heading out on a cruise, the privateers' chief obstacle was the customs house. All vessels arriving from abroad had to submit to an inspection so customs agents could assess duties on any imported goods.

Customs agents required inventories of prize goods, though it was not their job to decide if the goods had been obtained legally. They simply wanted to make sure nothing was disembarked without paying taxes. Still, if a captain showed up with a vessel full of Spanish merchandise and no explanation for how he got it, then that information could be turned over to the U.S. district attorney, prompting an inquiry.

Privateers devised a number of strategies to land their goods. Most simply, there was smuggling, though it was never as extensive or as sophisticated as in Louisiana. Captain Ewing, of the *Liberdad*, for example, stopped on the Virginia side of the Chesapeake and disgorged his cargo, giving twenty packages of clothing, shawls, and ribbons to John Willoughby, a nearby dry goods seller. The swag ended up buried on Willoughby's property, hidden under his wife's bed, stashed under his kitchen floor, and concealed in his attic. Willoughby was no Jean Laffite.[30]

More often, Baltimore privateers used weakness in the law, their knowledge of mercantile procedure, and their international connections to change the apparent ownership of their prizes before sending them into U.S. ports. For example, Robert M. Goodwin and the *Republicana* group, which sent its vessels to St. Bart's after leaving Baltimore, laundered their prize goods abroad before bringing them to Baltimore. Establishing a temporary base at St. Bart's, Clement Cathell took the new *Republicana* (the former *Athenian*) to the Azores for a cruise while Goodwin remained behind. The old *Republicana* he renamed *Mary*, and through some chicanery with a fake sale, obtained a Swedish registry for the vessel. Cathell sent the prizes he captured to the Five Islands, where Goodwin transferred their cargoes to the *Mary* and other vessels. Goodwin next sent the goods to St. Thomas, a Danish possession, and sold them to the Souffron and Company merchant house. Souffron, in turn, sold the goods to Nathaniel Levy, the U.S. consul in St. Thomas. Levy, acting in his private capacity as a merchant, then placed the goods aboard still other vessels and shipped them to Baltimore, consigned to Robert Goodwin's relative, Lyde Goodwin, who would sell them in Maryland. By this time, the original ownership had been obscured after passing through a Swedish island, a Danish island, a Danish merchant house, a U.S. official, a U.S. merchant, and multiple merchant ships. Everyone involved, except Cathell and Robert Goodwin, could say they had bought the goods in the regular course of business.[31]

Colonel Richard Dennis, owner of the *Hornet*, employed a similar scheme. In one incident, the privateer's captain sent a prize to the Bahamas under the care of a prize master named John Smith, a Bahamian planter. Dennis ultimately wanted the goods landed in Savannah, Georgia, since, a sailor testified, "he had agents at that place to protect the prizes & sell them to the best advantage." Accordingly, a Georgia pilot met Smith in the Bahamas, loaded a cargo, and brought it to the United States, entering officially at the Darien, Georgia, customs house, thereby allowing Dennis to claim that he had bought the cargo in the regular course of trade.[32]

In a variation, other privateer captains put their prize cargoes aboard merchant vessels they met at sea, hiding them in plain sight alongside the rest of a merchantman's cargo. Taylor had done so while cruising near Haiti, when he happened across the American brig *Huron* and contracted with its captain to transport some $35,000 of prize goods back to the United States. The *Huron* carried them to Boston with the rest of its goods. Later, Taylor also put $10,000 on the *Traverse the Ocean*, and he sent slaves, tobacco, and dry goods to Baltimore on *La Cât*. Taylor made these arrangements opportunistically. He was fortunate enough to encounter compliant merchant captains. But it could also be done by prearrangement. David Burke and John La Borde, for example, sent several vessels out to the gulf to pick up a load of sugar, claret wine, logwood, and mahogany captured by their *Paz/Patriota*. The *Baltimore Price Current*'s shipping news lists the goods as arriving from New Orleans, consigned to Burke and La Borde like any other shipment.[33]

Merchants knew that prize goods would rarely be seized unless they could be identified as having come from a Spanish or Portuguese vessel. That would happen only if U.S. authorities or a foreign consul received timely intelligence. Baltimore merchants Richard and William Douglass bought goods from a privateer docked in Haiti, although they worried about potential legal entanglements. "It is the opinion of some of our ablest lawyers," the Douglasses wrote to their agent, "that the prize goods which may be introduced here from Port au P., *if identified*, would or could be legally claimed by the original owners." But they were not deterred: "We are still of opinion that purchases might be made & shipped to this country before any proofs could be produced from the place of residence of the former owners, in which case no difficulty would occur." As an extra precaution, the Douglasses instructed their man to change the marks on the goods' packages "in a way that will prevent if possible their being identified here."[34]

As in New Orleans, the distress exemption to port-entry laws was a popular loophole. The law of nations as well as U.S. law allowed foreign vessels to enter neutral ports to receive shelter from the common dangers of the sea, and vessels so accommodated were supposed to leave with the same cargo, arms, and manpower with which they entered, less those goods sold to finance repairs, as approved by authorities. Still, access to port was sometimes all a privateer needed. For instance, Captain Danels deposited tens of thousands of dollars of specie in banks "for safe keeping," as he claimed. But could he be expected to risk taking all that money out again on the dangerous sea? Probably best to let it stay where it was, in a bank close to home. Distress also provided cover to the merchant captains who transported prize goods for privateers. In one instance, the owners of the schooner *Cora* claimed that their vessel, bound from Maine to Halifax with lumber, had been "driven by the stress of weather into the island of St. Bartholomew's in the West Indies." It must have been some storm to take the ship so far off course. The plucky captain then sold the lumber (fortunately finding a good market) and purchased a cargo of sugar that had come from a privateer. The captain swore he had no idea anything was amiss.[35]

Not all claims of distress were calculated. Some captains who fell in with privateers or prizes thought they were helping save a cargo from destruction in the best tradition of rendering assistance at sea. The American brig *Jerome*, for one, picked up a cargo from the prize *Rayhna dos Mares* because the vessel was leaking, "the worms having ... eaten her bottom," one sailor said. Likewise, there were cases of prizes entering port with real damages. The prize *Divina Pastora* ended up in New Bedford, Massachusetts, when its prize master fell ill "with an inflammation of the eyes" that left him blind for several weeks. Sailing into a cooler climate relieved his suffering, and the prize master recovered enough to direct the *Divina Pastora* into port, where an inspector found it needed $2,500 in repairs.[36]

These situations made the distress exemption powerful. Customs collectors knew to be suspicious of foreign privateers claiming distress, but Washington never instructed them to take any extra precautions. As in New Orleans, abuse of the distress exemption could have been prevented by barring all Spanish American vessels from port. But doing so would have invited retaliation from Spanish American governments closing their ports to distressed U.S. ships. It seems customs agents had to tolerate some abuse.

Despite the advantages enjoyed by the law's pliability, there were occasions when Baltimore privateers would have wanted it to be stricter. They experienced serious problems with prize crews and masters who ran away with their vessels, rather than sailing them to port as assigned, because no law could stop them. Prizes received small crews, just enough to work a vessel, so as to not deplete the privateer's main force. If even a few men got out of hand or decided they would rather keep the spoils for themselves, they could easily take the ship. Some crews did just that. The crew of the prize *Industria Rafaelli* rose on their officers, deposited them in a boat, and sailed for Maine, the ringleader's home. Soon, newspapers reported sightings of salty men traveling New England with Spanish gold. Captain George Wilson lost one prize when the crew took it to Philadelphia and another when the crew got drunk celebrating the Fourth of July, murdered their captain and first mate, and took the ship for themselves.[37]

Prize masters were no more reliable. James Chaytor lost a prize to a master who took his charge to Wales, turned it over to British authorities, and claimed salvage for having rescued the vessel from robbers. The prize master had either gotten cold feet about the legitimacy of his Spanish American commission or decided he could do better with salvage than prize money. Robert M. Goodwin lost two captured vessels to disloyal prize masters. One landed in Maine rather than the assigned rallying point at St. Bart's, and another sailed to the Virgin Islands, where the officers sold it for $35,000. They later moved to Norfolk and started a steamboat company.[38]

In other circumstances, runaway prize masters could have been sued or prosecuted for violating their nation's prize code. This was not an option for Spanish American privateers operating from the United States. Goodwin, a U.S. citizen, could not walk into the Baltimore federal court and ask for help retrieving the property he acquired by breaking U.S. federal law. Spanish American courts had jurisdiction over their own privateers' conduct, but with the rogue officers living thousands of miles away in Norfolk, they could not help. Without the law, then, trust and a few extra shares of prize money were the only incentives for prize masters and crews to do their jobs.

Opposition and Decline

The *Fourth of July* group fell apart in 1818. Changes began in January when Taylor, anchored in the Río de la Plata, secured an Oriental Provinces commission and turned command over to John Chase, who renamed the vessel *Fortuna* and embarked on a cruise that yielded several rich prizes. The group should have been elated, but at a shareholders meeting in July, some members grumbled against Karrick's management. He had declared a measly dividend of one thousand dollars per share. Where was their money going? Suspicious, the investors appointed two outsiders to monitor Karrick.[39]

More trouble emerged later that month when customs agents seized the *Fortuna* for neutrality violations. Karrick and John Gooding, an associate but not a group member, posted a sixteen-thousand-dollar bond to secure the vessel's release pending trial. At the same time, John Sands demanded to be reimbursed for all the expenses he had paid out of his own pocket when the vessel was first fitting out—more than three thousand dollars. Karrick refused to pay. Sands felt used. "They had made a tool of me to cover their faults," he complained. When Sands threatened a lawsuit to get his money, Karrick scoffed, knowing Sands could not go to court without incriminating himself. "Sue and be dam'd," he told Sands. With only one move left, Sands took his payment in revenge and revealed the group's business to the press, the courts, and the State Department. As the members were rounded up to face indictment, their privateering business was defunct.[40]

Criminal indictments, civil law suits, rising costs, and dissension among investors—Taylor's experience reveals the factors that led to the decline of Spanish American privateering from Baltimore. Beginning in 1817, the U.S. government revised its criminal code to close the loopholes that had allowed privateers to operate out of U.S. ports. But criminal enforcement was not the most effective deterrent. Rather, measures that made the business more costly provided the greatest obstacle to Spanish American privateering. Few investors could tolerate the mounting losses. Tensions ran high, and investors turned on each other. Ordinarily, businessmen would have sued each other and let the courts sort out their differences. Now, because of the illegal nature of their business, that door was closed to them. By 1820, Spanish American privateering was on the decline and nearly forced out of Baltimore.

When Spanish American privateers began operating from the city in 1816, existing neutrality legislation gave authorities little power to stop them. Small naval vessels occasionally patrolled the Chesapeake, and if the customs collector received word that privateers were smuggling prize goods ashore, he would send the revenue cutter out to stop them. However, to really control the problem, authorities needed to stop privateers as they were fitting out and before they captured any vessels. It was much easier said than done. By clearing as a merchant, supplying in the bay, and changing their purpose once at sea, privateers followed the letter of the law closely enough to prevent interference from authorities. There may have been suspicions, but under the 1794 and 1797 laws, suspicions alone were not legally sufficient to seize anything or arrest anyone. As Secretary of State James Monroe complained, the law worked only after the fact "upon the general footing of punishing the offence merely where, if there be full evidence of the actual perpetration of the crime, the party is handed over, after trial, to the penalty denounced." As a result, Monroe concluded, it was "extremely difficult, under existing circumstances, to prevent or punish this infraction of the law."[41]

In 1817, however, Congress directed customs officials to act preemptively with a new neutrality law. It required customs officers to collect a bond from any armed vessel owned in whole or in part by U.S. citizens before it cleared port to ensure the vessel would not violate U.S. neutrality. Likewise, any vessel arriving in port that appeared "manifestly built for warlike purposes"—that is, if its cargo were principally arms, if it carried a suspicious number of men, or if any other circumstances made it appear "probable" that hostilities were intended—then customs officers were to detain the vessel until bond was given to ensure good conduct. In either case, the bond was to be double the value of the vessel, cargo, and arms. For a thirty-five-thousand-dollar privateer, that was a hefty sum. Congress revisited the legislation a year later. Some imprecision in the law's language had been identified, and some sentiment emerged that the prescribed punishments were too harsh. Plus, having three separate neutrality laws in effect was unwieldy. The 1818 Neutrality Act thus repealed and replaced all previous neutrality legislation, articulated its provisions more clearly, and reduced punishments across the board—for example, the maximum prison sentence for owning an illegal privateer became three years rather than ten. The law also repealed the prohibition on U.S. citizens joining foreign privateers while overseas. At the same time, the requirement that all foreign armed vessels post bond remained in force. In 1820, Congress acted once more to curtail foreign privateering. It passed a law that allowed foreign warships to enter only a select list of U.S. ports. Baltimore was not on the list. By empowering customs agents to pursue privateering more aggressively, by making fitting out in the U.S. more expensive, and by removing any legitimate reason for their vessels to be anywhere near Baltimore, Congress had established the legal powers necessary to combat Spanish American privateering.[42]

The new powers worked. Baltimore customs collector James McCulloch instructed his officers to "examine, visit, and report to this office all and every privateer or ship of war under foreign colors." Officers searched the bay for law-breaking vessels rather than waiting for them at the docks. McCulloch told privateers to quit hovering in the Chesapeake; they either had to come into port and post bond or leave U.S. waters. Frequently abused by the Spanish consul and condescended to by John Quincy Adams (he "is a very honest man," Adams wrote, but also "an enthusiast for the South Americans, and easily duped by knaves, because he thinks all other men as honest as himself"), McCulloch enjoyed his new powers. They allowed him to answer his critics' "occasional ravings on the subject of South American cruisers."[43]

McCulloch's newfound aggression balanced Federal District Attorney Elias Glenn's miserable conviction rate. Between 1817 and 1820, so many privateering indictments were handed down that it seemed in some sessions that the Maryland circuit court dealt with nothing else. Glenn prosecuted fourteen owners, twelve captains and officers, and four shipping agents for their role in illegal privateering. Charges included neutrality violations, piracy, and, on two occasions, slave smuggling. Ordinarily, Glenn did not pursue common sailors; he left them alone in exchange for testimony against their leaders. Common sailors stood trial only when they were the primary perpetrators. In these instances, sailors had mutinied (sometimes murdering their officers in the process), run away with a ship, or attacked neutral vessels.[44]

Records are incomplete, but it seems Karrick was the only owner, captain, or shipping agent convicted, and his conviction was overturned, leading Glenn to discontinue prosecution. Common sailors were not as lucky. Between 1816 and 1820, at least 129 sailors from Baltimore privateers were tried. Records of verdicts in these cases are also incomplete, but it appears that thirty-one were found guilty of piracy because of their role in mutiny, murder, and attacking neutral vessels. From April to June 1820, seven of them were executed—in Boston, Baltimore, Charleston, and Savannah. Eventually, the rest had their sentences commuted to time served. These seven men were the only Spanish American privateers from Baltimore to suffer real criminal penalties.[45]

Prosecutions, then, had only a small impact on privateering. In fact, arresting wayward sailors actually pleased privateer captains and investors. "It will afford the govt. of South America much satisfaction," David De Forest informed Secretary of State Adams, "to learn that the U.S. will prosecute those mutineers; and punish such as are found guilty of crime, according to the law." De Forest wanted sailors who ran away with his prizes brought to justice.[46]

The civil courts were different, and the judges regularly ordered prizes restored to their original Spanish or Portuguese owners and pronounced privateer vessels forfeit to the United States. Of the thirty-three Maryland civil cases for which a decision can be found, the district court ordered a vessel or cargo restored to its former owner eighteen times, and it ordered privateering vessels forfeited to the United States three times. Thus, privateers won twelve cases. However, fifteen cases were appealed to either the Maryland circuit court or all the way to the U.S. Supreme Court. Outcomes at the circuit court level can be found for eight cases, and the picture did not look good for the privateers. The court affirmed two of their victories, but it reversed another and affirmed an order of restoration in five other cases. Before the Supreme Court, it got worse. Of the seven cases for which a decision can be found, the Court ordered property restored to its former owners all seven times, including one instance in which a privateer victory was overturned. Thus, of those twelve Maryland district court victories for privateers, only eight remained intact.[47]

The numbers in other jurisdictions tell a similar story. Privateers fared better in the New York district court: four of the five cases for which a decision can be found went their way (and, apparently, none were appealed). But they were blanked in Maine, where they lost in the one case (out of the three) for which a decision can be found. They were crushed in Virginia: six losses out of seven cases with two appeals, one ending with a restoration affirmed, and one resulting in a condemnation reversed (bringing their record up to two wins and five losses). They were routed in Georgia: four full victories and two partial ones in the seventeen cases for which an outcome can be found. They were shut out in Massachusetts: all six cases went against them, with the one appeal resulting in an affirmation of the lower court's ruling. In the end, then, privateers lost their property most of the time.[48]

If privateers lost so often in civil court, then why were they not convicted of crimes more often? No evidence exists to explain why juries voted the way they did. In the absence of such evidence, it is tempting to believe that public sympathy was responsible. In the civil court, cases were heard according to admiralty rules of procedure, under which there were no juries and the judge alone decided the outcome. Criminal cases, by contrast, were decided by juries, and since Spanish American independence was popular in Baltimore, juries may have turned a blind eye to the transgressions of men who violated an unpopular law.[49]

Yet, a fuller understanding of the law may offer a better explanation. For example, piracy law was unsettled and confusing, a flaw exposed by Spanish American privateering. Even the best legal minds of the day debated what, exactly, piracy was and when, precisely, the United States had jurisdiction to punish someone for the crime. Between 1818 and 1820, the Supreme Court heard a series of cases involving Spanish American privateers accused of piracy, and Congress passed a new piracy law aimed at achieving a clear definition. But they mostly achieved a muddle. On the one hand, Associate Supreme Court Justice Joseph Story embraced an expansive definition, known as general piracy, in which piracy was robbery at sea committed with the intent to steal. In this view, pirates were the enemies of all mankind and could be tried wherever they were arrested. A specific law defining what actions constituted piracy or granting the United States jurisdiction was unnecessary. Chief Justice John Marshall, on the other hand, subscribed to a narrower view, known as statutory or municipal piracy, in which only those acts that a state had specifically defined as piracy could be prosecuted and only in those circumstances specifically defined by statute. Meanwhile, in 1819 Congress passed a law that defined piracy according to the general definition of the crime offered by writers on the law of nations. In other words, statutory piracy had become general piracy.[50]

Disagreements between the two positions continued. In one decision, Story held that "there is scarcely a writer on the law of nations, who does not allude to piracy as a crime of a settled and determinate nature," and Marshall continued to wonder "whether any nation punishes otherwise than by force of its own statute." If Story and Marshall could not agree, then how could an ordinary jury reach consensus except in the most aggravated circumstances of mutiny, murder, and attacks on neutrals? Piracy was a hanging offense, and if juries hesitated imposing the ultimate penalty, it is understandable for reasons other than an enthusiasm for Spanish American independence.[51]

The experience of Spanish and Portuguese diplomats also suggests that structural challenges rather than sympathy explain the greater effectiveness of the civil courts. Spain and Portugal were represented in the United States by ministers Luis de Onís and José Correa de Serra, respectively, as well as by consuls stationed in Baltimore, Norfolk, and other cities. They deluged Secretary of State Adams and local customs collectors with reports of illegal privateering and demanded the arrest of the men involved. Everyone knew, they said, that Spanish American vessels arrived in U.S. ports and that officials would do nothing to stop them. Their complaints largely fell on deaf ears, but not because U.S. officials let their sympathies cloud their judgment. Rather, the Spanish and Portuguese lacked proper evidence. As Norfolk customs collector

Charles K. Mallory wrote, the Spanish consul based his arguments on the claim that the privateers' misconduct was "of too great public notoriety to require any thing like demonstration." Public notoriety was not enough for Mallory to act on. James Monroe, while still secretary of state, answered Spanish demands even more strongly. "This government is under no obligation, nor has it the power, by any law or treaty, to surrender any inhabitant of Spain, or the Spanish provinces, on the demand of the government of Spain," he wrote to Minister Onís. Spanish officials could call for arrests all they wanted, but the United States would not act without proof that would stand up in court.[52]

At the same time, Spanish and Portuguese consuls brought dozens of civil suits against privateers and their prizes. The consuls attached property they suspected had been stolen, and then proved it by swearing out libels, securing testimony from sailors, and obtaining information from a vessel's original owner that could be used to identify where particular goods had come from. Without their efforts, the privateers' intricate smuggling and laundering operations would not have been revealed. The consuls also faced a different burden of proof than in criminal prosecutions, since they did not need to prove intent, but only that a vessel had violated U.S. neutrality in some way—by being owned by Americans, fitting out in Baltimore, taking aboard arms in the Chesapeake, or adding sailors in Norfolk. The property would then be restored.

Portuguese consul Joaquim José Vasques knew the difference between criminal and civil penalties firsthand. He watched as juries acquitted the *Fourth of July* group—Taylor, Skinner, Murray, Sands, Chase, Watkins, and Holmes—of piracy and neutrality violations. Vasques may have been satisfied that Karrick was convicted on two counts of neutrality violations, but Karrick appealed, the convictions were overturned on a technicality, and the district attorney decided to drop the charges. On the other hand, Vasques triumphed in civil court. He instituted eight libels against the *Fourth of July*'s prizes, in Baltimore and New York, and he prevailed in the seven cases for which a decision can be found. Vasques recovered hundreds of thousands of dollars, and even if no one went to jail, they were forced out of business.[53]

Civil suits disrupted privateering more than criminal prosecutions did. Returning their captured goods and losing their vessels made privateering too costly to sustain. The civil courts had made Spanish American privateering a bad investment. Even De Forest, who was as committed to the revolution as anyone, began feeling financial pressures. "You do not appear to know," he wrote to Lynch and Zimmerman, "how much anxiety I have had on acct. of my fears of suits brought by Spanish claimants, although I have openly pretended to the contrary." To get by, De Forest turned to "the needful economy."⁵⁴

The losses could not have come at a worse time for Baltimore investors. The Panic of 1819, caused in part by a scandal at the Maryland branch of the Second Bank of the United States, devastated the city's merchants. By July more than one hundred merchants had failed, including privateer investors and agents John D'Arcy, Henry Didier, John Gooding, Lyde Goodwin, Joseph Karrick, Thomas Sheppard, and Nicholas Stansbury. To cope, Gooding rented out his Baltimore home (a "large three story Dwelling House" with stables), but eventually the chancery court ordered his country house and farmland sold to satisfy creditors. Meanwhile, Karrick put his house on the market, advertising that it contained "every comfort and convenience that a family could desire." He meant, of course, every comfort and convenience his family desired before he lost their money.⁵⁵

Because their financial interests were tied together, the problems of Baltimore investors spread throughout the network of South American merchants that made privateering possible. D'Arcy and Didier argued with Juan Pedro Aguirre, John Higginbotham, and William P. Ford, whom they not only called a scoundrel, but "as great a scoundrel as Higginbotham." Gooding importuned De Forest for payments from the capture of the Spanish brig *Sereno*, even though they had already settled accounts from their privateering business. "He calls all [his] unsettled & troublesome business, my business; and he has written me several insolent letters," De Forest complained, later adding that "Gooding & co. are all bankrupts and he shows a strong disposition to involve me in the same ruin."⁵⁶

Normally, De Forest could have sued Gooding and allowed the courts to decide who owed what to whom, but since this was an illegal business, the courts could provide no relief. Gooding could only write insolent letters while De Forest gossiped about him to other merchants. This was not a solution. In the end, De Forest wound up owing fifty-four thousand dollars to the Spanish owners of the *Sereno*, most of which, he said, was really Gooding's responsibility. Privateering investors had no means to settle the conflicts that inevitably arise in any business. Operating outside the law had had its benefits, but it also had its costs.⁵⁷

Conclusion

Spanish American privateering from Baltimore was a business. It could hardly have been otherwise given the complex organization and operations involved. The ventures required a commercial network of entrepreneurs thousands of miles apart. A privateer was a costly investment. Defeating U.S. neutrality law required legal and business acumen. But this was a business embedded in an Atlantic geopolitics of newfound peace in Europe and the United States and changing strategies in the Spanish American Wars of Independence. Baltimore seafarers turned to privateering in the United Provinces, the Oriental Provinces, and Venezuela at a moment of geopolitical as well as economic transition. The immediate situation of the post-1815 world created the conditions in which Baltimore seafarers had their services to offer at the precise moment when Spain's rebelling colonies demanded them.

Thomas Taylor had come to Baltimore to spread privateering and to make a fortune for his investors. Privateering for the Spanish American republics became popular, and Spain's commerce was devastated, but as an investment, the *Fourth of July* failed. Baltimoreans who sailed aboard Spanish American privateers wanted to make money. Privateering was expensive, and sailing for Spanish America was no charity. Ultimately, most foreign privateering left Baltimore when new laws, the federal civil courts, and the Panic of 1819 made it unprofitable. Taylor, however, was not done. In June 1819, he and former associate John G. Johnson crossed paths in Charleston. He had bought the *Fourth of July* alias *Patriota* alias *Fortuna* from the others and located a new captain. Taylor asked Johnston for a new investment: the *Fourth of July* was heading back to sea.[58]

4 / Galveston and Amelia Island

New Orleans customs collector Beverly Chew had bad news for the secretary of the treasury in the summer of 1817. "I deem it my duty to state," he wrote, "that the most shameful violations of the slave act, as well as our revenue laws, continue to be practiced" by men sailing "under the Mexican flag, [but] being, in reality, little else than the re-establishment of the Barataria band." The Baratarians were back, smuggling, privateering, and slave trafficking like old. Except that they were not actually in Barataria. As Chew reported, they had "removed somewhat more out of the reach of justice" to the island of Galveston, located off Texas in a zone claimed by the United States, Spain, and Mexico. While not as convenient as the Louisiana coast, Galveston was a few days' sail from New Orleans and close enough for American vessels to visit, disposing of prize goods that found their way, just as surely as before, into the United States.[1]

At the same time, Thomas Wayne, a U.S. naval officer stationed near Spanish East Florida, also had bad news for his superiors. Gregor MacGregor, a Scotsman in the Spanish American service, had captured the Spanish town of Fernandina on Amelia Island and proclaimed it an independent republic. Barely a mile from the Georgia border, Amelia would be ideal for privateering, slave trading, and smuggling. Wayne was worried. Should the Spanish American privateers and smugglers "continue in Amelia Island," he warned, "the place will become a second Barataria."[2]

In 1816 and 1817, Galveston and Amelia Island arose as new centers for Spanish American privateering. In some ways, they followed the patterns previously seen in Baltimore and New Orleans. American seafarers, and foreign seafarers living in the United States, joined armed vessels or helped smuggle captured goods and slaves into the country. They attracted familiar faces, including some of the old Barataria men. The Laffites would be back. So, too, would French privateer Louis-Michel Aury, now a Mexican governor. But in other ways, Galveston and Amelia Island were different. At each place, privateers became linked to filibusters such as MacGregor who claimed to represent the governments of Spanish America. At Galveston and Amelia, these privateers and filibusters settled outside U.S. territory and established states of their own, issued their own papers, and demanded respect from U.S. authorities. Chew and Wayne were right to call them "Baratarias." But they were also new Baratarias: Baratarias outside U.S. borders.

Given their locations, Galveston and Amelia Island provide another perspective on Spanish American privateering and the United States. The geopolitics of the post-1815 world was again crucial to the rise, development, and fall of both Galveston and Amelia Island. By the time of their establishment, the Spanish Americans' bid for independence had reached a low point, especially in Mexico, where the king's troops were triumphant and the resistance was left in the hands of irregular forces such as filibusters and privateers. Meanwhile, the United States reignited negotiations with Spain over the limits of the Louisiana Purchase and other outstanding issues that, in time, resulted in the Transcontinental Treaty. Meanwhile, Spanish officials wrestled with the implications of Spanish American filibusters and privateers' close relationships with some Americans and whether it portended an encroachment on Spain's North American lands. Spanish American privateers and their allies knew of these tensions and did their best to exploit them. Because of their location and political status, Galveston and Amelia claimed powers never before possessed by privateers: the ability to grant their own commissions, operate their own prize courts, and issue the documents of international trade. Galveston and Amelia, therefore, became examples of former colonies asserting the sovereignty gained by independence not to separate from the web of Atlantic connections but to spin new ones that accessed American capital, markets, supplies, ships, and sailors.

Finally, the U.S. government's response to Galveston and Amelia shows the modesty of its control over events. These were crucial years for the negotiations with Spain that resulted in the Transcontinental Treaty. The United States expanded as a result. Yet, the government reacted to events at Galveston and Amelia by balancing the desire to obtain territory and to increase the nation's security with the obligations of a neutral. No master plan existed to manifest the nation's destiny but only the concerns and challenges of a president and his advisers working in the context in which they lived.

Galveston: Operations

Mexican patriots had long sought a port from which they could receive shipments of munitions and supplies from U.S. merchants, assemble forces to attack Mexico and Texas, and host privateers, whose prizes would finance more arms purchases and invasions. The first years of the war brought scant success, and as the king's forces tightened their grip on Mexico, the patriots counted Boquila de Piedras and Nautla, open beaches far down the Mexican coast, as their conduit to the United States across the gulf. The Mexicans needed something better if they hoped to persevere. A breakthrough came in August 1816, courtesy of Louis-Michel Aury, the former captain of the French privateer *Guillaume* and smuggler of slaves from the prize *Massavito*. Aury had entered the Mexican service earlier in the year after following a circuitous route through French privateering and the Cartagenan navy, in which he had earned the rank of commodore and had become an associate of Simón Bolívar, before a disagreement with the Liberator led him to seek a new employer.[3]

Taking charge of the search for a port on the Texas coast, Aury led a squadron to Galveston and settled on the island's northwestern tip, where Galveston Bay protected an anchorage from the gulf's open seas. Galveston was a long, narrow barrier island, more than twenty miles from end to end and twelve feet above sea level at its highest. The ground was mostly mudflats and salt marshes; few trees offered shelter. No one lived there permanently, though Karankawa Indians sometimes visited to catch fish, crabs, oysters, and turtles. Life on Galveston would be rough for Aury's men. It had once been called Snake Island—and not because a Mr. Snake discovered it. In September, José Manuel de Herrera, an official of the Mexican Congress, arrived from New Orleans with a contingent of filibusters to claim the island for Mexico. He named Aury governor and appointed a customs collector, judges and clerks for civil, criminal, and admiralty courts, a marshal, and a notary public. Then, according to one witness, Aury, de Herrera, and the filibusters raised the Mexican flag and swore an oath "to defend it unto death."[4]

In the following months, Aury used his power as governor to build Galveston into a privateering center where captains received commissions, brought their prizes before an admiralty court, and sold their goods and slaves to smugglers who would ship them to Louisiana. Aury commissioned around eighteen privateers, an enormous number given the short duration of his rule. At least three more armed vessels from other Spanish American republics also visited Galveston. Some privateers had begun their cruises in New Orleans, where they fitted out and then made for sea with the old trick of clearing customs in the city and then arming in the lower river. Galveston privateers were typically small vessels, sailing the gulf and prowling around Cuba and the coast of New Spain. Most of the time, they preyed on the little vessels of the Spanish coastal trade.[5]

Privateers flocked to Galveston, rather than reconvening in the swamps of Barataria, because Aury possessed something neither the Laffites nor their associates had ever had: the power to issue the documents on which maritime law and commerce depended. Wind may have driven the ships, but in any maritime nation, paperwork—registers, manifests, customs clearances, customs entrances, owner's instructions, crew lists, passenger lists, logbooks, and commissions—propelled trade and the law of the sea. Aury's papers gave legitimacy to Mexican privateers and to the merchants who dealt in their prizes. Mexican commissions looked just like the commissions of other nations, and they served both a practical and symbolic function. They were part form letter, with spaces for the name of the privateer vessel, its owner, and its captain; for the vessel's size; for the number of men or "hombres" in its crew; and for the number and type of its arms. Large, ornate documents, the commissions projected the authority of the nation that issued them. Some Mexican commissions were emblazoned with "Louis Aury Gobernador Político y Military de la Provincia de Texas" at the top; at the bottom, the gobernador signed his name with a flourish. Another example featured a drawing of a stout three-masted ship under full sail between the words "Provincia de Texas," as if to suggest the strength of Texas and its privateers, even though the vessel commissioned was a little coaster with one gun and twenty men. Aury's papers also protected traders of prize goods. When a privateer came into Galveston with a prize, an admiralty judge issued a certificate of condemnation. Then the goods were loaded aboard a merchantman, and papers—inscribed "Republica Mexicana, Provincia de Texas, Puerto de Galveston"—were signed and delivered by Galveston's customs collector. The merchantman then entered Louisiana, not on the sly, but openly as a Mexican vessel with a Mexican cargo and the papers to prove it.[6]

The American brig *Alonso* employed this strategy to introduce an assortment of dry goods captured from the Spanish schooners *Nueva*

FIGURE 4. Commission of the privateer *Esperancia* issued by Aury at Galveston, 1817. (From *Felipe Fatio* v. *The Schooner* Lameson *alias* Panchita. National Archives, Ft. Worth, Tex.)

Anna and *Liebre* into the United States. After being condemned at Galveston, the goods were shipped to New Orleans with an official manifest and clearance papers, signed by both the ship's captain and by the customs collector, just as would have been the practice at any port. The Spanish consul libeled the property as having been captured illegally, but this may have been an exceptional case. During the trial, former customs collector Pierre L. B. Duplessis admitted that according to the Treasury Department's instructions, "all vessels under the Mexican & other Independent flags" were treated "upon the same footing as vessels belonging to Old Spain." Indeed, Duplessis's boss had previously reminded him that "there is no principle of the law of nations, which requires us to exclude from our ports the subjects of a foreign power, in a state of insurrection against their own government." According to Beverly Chew, the current collector, there existed a "regular intercourse & trade between this port & Galveztown." Receiving papers signed by a Mexican officer also gave smugglers a way to separate themselves from the source of the goods they hoped to sell. For example, Jean Fabiani, a resident of New Orleans who had once owned Aury's *Guillaume*, transported a cargo of tallow, bear oil, bear furs, and raccoon skins into New Orleans aboard his schooner, *Matagorda*. When the *Matagorda* was libeled by customs agents, Fabiani claimed that while at Galveston he had purchased the vessel and a cargo, which he then traded to Indians from whom he obtained the tallow, oil, and pelts. Fabiani thus removed himself several steps from the actual capture of Spanish property.[7]

Using official documents to enter the United States may have helped slave smugglers as well. In March 1817, the Mexican privateer *Mosquito* was detained in New Orleans for attempting to land foreign slaves. The vessel carried a commission from Aury, a cargo manifest, and lists of the crew and passengers, which included ten blacks and six mulattos. Since none of the men carried papers documenting their citizenship or free status, they may have been slaves hidden on the ship's papers as passengers and crew. At the same time, it is possible that at least some of the men were, in fact, free since five of the sailors produced witnesses to vouch for their status as freemen. In the end, the court dismissed the case and allowed the *Mosquito*'s captain to go about his business. If he were attempting to smuggle slaves, the right paperwork had won the case.[8]

Despite the appearances of legitimacy, witnesses to life at Galveston found Aury's practices highly irregular. Juan Domingo Lozano, a Spanish captain imprisoned by the privateers, found the governor's methods suspect. "Prizes were condemned without any order, process, or formality," he observed, and the marks on the packages were "always removed from all the goods from prizes before leaving Galveston in order to prevent their being recognized and claimed by the real owners." Commerce was dedicated solely to privateering. As Lozano reported, the island had "no other traffic than what consisted in Spanish prizes." Even worse, chaos reigned. A Spanish prisoner named Lopez reported seeing "a great disorder at Galvestown," including "frequent stabbings." No one respected Aury. As Lopez said, "one could insult the Governor."[9]

Governor Aury was a divisive leader and spread discord throughout his settlement. The problems started on approaching the island for the first time when Aury discovered—the hard way—that a sandbar guarded the entrance to Galveston Bay. The lead vessel became stuck, and the second became stuck, too. Then another. And another. Until five vessels piled up. Things got worse before the first month passed. There was a mutiny when two hundred black men, whom Aury had recruited in Haiti, became angry that he had put them to work salvaging the wrecked ships' cargo and building a fort and shelters rather than cruising for

Spanish gold. One night, they rushed into Aury's house, violent words passed, and one mutineer shot the commodore, wounding him in the hand and chest. The mutineers collected the prize goods they had salvaged and took off with two ships. On the way out they met another of Aury's vessels, captured it, and sailed home.[10]

Aury's struggles mirrored the difficulties experienced by other Mexican filibusters. Indeed, the Galveston project was only the latest, and certainly not the last, in a series of invasions of Spanish Texas. For example, in 1812 and 1813, a force led by Jose Bernardo Maximiliano Gutierrez de Lara, a Mexican blacksmith and merchant, and Augustus W. Magee, a former U.S. Army officer, marched from Louisiana into Texas. About five hundred men strong, the band captured San Antonio and held it for five months until the Spanish counterattacked, driving the filibusters out of Texas. That was the most successful filibuster expedition. Between 1813 and 1816, six subsequent expeditions were launched from Louisiana against Texas, including one led by John Hamilton Robinson, an American doctor and explorer who apparently found the prospect of liberating Mexico attractive; one organized by two former officers in Napoleon's service, General Jean Joseph Amable Humbert and Colonel Irenee Amelot de Lacroix; a new expedition led by Gutierrez; one commanded by Jose Alvarez de Toledo y Dubois, a Cuban-born former Spanish naval officer and member of the resistance Cortes; another involving Gutierrez, this time in tandem with Humbert; and a final effort that brought together Toledo, Humbert, and Henry Perry, a Connecticut native who had left the U.S. Army to join the Gutierrez-Magee expedition. In each case, success was elusive. Men recruited to fight lingered in Louisiana for months of preparations. Texas border towns, such as Nacogdoches, fell easily but better-defended targets farther inland offered stiffer resistance. Divisions in leadership turned to bickering, then to antagonism and outright opposition.[11]

Aury's experience was no different. At Galveston he had cobbled together a loose assemblage of veterans of previous expeditions, such as Perry, and newcomers such as himself. The group had a chain-of-command problem, made worse because the only link to the Mexican government came through their unacknowledged ambassador to the United States, Father José Manuel de Herrera. De Herrera had ties to many would-be filibuster leaders as well as to the New Orleans merchants who helped equip the expeditions (while helping to lighten de Herrera's purse). Conditions frayed even more when a new filibuster band dropped anchor at Galveston unexpectedly in November 1816. Led by a charismatic, young Spanish liberal named Francisco Xavier Mina, the expedition had left Baltimore intending to attack Mexico directly until problems at sea forced Mina to seek assistance. The presence of yet another rival—one hoping to take command of Aury's forces— disillusioned the commodore on Galveston. When Mina went to New Orleans to meet with a group of merchant backers, he began preparing to abandon Galveston and move operations to Matagorda. Perry objected, however, saying he wanted to keep all the forces together. Facing a challenge to his rule, Aury stationed cannon in front of his house. When Mina returned from New Orleans, he worked out a compromise with Aury. The commodore would help sail his men to Mexico, and then they would go their separate ways. In the end, Aury lacked the authority he needed to enforce his rule. Given that the Mexicans were nearly defeated in 1816, it could hardly have been otherwise. After all, if Mexico could have fielded an army, it would not have needed informal expeditions of filibusters.[12]

Although Aury's ineffectual leadership doomed Galveston, his documents told a different story, at least to U.S. officials guided by a government policy of neutrality. Only court proceedings uncovered the truth, and in the meantime, the official-looking papers issued at Galveston emboldened privateers to capture Spanish prizes and gave them cover when transporting their goods to market in New Orleans. To a customs officer, Galveston could appear to be as legitimate as any port in the world.

Galveston: The Laffites Take Over

Aury was not long for the governorship of Galveston, given the divisions forming between the men on the island and the external threats always present from Spain and the United States. Still, Aury was forced out not because of the divisions or the enemies, but because of the machinations of two French brothers whose superior grasp of the geopolitics of their world allowed them to reopen their old business.

The Laffites had kept a low profile following the Battle of New Orleans. The U.S. Navy had destroyed their Barataria headquarters, and peace in Europe and the United States was bad for a business that thrived on wartime trade restrictions. Nevertheless, they found a new line of work late in the year: spying for Spain, the nation they had so recently antagonized. The Spanish intelligence service, fearing Mexican filibusters and privateers, wanted moles to penetrate Galveston. Spanish agents recruited first Pierre, in New Orleans, and then Jean, who had traveled to Philadelphia to pursue business opportunities in the East. In return for their secret services, the brothers received a pardon from the king of Spain, payment for the information they gathered, and permission to trade munitions to the Mexicans as a way to gain their trust. Pierre may have also received permission to operate privateers. Throughout 1816, as Galveston grew, Jean and Pierre spied. Pierre passed along intelligence gleaned while shipping arms to Mexico and from the meetings he attended with the filibusters' New Orleans backers. Jean received an assignment to explore the northern edge of Spain's empire in North America. Along with Arsène Lacarrière Latour, a U.S. Army engineer at the Battle of New Orleans, Jean traveled the Arkansas River, through what are today the states of Arkansas and Oklahoma, drawing maps, scouting out who occupied the territory, and observing where local sympathies lay. Jean and Latour gathered valuable information for Spanish officials to assess the future. At the moment, though, the danger posed by the filibusters and privateers was their chief concern, and Spanish officials wanted something done about Galveston. Giving the Spanish what they wanted provided the Laffites with an opening.[13]

The Laffites gained control over Galveston through a series of moves. First, they learned of the disharmony on the island and began planning a way to turn it to their advantage. Pierre perceived the rifts between the filibusters in February 1816, when Mina came to New Orleans. Pierre attended Mina's meeting with his supporters, watching as one faction encouraged the young general to continue in Texas while another tried to persuade him to attack Pensacola instead, apparently in the hope of capturing the town and selling it to the United States. Mina denounced the latter idea as "merely a mercantile speculation, from which no advantage would result [for Mexico]," according to one of his followers, and he returned to Galveston.[14]

After the meeting, the Laffites sent Latour to Havana to inform the Spanish that they were developing a plan to strike Galveston and destroy all the filibusters and privateers. Latour was to stress that only the Laffites, with their unique talents, could pull off the scheme—and only if Havana provided the necessary financial support. While Latour lobbied the Spanish, Jean sailed to Galveston for a closer look. He found Aury and Mina feuding. Jean visited Mina and then Aury, and both men gave him an earful of their troubled relationship.[15]

Next, Jean and Pierre coped with the unexpected and seduced the Spanish. Aury and Mina sailed in early April, and in the governor's absence, some of the men left behind staged a coup. They elected a new governor, named a new slate of officers, swore a new oath of loyalty to Mexico, and began passing new laws. Jean had landed by this point, and he later told the Spanish that the coup was his idea—he said it would keep the privateers and filibusters congregating there so that they could all be destroyed at once—but the evidence is not clear. Jean had reason to embellish his control over events to impress the Spanish. Jean was not named an officer, and although he may have hoped to exert power indirectly, he soon returned to New Orleans. It would have made more sense to stay at Galveston, especially since Aury returned there in early May and began reasserting himself. Whatever the case, Jean now saw Galveston's vulnerability.[16]

When Jean arrived in New Orleans, he found that Latour had been persuasive. Havana had appointed Felipe Fatio to replace Diego Morphy as consul and empowered him to run—and fund—the Laffites' antirevolutionary operations. Jean and Pierre then unfolded their plan to destroy Galveston. They would need five vessels (six would be better). Three vessels would approach Galveston flying the Mexican flag, pretending to be privateers. The other vessels would trail behind, flying the Spanish flag below the Mexican flag so as to look like prizes. Once the vessels passed over the sandbars and entered the bay, the men aboard would spring a trap and demand the Mexicans' surrender. They would not have to fire a shot. "In this way," the Laffites wrote, "the project will be realized without any risks and with great ease." Spanish officials loved the idea. Fatio called the project "the most effective one for striking a blow at the root of the evil we have been enduring for such a long time." He saw no reason to doubt the Laffites.[17]

Finally, Jean and Pierre maneuvered Aury out of the way, returned to privateering and smuggling, all while convincing the Spanish that they still wanted to destroy Galveston. The first step of the brothers' plan called for more observation of Aury's latest movements, and in June, Pierre sailed for Texas. By this time, Aury, mysteriously, had begun moving his operations ninety miles south to Matagorda Bay. When he arrived, he again wrecked his ships traversing a sandbar, and he decided to go back to Galveston. Pierre trailed behind, observing Aury's misfortunes. Pierre then landed at Galveston, established his own settlement on the island, and started luring men away from Aury. At the end of July, Aury gave up on the Texas project entirely, though not privateering and filibustering. He abandoned Galveston and headed for Florida. Pierre wrote his brother with the good news: "I am like the Chief and father of Galveston."[18]

With Spain's man in charge, Galveston should have been evacuated, giving it back to the turtles and snakes and occasional fishermen. But it persisted as a haven for privateers as the Laffites played the Spanish and the filibusters against each other for their own benefit. At one moment, they promised Spanish officials that their plan to destroy the privateers and filibusters was still viable. In fact, they contended, it would work even better with them in charge. Some Spanish officials doubted the Laffites' usefulness, but even a year later Fatio still believed that Jean "has always transacted with us in the greatest sincerity and shows us now that he desires to cooperate in the destruction of that gang of adventurers." At the same time, the Laffites allied themselves with new filibusters who arrived in Texas, and Aury's privateers were still welcomed at Galveston, even if their leader were not. Drawing on their old skills, the brothers made money for themselves outfitting vessels and smuggling slaves. The Laffites were back.[19]

Amelia Island: Operations

East Florida was an inviting target for Spanish American partisans. Although small (fewer than four thousand whites, free blacks, and African slaves lived there) and struggling (it survived only with money sent from Mexico City and troops deployed from Havana), it was strategically vital, since it provided a buffer against Anglo-American encroachments from the north and protection for vessels bound home to Spain from the Caribbean and the gulf. If attacked, Spain would be forced to defend it, a beachhead for further invasion could be established, and a new front in the Wars of Independence could be opened.[20]

In the summer of 1817, Gregor MacGregor, a Scotsman in the Spanish American service, intended to do just that. MacGregor had come to South America after a promising career in the British army ended in disappointment. He had served as an officer in Portugal during the Peninsular War until a barroom quarrel with another officer led to a transfer to an unattractive posting. MacGregor refused and resigned his commission. Joining the Venezuelan army around 1811, MacGregor became a general and fought in Venezuela, New Grenada (including at the siege of Cartagena), and in Venezuela again during Bolivar's first Aux Cayes Expedition. In 1816, MacGregor, upset about being passed over for a command, once more resigned his commission and struck out on his own, this time heading for the United States to prepare an attack on Florida.[21]

FIGURE 5. General Gregor MacGregor. (From Thomas Strangeways, *Sketch of the Mosquito Shore* [1822].)

MacGregor gathered supplies and men in ports from New York to Savannah and, after convening with three Spanish American agents, decided to target Amelia Island. About thirteen miles long and four miles wide, Amelia featured several commodious anchorages. For filibusters, privateers, and smugglers, Amelia combined the most useful aspects of Barataria and Galveston. It was outside U.S. jurisdiction but very close to U.S. markets and sources of supply. The St. Marys River, the southern boundary of Georgia, emptied off the island's northern tip. A strong swimmer could make it to the United States. Unlike Barataria and Galveston, however, Amelia Island was occupied. More than a thousand people lived there, and the town of Fernandina, a small but active port defended by a fort and fifty Spanish soldiers, lay in the northwest corner.[22]

On June 29, 1817, MacGregor landed one hundred men on the island's east side and marched toward Fernandina. The Spanish commander, paralyzed by rumors that MacGregor commanded a thousand men and a half-dozen warships, surrendered without a fight. Announcing himself as "Brigadier General MacGregor, commander-in-chief of all the forces, both naval and military, destined to effect the independence of the Floridas," MacGregor accepted the Spaniards' surrender. He raised a new flag, the Green Cross of Florida (apparently his own design) and proclaimed the island free from Spanish oppression.[23]

MacGregor attempted to run his new government as a regular, legitimate one. He established a post office and a police force. He consulted with a mayor and board of aldermen to make laws, including a curfew law for slaves meant to better regulate their movements. He issued naturalization papers for anyone wanting to become a citizen of the "Free Floridas." MacGregor also distributed privateering commissions and created an admiralty court, with a Charleston lawyer sitting as judge. For the government's revenue, MacGregor planned to levy duties on prizes and charge fees for his court's services. MacGregor also raised money by selling the thirty-one slaves left behind when their owners fled the invasion.[24]

MacGregor's plans, however, never materialized. He issued no more than nine privateering commissions, a number that includes two or three given out as he was leaving Amelia in early September and a commission sent to New York that may not have been used. Privateers from other nations arrived periodically, but just four or five MacGregor privateers put to sea while he commanded. They did little damage. For example, the *Challenger*, an open boat armed with one swivel gun and thirteen men, attempted to raid plantations for slaves. While ransacking a planter's house, breaking open drawers and rifling through trunks, the privateers were spotted by the planter's neighbors, who raised the alarm. A detachment of Spanish troops, including several black soldiers, found the privateers and opened fire, killing three and taking the rest prisoner.[25]

MacGregor failed to invade mainland Florida. In fact, he struggled to maintain his hold over Amelia, and a combination of legal adversities, geopolitical realities, and personal failings eventually ended his rule, barely two months after his arrival. While planning the initial invasion, MacGregor had made arrangements with Ruggles Hubbard, a New York lawyer and politician, to bring a shipload of supplies and reinforcements. Unfortunately for MacGregor, U.S. officials grew suspicious and prevented the vessel from sailing until the supplies and crew were reduced to a level that officials deemed appropriate for a vessel on the merchant voyage Hubbard claimed he intended. When Hubbard dropped anchor at Fernandina in late August without the full complement of men and supplies, MacGregor was crestfallen.[26]

At the same time, the Spanish regrouped at St. Augustine for a counterattack, and rumor had it that five hundred Spanish soldiers were on the way. Meanwhile, MacGregor's followers grumbled. Throughout July and August, men deserted and others fell ill with yellow fever and died. Officers quarreled with each other and with MacGregor. On September 3, MacGregor gathered his officers and announced his intention to abandon the island. MacGregor had chosen Amelia for its location: in Spanish territory but close to the United States. In time, he could have pursued strategies similar to those employed by Aury at Galveston. But he never got the chance. With supplies running low, men growing surly, and a force of Spaniards on the way, MacGregor gave up. He boarded a ship and prepared to depart.[27]

Many of MacGregor's men remained on the island, however, and the privateering and filibustering settlement at Amelia entered a second phase with a tumultuous week in early September. Without MacGregor, Ruggles Hubbard and Jared Irwin, a former Pennsylvania congressman, postmaster, sheriff, and colonel in the Pennsylvania militia, took charge of Fernandina—just in time to defend against the Spanish counterattack. Irwin galvanized the remnants of MacGregor's men into an effective band of resisters. After a few days of fighting, the Spaniards gave up their assault. Hubbard and Irwin then formed a new government with Hubbard as civil governor and Irwin as military commander. Their rule lasted two days.[28]

On September 17, Commodore Aury sailed into Fernandina aboard the *Congreso Mexicano*, this time without wrecking on any sandbars. Stepping ashore, Aury seized power over the sick, hungry, battle-weary group, and pushing aside Hubbard and Irwin just as the Laffites had done to him. Aury had learned of MacGregor's conquest, and, after departing Texas, he sailed to Florida, stopping at Haiti to acquire more men and along the way capturing a few prizes. Aury brought much-needed supplies, which made his claim to power irresistible. Aury, Hubbard, and Irwin worked out an arrangement that made Aury commander of the island's naval and military forces, Hubbard civil governor, and Irwin the military's second in command. Still, Aury claimed preeminence. After all, Aury said, he was "a chief of the Mexican Republic," and he expected to be treated as such. On September 20, he announced that henceforth Amelia Island would be a province of the Mexican Republic. The next day, Aury hauled down MacGregor's Green Cross of Florida and raised the Mexican flag.[29]

Soon it was just like old times for Aury—privateering and smuggling, organizing a government and wrangling with rival leaders. Some privateers followed him from Galveston, while new vessels arrived in search of commissions or to dispose of prizes. "Armed vessels were arriving daily [from the United States] for the purpose of obtaining commissions," one privateer reported, while a U.S. Navy officer observed eight large prize ships sail for Amelia in October alone. In the first two months of Aury's tenure, one newspaperman estimated, more than $500,000 of goods had already passed through the island. Aury knew how to attract privateers.[30]

Because Amelia was located so near the United States, legal loopholes abounded there. Aury obtained arms and munitions in Georgia and had them brought over in rowboats. U.S. customs law required official clearances for vessels larger than five tons. Anything smaller could not get very far and would not have carried enough contraband to be worth stopping. Thus, rowboats could come and go as they pleased, and neither the customs service nor the navy could do anything about it. In fact, when the U.S. brig *Saranac* did seize a small boat transporting naval stores, the collector at Savannah let the vessel go. It had broken no law. Small boats and borders also came in handy for slave smugglers. On some occasions, slaves were rowed to Georgia, with the slaves themselves sometimes assigned to do the rowing. Thus, reported John H. Elton, commander of the *Sarnac*, "they can smuggle one or two at a time without detection." Other times, slaves would be sold to dealers who took them to the mainland and followed the St. Marys River on the Spanish side of the border for fifty miles or so before crossing into the Georgia backcountry, far from the eyes of customs officers.[31]

Vessels operating out of Amelia were protected also by a measure of sovereignty and the United States' commitment to neutrality. In one instance, Elton spied a prize headed into Amelia. "I would have taken her out immediately," he informed the secretary of the navy, "but I considered it neutral ground, and it was the wish of [the] government not to infringe." Over and over, Elton asked the secretary for guidance. "I have several times written for instruction how to act as regards the patriots or people of Amelia, & particularly whether I am expected to detain vessels freighted with slaves," he wrote in October, 1817. Without instructions, Elton confessed, "my judgment would dictate that I had no right [to] interfere, particularly if we consider the place a neutral place." When Ruggles Hubbard asked Elton to assure him that the navy would not seize his vessel, Elton could only give one answer. He promised to treat MacGregor's flag "as the flag of a Neutral and unless some very flagrant cause should exist [I] have not any directions to interpose with it."[32]

Just as at Galveston, Aury attempted to run Amelia as a regular government. Together with Hubbard and Irwin, he created a temporary governing body called the "Supreme Council of the Floridas," which included eight members and made laws, such as offering land bounties for soldiers, and issued proclamations, such as one that assured Georgia slave owners that runaway slaves would be returned promptly. In October, these efforts received a boost when two veteran Spanish American agents arrived to help establish the government: Vincente Pazos, a former newspaperman in Buenos Aires, and Pedro Gual, a one-time governor of Cartagena and longtime Spanish American operative in the United States. By December, the two had begun drafting a constitution. Modeled on the U.S. Constitution and the *Federalist Papers*, Amelia's government would include a single executive, an elected legislature, and a judiciary. The military would be subordinate to civilian authority. Freedom of the press and liberty of conscience would also be guaranteed.[33]

Though the vision was noble, the reality looked different, as the settlement was riven by factionalism. Not surprisingly, Aury chafed against Irwin and Hubbard, and their tensions simmered. A racial component to the ill-feelings emerged since the white followers of Irwin and Hubbard, some of whom MacGregor had recruited in Charleston and Savannah, did not want to serve with the black sailors Aury had enlisted in Haiti. As one newspaper reported, Aury's men "insist[ed] upon equal rights and privileges with the whites, and otherwise [are] very insolent;

indeed, [even] so as to assume equal command." The whites rebelled. They were "so enraged at the attempt of the blacks to command them that they would have died in the contest." As time passed, the chaos only increased. Hubbard died in late October, succumbing to an illness. A few days later, thirty former British officers arrived in search of MacGregor. The men had crossed the Atlantic to serve the patriots in Venezuela, but when hearing that a countryman had a Spanish American republic of his own, they sailed to Amelia. Just as Mina had done at Galveston, the British soldiers showed up unexpectedly and complicated Aury's rule. Some newcomers sided with Irwin, while others joined Aury. A Colonel MacDonald tried to insinuate himself into Aury's good graces by spying on Irwin, which was only fair, since the other Brits were encouraging Irwin to stage a coup.[34]

A measure of peace returned when Aury declared martial law on November 5. He denounced the "mercenaries, traitors or cowards who abandoned the cause of republicanism in the hour of danger." Aury then banished some of his harsher critics. But Aury was no dictator. Two weeks later, he held elections to settle the island's leadership democratically. A council of nine would be selected to put the settlement on a more permanent footing, and military men were excluded from voting, thereby removing the angriest element from the decision. In the event, five of Aury's supporters were elected, outnumbering Irwin's by just one. Tensions continued. Amelia Island resembled Galveston even more.[35]

The U.S. Response: Amelia Island

Aury's reign over Amelia Island ended with a whimper. In late December 1817, six U.S. warships and two hundred American soldiers approached the island, and the commanding officers ordered Aury to surrender. "We propose to land a force to-day, and to hoist the American flag," they announced. Preparations to seize Amelia had begun in late October, when President Monroe's cabinet met to discuss Spanish American affairs, including what to do about Amelia Island and Galveston. Secretary of State John Quincy Adams was blunt. "The marauding parties at Amelia Island and Galveston ought to be broken up immediately," he said. The president agreed, and orders went out to the army and navy to begin planning an attack. When the day arrived, Aury had no choice. He yielded to the Americans, who marched ashore playing "Yankee Doodle" and "Hail Columbia" before raising the Stars and Stripes. A month later, Aury departed in search of another project to advance the independence of Spanish America.[36]

Spanish American privateering, smuggling, and filibustering at Amelia Island stopped for a simple reason: U.S. forces showed up and took over. Nevertheless, the significance of seizing the island—an island, after all, located in foreign territory that the United States had long desired—and the Monroe administration's justification for the action demonstrate that the immediate circumstances determined the American response.

Four lines of thought converged among U.S. policy makers to argue in favor of seizing Amelia. First, MacGregor and Aury encouraged violations of U.S. neutrality, customs, and slave trade laws. For example, a House Committee investigating Amelia Island condemned "the spoliation of peaceful commerce upon and near our coasts by piratical privateers, the clandestine importation of goods, and the illicit introduction of slaves within our limits." Aury's slave dealing warranted particular attention, as the House Committee announced it "but too notorious that numerous infractions of the law prohibiting the importation of slaves into the United States have been perpetrated with impunity upon our southern frontier." The congressmen were right. Slave smuggling was one of the most important activities on the island. MacGregor had barely taken control when a dozen slaves left behind by the Spanish were put aboard a small sloop and sent to Georgia. In the following months privateers brought at least eight slave vessels to Amelia. The U.S. Navy seized a good number of them, although that generally did not preserve the captured people from a life of servitude since they were sold in Georgia by the government. Altogether, approximately 450 slaves were landed at Amelia successfully with another 500 intercepted by the United States. It is possible that the number of vessels landing slaves was actually higher, given that naval officers often complained about not being able to detain privateers and their prizes coming into Amelia.[37]

Not all of the agitation caused by the slave trade through Amelia was humanitarian. Georgia planters alternately feared that their slaves could seek refuge in a patriot settlement and that Aury would introduce rebellious West Indian slaves. In his First Annual Message to Congress, Monroe voiced the concerns of all constituencies when he denounced "the island being made a channel for the illicit introduction of slaves from Africa in to the United States, an asylum for fugitive slaves from neighboring states, and a port for smuggling of every kind. After the invasion had succeeded, Monroe emphasized the peril posed by smuggling slaves "of the most odious and dangerous character." In this way, the

TABLE 3. Slave landings at Amelia Island, 1817–1820

Year	Vessel	Number of slaves	Outcome
1817	Fire Fly	11–12 at Amelia Is., captured by MacGregor	Seized by U.S.
1817	Jesus Nazareno	95	Landed at Amelia Is., sold to Georgia; seized by U.S.
1817	Isabelita	112	Landed at Amelia Is.; 95 taken to Georgia, seized by Georgia
1817	Nuestra Senora de Montserrat	256	Undetermined number of slaves landed at Amelia Is.; vessel seized by U.S.
1817	Tentativa	146	130 seized by U.S.
1817	Poletina	109	Seized by U.S.
1817	Prize to Morgiana	118	Seized by U.S.
1817	Syrena	72–160	Seized by U.S.
1818	Nuestra Senora de Belin	—	Seized by U.S.
1819	Captured by Puerrydon/Tigre	16	Seized by U.S.
1820	Vessels captured by Colombia (including Antelope/Gen. Ramirez)	280	Attempted landing 259 at Amelia; seized by U.S.; 16 freed; 100 sent to Africa by American Colonization Society

SOURCES: *U.S.* v. *The Pilot Boat* Fire Fly, GA Adm.; *Miguel de Castro* v. *Ninety-five Africans*, GA Adm.; *John Madrazo* v. *Slaves, the Cargo of the* Isabelita, GA Adm. *Voyages Database* no. 5050; *U.S.* v. *The Brig* Montserrat, GA Adm.; *John H. Elton, on Behalf of the United States* v. *The* Tentativa *and Slaves*; *John H. Elton, on Behalf of the Officers and Crew of the* Sarnac v. *The* Tentativa *and Slaves*; *The Spanish Consul* v. *The* Tentativa *and Slaves*; *M. Lavignon, on Behalf of the Brutus Privateer* v. *The* Tentativa *and Slaves*, GA Adm.; *Charles Mulvey* v. *109 Slaves, Cargo of the Politina*, GA Adm.; John H. Elton to Benjamin Crowninshield, Dec. 6, 1817, Commanders' Letters; *John H. Henley* v. *The Schooner* Syrena; *U.S.* v. *The* Commodore Champlin *and Her Prize the* Syrena, GA Adm.; *U.S.* v. *The Ship* Nuestra Senora de Belin, GA Adm.; *U.S.* v. *Samuel Franklin*, Md Crim.; *John Jackson* v. *The* Antelope *or Gen. Ramirez*; *Charles Mulvaney* v. *150 African Negroes, Part of the Cargo of the* Antelope; *Francis Sorel* v. *130 Slaves, Part of the Cargo of the* Antelope, GA Adm.; *Voyages Database* no. 41885, 41892, 41893, 41894, 41895, 41896; Landers, *Black Society in Spanish Florida*, 181–182.

politics of the response to slave dealing at Amelia Island resembled previous debates on limiting the foreign slave trade. Antislavery forces, who opposed the trade on moral grounds, found themselves on the same side as planters, who wanted to preserve their bondsmen from the perceived malign influence of foreign slaves and foreign laws. Aury's misfortune was to make enemies on all sides.[38]

Second, with the rise of yet another center of Spanish American activity near U.S. territory, the problem of foreign privateering seemed to metastasize. Again and again, U.S. policy makers linked Amelia Island to the broader context of privateering, smuggling, and filibustering. The connection to Galveston was especially important. Aury was at both settlements; both operated similarly; and Aury claimed to govern Amelia with the authority he received in Texas. Anxiety over the growth of foreign privateering was understandable. For seven years now the problem had deepened. First New Orleans and the Louisiana coast, then Baltimore and Galveston and Amelia . . . where would it end?, President Monroe must have wondered.[39]

Third, in a departure from previous policy, the administration decided not to respect the legitimacy of the governments formed by MacGregor and Aury. Generally U.S. officials were admonished to observe a strict neutrality between Spain and its former colonies, which had given privateers access to U.S. ports. In the fall of 1817, confusion reigned at Amelia among naval officers, who could never be sure how to treat the flags of MacGregor and Aury. But the more Washington officials learned about MacGregor's and Aury's lack of connection to any actual Spanish American government, the more dubious they became. MacGregor, for example, based his legitimacy on a commission he had received from government agents of Venezuela, New Grenada, Mexico, and Buenos Aires. However, MacGregor received the commission while in Philadelphia, a violation of U.S. neutrality law, which prohibited anyone, including foreign nationals, from receiving a foreign commission to attack a nation at peace with the United States while on U.S. soil. MacGregor's commission itself ended with the words "signed, sealed, and delivered, at the city of Philadelphia, the thirty-first day of March, 1817"—making it signed evidence of a felony. Aury, meanwhile, had received the blessing of a representative of the Mexican government to establish Galveston. He was named governor of a province in Texas, and it is dubious how this empowered him to rule an island in East Florida. Both men displayed a personal attachment to the Spanish American cause, but the legitimacy of the Amelia Island settlement was a question separate from

MacGrergor's and Aury's feelings. Legitimacy exists, partly, in the eyes of other nations. Given the source of MacGregor's and Aury's power and the conduct of their privateers, U.S. officials had good reason to look askance at Amelia.[40]

Fourth, President Monroe and his advisors believed that U.S. laws authorized a strike against a foreign presence in the Spanish Floridas in the present circumstances. In 1811, Congress had enacted the No Transfer Resolution, which empowered the president to occupy any Florida lands in danger of falling under the control of any power other than Spain. Though Spanish American adventurers were certainly not the danger first envisioned by the resolution's authors, the diplomatic context warranted its application to Amelia. Secretary of State Adams had taken up his post in the fall, and negotiations with Spain over the long-standing issues between the two nations resumed in December. If the Spanish lost control of Florida, they would not have it to give to the United States. As Monroe said in his message announcing the suppression of Aury, "Care will be taken that no part of the territory contemplated by the law of 1811, shall be occupied by a foreign government of any kind."[41]

In spite of the justifications the Monroe administration offered for its decision to seize Amelia Island, many scholars remain doubtful. They see the words of U.S. officials as verbal cover for a land grab. Monroe's Amelia policy, the argument goes, was part of a long-running government program of undermining Spanish rule over Texas and the Floridas through secret agents, filibusters, and pretexts for intervention. For example, William Earl Weeks maintains that Adams deliberately placed both diplomatic and military pressure on Spain, hoping to show the Spanish that the United States was prepared to take by force what it could not obtain by treaty. Similarly, Frank Owsley and Gene Smith believe that although "the operation at Amelia Island was not as clearly identifiable as a planned expansion attempt, . . . the silent hands of the government seemed to have touched all of these adventurers."[42]

But such a view is not supported by the evidence. Weeks, for example, argues that U.S. officials denied the legitimacy of Spanish American privateers in general and Aury's settlement in particular because it really was legitimate and therefore a threat to U.S. designs on Florida. As a result, Secretary of State Adams perpetrated three deceptions. First, according to Weeks, Adams carefully labeled Aury's men pirates to undermine their legitimacy. Then, he responded to a congressional request for information on Amelia with a report that deliberately confused the issue by focusing on unrelated developments at Galveston. Finally, Adams overestimated

FIGURE 6. Commission issued by Aury at Amelia Island, 1818. (Amelia Island Papers, National Archives, Atlanta, Ga.)

the scale of the slave trade through Amelia to incite support for immediate action. However, none of these charges withstand scrutiny. Adams did call Aury a pirate, and he no doubt meant it to reflect badly on the commodore's legitimacy. But for Adams this was no cynical trick. He regularly denigrated all Spanish American privateers as pirates—his favorite appellation was "piratical privateers"—because that is the way he felt about them. Adams's contempt was sincere. Why Adams reported on both Galveston and Amelia is easily explained: Congress specifically asked for a report on both places, a natural request given the similarity between the two. Meanwhile, the slave trade through Amelia Island was real and damaging.[43]

The contention that the seizure of Amelia was part of a standing U.S. policy of undermining Spanish rule also rests on the similarity of this episode with four other incidents in the Spanish borderlands: the West Florida uprising of 1810, allegedly orchestrated by American agents and which precipitated the region's annexation by the United States; the so-called East Florida Patriot War of 1811–12, said to have been instigated at President Madison's behest; the 1812–13 Gutierrez-Magee expedition into Texas, supposedly organized with U.S. government aid; and Andrew Jackson's 1818 invasion of Florida. But J. C. A. Stagg and others have challenged the degree of U.S. government involvement in each action, instead showing that they occurred without government sanction and involved Americans, sometimes in government employ, who exceeded their orders and took matters into their own hands.[44]

Ultimately, the idea that U.S. officials sought to take Spanish lands by force contradicts the Madison and Monroe administrations' commitment to obtaining the Floridas by means that would be respected by the community of nations. Only then would America's title to the Floridas be seen as legitimate. U.S. officials exercised less control over events than some diplomatic historians have given them. U.S. policy makers did not deftly manipulate international conditions to the nation's advantage. Instead, their response to the challenge posed by Amelia Island depended on the legal and geopolitical conditions that existed at the time decisions were made.[45]

The U.S. Response: Galveston

As Amelia Island rose and fell as an independent port, the Laffites continued building their Galveston privateering, smuggling, and slave-dealing business, while also hiding from U.S. authorities and presenting a loyal face to the Spanish, in whose service they remained. Still, Jean and Pierre would have done well to pay close attention to the events at Amelia. President Monroe, in his message to Congress announcing the successful occupation of Amelia Island, had a warning. The suppression of Galveston, he said, "will soon follow."[46]

A raid on Galveston seemed attractive to officials in Louisiana, since traditional law enforcement methods had not worked. The navy patrolled the coast. Customs agents scoured the bayous and investigated planters rumored to have received illegal slaves. Both services made a handful of captures. But customs had still not figured out how to stop foreign armed vessels from abusing the law's entry-in-distress provision, and the navy's low morale persisted. A sullen Charles Morris, captain of a vessel cruising against slavers, informed his superiors that "every exertion will be made to intercept them, but I have little hopes of success."[47]

The failure of U.S. officials to stop privateers, smugglers, and filibusters operating from Galveston has, as before, been assigned to their negligence. In this view, officials allowed illegal activities to persist either because they were implementing a government policy to go easy on anyone who harmed Spain (and thereby pressured the Spanish to negotiate with the United States) or because they were too timid or too lazy to do their jobs in the face of a local population sympathetic to the Spanish American cause. U.S. law enforcement's shortcomings were real. But to blame officials' failures on their lack of will or their involvement in a policy of diplomatic pressure misjudges the way they operated.[48]

As Aury built Galveston and the Laffites restarted their operations, U.S. authorities amassed a terrible record in criminal court. Between 1815 and the first half of 1819, thirteen men were indicted for their alleged violations of piracy, slave trade, and neutrality laws. None of the indictments produced convictions. In the second half of 1819, the losing streak ended. Twenty-three men were indicted for piracy or accessory to piracy. Twenty-two were found guilty, and the outcome of the remaining case is unknown. When the government secured convictions, it had an enormous impact on the viability of privateering. But for the first few years of Galveston's existence, privateers operated freely.[49]

On the civil side of the Louisiana federal court, the privateers' enemies found success. After the Battle of New Orleans, Mexican privateers and filibusters produced thirty-three case files assigned a unique case number. Since multiple parties sometimes filed separate suits contending for the same property, it makes sense to combine these instances into one case. Thus, there were eighteen cases in which different prizes or privateers were involved. Outcomes can be found in thirteen. The results: privateers were able to keep their property—either prizes or armed vessels—six times, although one of these was later reversed on appeal. Spanish merchants received their property back five times, either when the court ordered restoration or when the United States gave up its claim to a vessel. The United States saw one privateer vessel condemned to the government. Finally, another case resulted in a divided outcome. The privateer, *Aguila*, was condemned to the United States; the prize goods it captured were returned to the Spanish; and although the prize vessel *Santa Rita* was also awarded to the Spanish at first, it was later divided between the parties to avoid an appeal. The final scorecard, then, reads: five privateer victories, six Spanish victories, one U.S. victory, and one case where everyone got something. The privateers lost nearly 60 percent of the time. If U.S. authorities or the Spanish consul could libel privateers' property, there was a good chance they would prevail.[50]

Nevertheless, the chances of capturing a privateer, its prize goods or slaves, and bringing them into court may have been hampered by the corruption of authorities and the legal process. For example, James Bowie, the man who invented the famous knife and later died at the Alamo, operated a slave-laundering scheme with the connivance of officials. With his brothers John and Rezin, James bought slaves from the Laffites and then moved them to Louisiana. Rather than selling the slaves immediately, however, the Bowies turned them over to authorities, claiming they had discovered a violation of the slave law and had taken it upon themselves to perform their civic duty by chasing the contrabandists away and seizing the slaves. According to the law, smuggled slaves were sold at auction, with half the proceeds going to the government and half to whomever provided the information leading to their seizure. Since anyone could bid, the Bowies bought the slaves back, and with their share of the sale, they effectively received a 50 percent discount. They also received legal title to the slaves, making it possible to sell them again and demand a higher price, since with the title in hand a buyer could be confident he had bought the slaves legally.[51]

Even worse, Commodore Patterson allowed U.S. Navy vessels to escort merchantmen transporting arms to Mexico, and sometimes he also arranged for the navy to do the transporting itself. The U.S. schooner *Firebrand* and the U.S. ketch *Suprise* brought dispatches, a printing press, and guns to Mexico and returned to New Orleans with money to pay the filibusters and their backers. Between 1815 and 1816, U.S. naval vessels completed six trips to Mexico. Patterson stopped only when an escort of a merchantman and a Mexican privateer nearly provoked hostilities with Spain. Three Spanish men-of-war, believing the American vessel and its charges to be privateers, captured the *Firebrand*. Though they were soon released, the attack on a U.S. naval vessel brought cries for war.[52]

Patterson's actions are suspicious. He was said to be a supporter of Mexican filibustering and privateering, and his association with these men suggests he was up to something unsavory. Still, he opposed privateers and smugglers throughout his tenure in New Orleans, and even while some naval vessels delivered munitions to Mexico, others cruised against smugglers and illegal privateers. Patterson may have actually aimed to prevent just the kind of incident that the *Firebrand* provoked. The law allowed Spain to capture neutral vessels trading munitions to an enemy, but American merchants would not be happy about the loss and would demand a response from the United States. As long as New Orleans merchants were sending arms to Mexico, perhaps they needed a chaperone. Yet, Patterson crossed a line by having the navy convoy a foreign armed vessel and transport materiel. U.S. commanders occasionally had a problem with how to proceed. Military and naval commanders received wide latitude from their superiors in Washington, allowing them to deal with foreign governments as circumstances developed rather than waiting for instructions. Sometimes they got carried away, especially in distant posts such as New Orleans. When Madison learned of Patterson's dealings, he wrote new instructions for naval commanders circumscribing their ability to act on their own judgment. In the end, it seems Patterson acted foolishly but not maliciously.[53]

Policing the gulf and the bayous was hit or miss and failed to sever the link between Galveston and Louisiana. The civil courts raised the cost of doing business, but the criminal courts failed to convict anyone. Privateers continued to cruise the gulf. Illegal goods and slaves still found their way into Louisiana. And yet President Monroe never ordered an Amelia-like seizure of Galveston.

Texas was different from Florida geopolitically. Florida had long been the priority for U.S. policy makers. Its geography complemented the southern states, providing river access to the gulf for Alabama and Mississippi, security against foreign incursions for Georgia and Louisiana, and a barrier to slaves who hoped to escape to Spanish freedom. Thus, there was no Texas counterpart to the Florida No Transfer Resolution that could be called on to justify a strike against Galveston. Moreover, officials felt that Texas was not worth angering the Spanish over. As early as 1816, Madison and Monroe were ready to give up Texas if they could obtain the Floridas. Finally, U.S. officials did not possess the same kind of information on Galveston as they had on Amelia. Reports of activities at Amelia Island had circulated regularly in American papers, and Georgia officials could observe from barely a mile away. But for Galveston, even Customs Collector Chew was at a loss. In his reports to the treasury secretary—written in August 1817, a year after Aury had arrived—Chew appeared to have a rudimentary understanding of the situation at Galveston, and given that the Laffites were then consolidating their power, the intelligence was worthless.[54]

Ultimately, the United States did not need to invade Galveston to end the problems it caused. Between 1818 and 1820, changes on the ground in Texas and the way those changes interacted with shifts in the law and geopolitics increased pressure on the Laffites. In time, their strategies no longer worked, and they chose to abandon Galveston on their own.

The first sign of a shift came in spring 1818 via a new filibuster expedition, this time led by Charles-Francois-Antoine Lallemand, a former

French general and close associate of Napoleon who had fought in Italy, Egypt, Haiti, Spain, and Belgium. At war's end he left the French army and traveled to Turkey, Persia, and Egypt to offer his military expertise (he found no takers) before sailing to America. There he met his brother Henri, also once a French general, and conceived the idea of establishing a refuge in Texas for fellow veterans of Napoleon's service. Lallemand drew particular support from a group of French and French-Haitian émigrés known as the Society for the Cultivation of the Vine and Olive who owned land in, of all places, Alabama. The Society had received a land grant from the U.S. government in the hope that they would occupy territory recently won from the Creek Indians while also developing an American wine industry. Lallemand politicked his way to the Society's presidency and persuaded many of its members to sell their lands to finance his expedition. Thus, unlike other filibuster expeditions, Lallemand did not aim to open a port for the Mexicans or establish a new independent republic. He attracted eighty or ninety followers and established a settlement near Galveston, calling it Champ d'Asile, the field of asylum. Jean and Pierre used this expedition as an opportunity to revive their plan to gain the filibusters' trust while promising the Spanish to turn them over, thereby earning protection for their other activities. Lallemand played into their hands. Champ d'Asile struggled (it provided asylum only from things like regular meals, freshwater, and good health), and before long Lallemand and his men abandoned it to live at Galveston.[55]

But the Laffites miscalculated. Lallemand's filibuster posed a new challenge to the geopolitics of the gulf. He was not a Mexican revolutionary but a Bonapartist seeking to build a haven for other Bonapartists at a time when rumors swirled that Bonapartists were plotting to rescue their emperor from exile and begin a new campaign. Champ d'Asile threatened to destabilize the region. Lallemand had cultivated contacts with both U.S. and Spanish officials, creating suspicions all around. He also threatened to invite British and French interference in Spanish American affairs. Britain and France did not want Napoleon partisans gaining a foothold in Spanish America, but they also did not want the United States to use Lallemand's presence as a pretext to take territory from their Spanish ally. Either situation could require military intervention. For the United States and Spain, bilateral negotiations were complicated enough. They would grow harder—and, from the U.S. perspective, more dangerous—if other European powers got involved. Lallemand had to go, and his protectors, the Laffites, would be caught in the crossfire.[56]

Through the second half of 1818, Spain and the United States each took steps to counteract Lallemand, and the Laffites found themselves boxed in. That summer, the viceroy of New Spain ordered an attack on Galveston. Clearing out Lallemand was the first priority, but Spanish officials had also caught on to the Laffites and their "double dealing," as the captain-general of Cuba wrote. Jean and Pierre survived only because a hurricane struck the gulf and disrupted Spain's plans. In October, the Spanish tried again to destroy Lallemand, and again the Laffites survived through good fortune: the Spanish lacked sufficient boats to cross Galveston Bay.[57]

The U.S. response was less dramatic. President Monroe sent an agent, George Graham, to Texas with instructions to gather intelligence and order Lallemand to disperse. Graham arrived at Galveston in August, ahead of the hurricane. He met Lallemand, delivered his message, and secured the general's promise to leave. When Graham later sailed for New Orleans, Lallemand went with him, ending the filibuster expedition. Graham performed less admirably with Jean. At first, he was harsh. "The Government of the United States will not allow an establishment of any kind," he warned, "especially one ... so dubious as that which at present exists [here]." Nevertheless, Graham assured Jean that he could keep privateering as long as he did it somewhere else and did not violate U.S. law. Before departing, Graham secured Jean's promise to vacate Galveston, though they agreed that Jean and Pierre should have two or three months to settle their affairs. John Quincy Adams blanched when Graham reported his friendly interview with Jean. It was "all of Graham's own head," he wrote, and "not much to the credit of its wisdom." Jean and Pierre had once thrived by manipulating complex international tensions to their advantage. Now only luck and George Graham's poor judgment preserved them.[58]

The Laffites repeated their mistakes when a final filibuster, the eleventh since 1810, came through Galveston in 1819. The expedition was led by James Long, a twenty-five- or twenty-six-year-old American who had drifted between careers in business, medicine, and the military before falling in with a group of hotheads angry that the Transcontinental Treaty surrendered America's claim to Texas. Long and his followers aimed to protect the land from "all those exactions which Spanish rapacity is fertile in devising" and make Texas an independent nation under their own government. Long sought an alliance with the chief of Galveston. He named Jean governor and empowered him to issue privateering commissions. In the past, filibusters such as Long were the

Laffites' key to opening room for them to operate. Espionage pleased the Spanish, while the filibusters' aura of revolutionary legitimacy offered protection from U.S. law enforcement. In 1819, however, that strategy no longer worked. The Spanish viceroy sent another military force that spring, though it, too, failed because of weather, this time floods. Meanwhile, the U.S. Army cut off supplies headed out of Louisiana. Eventually a Spanish army routed Long and drove him back to the United States. With the Transcontinental Treaty now signed and awaiting ratification, Spain and the United States were united in opposition to Long. The Laffites had no more geopolitical openings to exploit.[59]

The law also turned against them. In November, the captain and crew of a Laffite privateer, the schooner *Bravo*, were convicted of piracy and sentenced to death. The *Bravo* had sailed from Galveston under the command of Jean Desfarges in August and captured the Spanish schooner *Filomena* off Florida before both vessels were overhauled by two U.S. Customs cutters. As in most cases, no record survives to explain why the jury reached its conclusion. But there are hints. Newspapers reveal the defense's strategy was to claim that the *Bravo* was a regular privateer—owned by the Laffites, outfitted at Galveston, commissioned by the Independent Government of Texas—that had captured a prize in the regular course of war. The prosecution's jurisdictional burden was eased by a new piracy law, passed in March 1819, that embraced the broad, "general piracy" definition of the crime as murder or robbery at sea that any nation could punish. Still, to secure a conviction, prosecutors needed to show that the crime was committed *animo furandi*, that is, that Desfarges and his men knew their commission was invalid and attacked the *Filomena* anyway. The Laffites' notoriety could not have helped Desfarges's cause, and Long had no connection to any Spanish American republic. What's more, the paperwork filed as evidence did not support the defense's story. The commission had been issued to a Juan Salvador de Torres, not a Laffite, and it had been granted by General Humbert, not James Long.[60]

The Laffites were astute readers of their situation, and they saw that the geopolitical tensions that they had exploited for over a decade no longer worked in their favor. In the spring of 1820, Pierre packed up their belongings in New Orleans and Jean razed their buildings at Galveston as the U.S. Navy watched in the distance. The Laffites ended their smuggling days in the United States and headed deeper into the Caribbean to attempt to revive their business, with Jean becoming a privateer captain himself—unsuccessfully. As time went on, the wars wound down and the major sponsors of privateering had less and less use for new captains. As the Laffites were learning, the geopolitics that had driven their business had changed.[61]

Conclusion

The rise and fall of Galveston and Amelia Island is a three-part story that reveals the multiplicity of geopolitical influences along the U.S. borderlands. The privateers and filibusters who sailed from Galveston and Amelia depended on borders and the privileges accorded to states. They chose these islands because their leaders acted like the officers of an independent government rather than a collection of outlaws. They issued their own papers, which the United States, because of its policy of neutrality, often chose to respect.

The U.S. government's response forms the second aspect of the story. U.S. policy makers sought to preserve neutrality and to settle relations with Spain in a way that achieved security amid fears that a new European war would follow the recently concluded one. U.S. officials hoped that Spain's loss in North America would be the United States' gain, and the invasion of Amelia Island expanded the nation. Still, the immediate geopolitical context—the status of negotiations with Spain and the threat posed by smugglers, slave dealers, and privateers—drove U.S. policy.

Then there are the Laffites. Jean and Pierre donned new loyalties for a while, but they played the same game: manipulating conditions to their favor. Only when the Transcontinental Treaty brought calm to U.S.-Spanish relations did the Laffites begin their losing streak. The geopolitics that had created foreign privateering evaporated, driving the Laffites, and most other Spanish American privateers, out of the United States.

5 / Service and Toil in Spanish America

As the Wars of Independence drew to a close, James Chaytor was back in South America, and even though he had aided the victory, he was unhappy. Chaytor had been invited to assume a position in the Colombian navy, but after arriving in Bogota to take office, an earthquake struck, and he injured his back when his house collapsed. By the time he recovered, President Simón Bolívar was cutting back the navy, and Chaytor, fearing "the mortification of being laid on the shelf," resolved to come home. Chaytor's final turn in South America was frustrating. "Here," he wrote from Bogota, "nothing is expeditiously done[;] 'poco a poco' is the 'sine qua non,' and he who possesses most patience generally succeeds best." Chaytor still took pride in Spanish American independence, but he was conflicted. Writing to his son-in-law, W. G. D. Worthington, Chaytor reflected on his "more than 13 years of ~~service~~ toil in the noble cause of South American emancipation." He wrote "service" but changed it to "toil."[1]

Chaytor's feelings toward Spanish America were complex. He first joined a privateer as an alternative to an unsatisfying merchant voyage, but soon after there was something different about him. He started claiming that he preferred speaking Spanish to English. He began calling himself Diego, the Spanish version of his name. He signed his letters "Diego Chaytor" and "DC"—even when writing his wife. He once yearned for Buenos Aires to be free. "My whole soul is devoted to the cause," he said. Nevertheless, a measure of bitterness slipped into his thoughts as time went on, sacrifices went unacknowledged, bills went unpaid. He worried about financial security and how his family was coping during his absences. "I am fearful," he wrote of his wife, Sarah, "that her pecuniary distress will be equal to my own." He groused, too, that his true talent was not appreciated, on one occasion telling Worthington that "the marine service in this section of America is so clogged with ignorance & ambition only to obtain the *gold lace*" that he would never advance, "so that the *association*, when the limits of rank is considered, will cause more pain than profit." Spanish American held so much promise for Chaytor, promise that was only partially fulfilled.[2]

Chaytor's ambivalence embodied the larger, tangled pattern of motives found in those who left the United States to fight for Spanish American independence. For many, money was the primary motivation. Privateering was a business. The point was to seize ships and cargoes and sell them for a profit. But for others, fighting for independence mattered, too. The motivations of Spanish American privateers were multifaceted, varying from one man to the next and even for the same man from one moment to the next. Records are fragmented and cannot provide a universal view of why the thousands of Spanish American privateers sailed, but patterns emerge from piecing together their stories. This chapter examines the motivations of privateers and their associates in the key positions of captains, investors, sailors, and filibuster allies, men such as Joseph Almeida, a sea captain out for revenge against Spain; Jean and Pierre Laffite, the businessmen-privateers of the Gulf Coast; Jonathan Falconar, a young man in search of money and adventure; and Gregor MacGregor, the filibuster-dreamer who conquered Amelia Island as a haven for privateers. The chapter looks closely at their decisions to become involved in the Spanish American wars, their decisions to persist or give up, and their reflections on what it all meant. Taken together, the work of these men in Spanish American privateering, along with that of many others, reveals that the desire for money and power commingled with the desire to advance the cause of Spanish American independence while also mixing with the personal, idiosyncratic desires of each.

Captains

Captain Joseph Almeida wanted revenge. In December 1815, he had sailed a merchant vessel to Cartagena expecting to find a profitable market only to discover—too late—that the city had fallen to the Spanish, who seized his ship and threw him in jail. Although the U.S. State Department eventually secured his release, Almeida was embittered.

"Cartagena [is] ever memorable to me by the cruelties which I received from [Spanish General] Morillo and his army," he once wrote. "I lost my property, suffered imprisonment and was discharged with my life only." "Resentment for lost property and personal injury," he explained, "carried me into the South American service." For the rest of his life, Almeida battled the Spanish, even after Spanish American independence had been achieved. In the end, Almeida lost to his enemy. In 1829 a mutinous crew turned him over to Spanish officials in Puerto Rico, where he was executed as a pirate.[3]

Almeida burned with resentment, a hatred born of his lost property and lost dignity at the hands of the Spanish, a hatred that ultimately led to his death. Almeida's feelings were unusually intense, but they were not unique. For some, such as Almeida, commanding a privateer was personal. For others, privateering held out a path to prosperity. For others, privateering promised a kind of patriotism for an adopted home. And for others still, privateering was all three at once.

Captains often displayed an attachment to Spanish American independence. Thomas Taylor, for example, wore a uniform and, according to one sailor, had his crew take "the oath for the Independence of South America" before sailing. Taylor also nursed a bitter hatred for the Spanish consul in Baltimore, Pablo Chacon, reportedly promising a thirty-thousand-dollar reward to anyone who would help him kidnap his adversary. Taylor supposedly wanted someone to lure the consul onboard his *Fourth of July* by saying it was a Spanish vessel recently stolen by privateers. Taylor then planned, a sailor testified, to "confine the Consul and carry him out in the vessel and deliver him to the patriots."[4]

Meanwhile, French privateer captains Charles Lominé and Jean Monier demonstrated their commitment through their service. Both accepted Cartagenan commissions and cruised against Spanish shipping, Lominé sailing the *Piñérez*, named for Gabriel Piñérez, the vice president of Cartagena, and Monier commanding the *Constitution*. When Spanish forces closed in on Cartagena, the captains evacuated the city's residents, running them through the blockade and on to safety in Haiti. Lominé and Monier were close to Simón Bolívar, assisting at the January 1816 Aux Cayes meeting, in which Bolívar developed a plan to liberate South America, and sailing on the first Aux Cayes expedition to Venezuela. Bolívar entrusted Monier with a special task: fetching Bolívar's mistress, who had arrived in Haiti after the expedition sailed. If, as it was once said, that "wherever Bolívar was, there the republic existed," then those men closest to him were closest to the republic he founded.[5]

Captain John Chase never met Bolívar, but he loved Buenos Aires, delighting in the memory of commanding a Buenos Aires privateer. "I shall ever rank among the proudest reminiscences of my life," he wrote in 1832, "that I have been able to do the state of Buenos Ayres 'some service.'" Chase bristled at the suggestion that he acted from any other motive. In 1828, he became embroiled in a controversy with a U.S. naval officer, Josiah Tatnall. Chase had told a newspaper that Tatnall's vessel had illegally stopped a Buenos Airean privateer. Taking offense, Tatnall denounced Chase as a man who "expatriate[d] himself with the base purpose of pecuniary exaction" and who was "deservedly more execrable than the avowed buccaneer, who boldly displays the red banner of rapine, and jeopards his neck unprotected by *colourable* rights or prostituted flags." An anonymous pamphleteer joined the fray, condemning Chase for following "the advice of the old man to his son: 'to make money honestly if he could, but if he could not make it honestly, to make it anyway.'" Chase fought back, promising two hundred dollars for information leading to the identity of the anonymous author (he discovered it was a Baltimore lawyer) and publishing a pamphlet of his own in which he challenged Tatnall to a duel. "I pronounce JOSIAH TATTNALL a calumniator without provocation, an officer without courage, and a man without honor," Chase asserted. He denied any but the purest motives. "I entered into the Navy of the government of Buenos Ayres and continued faithful to her interests during the whole of her struggles," Chase continued. "I have been influenced by higher considerations than 'pecuniary exactions.'" Tattnall, however, was unimpressed. He refused to give Chase satisfaction, making his own statement that Chase, whatever his pretentions to importance in South America, was beneath the standing of a gentleman officer of the United States Navy.[6]

Chase's protestations aside, some captains were driven by lower considerations, including "pecuniary exactions." Pierre Liquet, for example, drifted into Spanish American privateering, seizing the opportunity to keep working in a familiar field. Liquet commanded three French and four Spanish American vessels in almost fifteen years of privateering in the gulf and Caribbean. Other captains were more calculating in their choice of commands. Dominique Youx also got his start privateering for France in the early 1800s, sailing from Guadeloupe and Baracoa, Cuba, where many French exiles from Haiti had settled. Beginning in 1805, Youx commanded the *Superbe*, and over the next few years he also took the helm of the *Guerrie* and the *Pandoure*. In 1814, Youx commanded the Cartagenan privateer *Tigre*. He frequented Barataria and was one of the men arrested by the U.S. Navy in its September 1814 raid. Once released from jail, he joined the defense of New Orleans and manned an artillery position overlooking the Mississippi River. Because of this service, Youx has gained a reputation for American patriotism. However, he moved easily among the nations at war in the early nineteenth century, using the shifts in geopolitics to his advantage. He captured American, Spanish, and British vessels, depending on whom he served. Indeed, as a French privateer, Youx hunted American vessels sailing for Haiti. Following the island nation's declaration of independence in 1804, a lucrative trade in munitions sprang up, and although legal, French officials did not want to see the rebels fortified. Privateers like Youx helped stop them.[7]

Some captains had no allegiance at all. Bernard Lafon, for example, commanded a Spanish privateer against Britain and a French privateer against Spain. He sailed an American privateer out of Norfolk in 1812 and a Cartagenan privateer a year later. It was his fourth commission in less than a decade. Lafon felt no more loyalty to his new sponsor than he felt toward any of the others. When later hired by a Cartagenan merchant to sail his *Flora Americana* to New Orleans, Lafon ran away with the ship and went cruising without official sanction. He landed at Barataria, sold *Flora*'s cargo (including a thousand coconuts), and attempted to ransom the vessel back to its owners, with the Laffites brokering the deal. A Spanish official once accused Lafon of "going privateering whenever there was a war and he got any sort of chance." He was right.[8]

For sheer marauding, no one topped Baltimore captain Henry Ford. A former officer in the United States Marine Corps, Ford had been cashiered in 1816 and then went on to command the privateer *Buenos Ayres*, which he renamed *General Artigas*. Ford made prize of eleven Portuguese vessels and sacked three small towns in Brazil. In the first, he pillaged a church, stripping the altar and stealing the priest's vestments. In the second, he assaulted some "harmless and pious inhabitants returning from mass," the Portuguese consul reported, "and robbed and plundered [them] of their watches and trinkets." In the third town, Ford filched one hundred dollars' worth of silver pots and plates and some oxen and horses, which he had killed to provision the ship. Captain Ford did not treat his own men well, either. When some officers objected to what one called his "very irregular and piratical" conduct, Ford got rid of them. He made them prize masters and ordered them to sail a vessel into what he knew was an enemy port. The officers were never heard from again. For Ford, privateering was a chance to plunder.[9]

Ideology, convenience, and personal gain—captains who displayed each of these motivations can be found among the men who sailed French and Spanish American privateers from the United States. These motives can also be found mixed within the same person, as the examples of Captains Rene Beluche and John D. Danels show.

Beluche was a committed revolutionary who sought wealth from his cruising and was not above trading slaves to get it. Born in New Orleans, he began his career sailing merchant vessels to ports such as Havana and Vera Cruz. In 1810, Beluche began privateering, first for France, then for the United States, Cartagena, and Venezuela. He was not overly scrupulous about the law. Beluche obtained a French commission by sailing to St. Bart's, a violation of U.S. neutrality for an American citizen, which Beluche would have automatically become with the Louisiana Purchase. As commander of the American privateer *Spy*, he smuggled goods through Barataria, much to the chagrin of the vessel's owner, who could have obtained the goods legally if his captain had brought them before a U.S. admiralty court. Yet, Beluche was also devoted to the cause of Spanish American independence. With the *Spy* renamed *Nuestra Señora de la Popa*, after Cartagena's patron saint, he support an 1813 assault on Santa Marta, a Spanish-held city just north of Cartagena. In late 1815, he delivered food and supplies to the beleaguered citizens of Cartagena, holding out against the Spanish blockade. In time, Beluche became one of Bolívar's trusted lieutenants. He joined the 1816 Aux Cayes meeting, alongside Lominé and Monier, and he continued in the service of Spanish America until independence was achieved, becoming a Colombian naval officer in the 1820s. When Bolívar decided to send a fleet to the Pacific in 1828, he knew who he wanted in charge. "I prefer Beluche," he said. "He is superior to all the others because of his rank, knowledge and ability, enthusiasms, etc."[10]

Captain Beluche believed in Spanish American independence. "I was born in the new world and acquired a love of glory in the defense of her liberty," he once remarked. "Scarcely had the cry of independence gone up from South America when I hurried to enlist myself among her defenders." Yet part of his service involved taking away the liberty of others. While commanding the Venezuelan privateer *General Arismendi*, Beluche apprehended the Spanish slave ship *Josefa Segunda*, with two hundred to three hundred slaves aboard. The vessel was later seized attempting to land the slaves in Louisiana. Like the others involved in privateering from Louisiana, Beluche was a worldly, cosmopolitan man who moved easily across national boundaries, and yet his relations with the world were ultimately shaped by his own personality, goals, and ambitions.[11]

For Captain Danels, the Spanish American wars provided a way to earn money and prestige, probably more of both than would have been available at home. Born in Maine, Danels had relocated to Baltimore and sailed merchantmen and U.S. privateers during the War of 1812. He was successful overall, escaping from shipwrecks, disloyal crews, imprisonment, and other vicissitudes of the sea with remarkable skill. Danels began Spanish American privateering in 1818 and made his richest prizes while hunting Portuguese East Indiamen between Africa and Brazil. Commanding the *Irresistable*, he nabbed vessels hauling specie worth $7,000, $10,000, $11,000, $26,000, and $400,000 (the last from the appropriately named *Asia Grande*). Two brigs, the *Guadeloupe* and the *Globo* brought a combined $160,000 worth of cotton, tea, coffee, ginger, sugar, salt peter, cinnamon, and rice. All told, Danels made off with more than $1.5 million in property—worth nearly $30 million today.[12]

Danels followed the rules when it suited him. On leaving Baltimore to obtain a commission in Buenos Aires, his vessel, the *Vacunia*, sailed directly to its destination, refusing to put into any port or attack any vessels on the way. He also refrained from stopping to speak to any passing ships as friendly captains so often did. Danels honed his crew's fighting skills, calling the men to quarters and practicing their gunnery. In Buenos Aires, he discharged the crew, dismantled the ship, and sold it to the government. Having given over his ship to the United Provinces, Danels next became a naturalized citizen. Now, with a commission for his vessel, to be called the *Maipú*, the site of a recent victory by General José de San Martín, Danels was ready for sea. Except that he changed his mind and secured an Oriental commission. Holding two commissions at the same time violated the law of nations and the prize code of the United Provinces. Just prior to sailing, several officers boarded his vessel for an inspection. Danels denied holding two commissions, and when asked to take a complement of Buenos Aires marines along for the cruise, he agreed, promising to wait for them to come aboard the next day. Danels sailed that night, without the marines, and returned the United Provinces commission via a ship he passed while exiting the River Plate. Buenos Aires officials declared Danels "a Pirate and a sea Robber" and seized the $10,000 bond posted by his *armadore*. Persona non grata in the United Provinces, Danels never returned.[13]

Danels also seems to have been indifferent to common sailors. While docked at Margarita, an island off Venezuela, he pledged his ships, the

Irresistable and the *Nereyda*, to an attack against a Spanish-held port. Needing additional men, Danels shanghaied the crew of a Buenos Aires privateer, the *Creolla*, lying nearby. He demanded that they enlist with him or be thrown in jail—if he did not first "hoist them to the yard arm," as one of the *Creolla*'s men recalled. The menaced sailors took matters into their own hands. They mutinied against their officers, rowed over to the faster-sailing *Irresistable*, wrested control from its officers and crew, and crowded sail to escape. Danels, spending the night on shore, frantically gave chase in the *Nereyda*. When he caught up with the *Creolla* mutineers in Baltimore, Danels "abused" them, according to one sailor, and shouted that "he would give them Five Dozen [lashes] apiece and that if he ever caught them in Buenos Ayres he would punish them." Another sailor remembered Danels snarling that "if ever he caught him in South America he would [put] a striped jacket on him and hang him up to the foreyard."[14]

Nevertheless, Danels persisted in the Spanish American service longer than many others and, given the size of his prizes, longer than his wallet demanded. In the 1820s, he joined the service of Gran Colombia and continued his ascent, participating in a blockade of Cumana and Laguaira in 1821. For his efforts, Colombia granted him citizenship and a commission in the navy. A year later, Danels traveled to the United States to buy a vessel for the Colombians. By 1823, he commanded a significant part of the republic's naval forces and received official correspondence addressed to the commander of "the Colombian Squadron."[15]

Danels enjoyed calling himself commodore; it likely made him feel important. In 1823, he took time to sit for a portrait: with a ship running before the wind in the background, Danels wears the uniform of the Colombian navy and holds a card in his right hand inscribed "Commodore J. D. Danels / de la Marina / Naval de Colombia / a la Guyara." Significantly, Danels chose to present himself with a distinctly Spanish American identity. He also emphasized his Spanish American connections when he commissioned a second portrait a few years later, this time of his children. In the painting, sons John, Lewis, and James, and daughters Eugenia and Elizabeth play alongside two boys of African descent: Manuel and Thomas Páez, the sons of Colombian general and future president of Venezuela José Antonio Páez. The Páez boys had been sent north to be educated at the elite St. Mary's College alongside Danels's own sons. Manuel and Thomas did not stay at the school long, unfortunately, as the families of white students complained about their race and they were dismissed. Danels, however, included them in his family portrait. Finally, Danels cemented his family's

FIGURE 7. Commodore John Daniel Danels. By Robert Street, 1822. (Courtesy of the Maryland Historical Society, 1976.57.1.)

connection to Spanish American independence in 1826, when he named his newest son Bolivar Daniel Danels (all the Danels sons received middle name Daniel, just like their father). He was not the only one to name a son for the Liberator, but unlike those other families, Danels participated in the Liberator's cause and may well have met him.[16]

FIGURE 8. Children of Commodore John Daniel Danels. By Sarah Miriam Peale, 1826. (Courtesy of the Maryland Historical Society, 1973.12.1.)

Owners and Investors

Privateer owner Jean Laffite claimed patriotism was his motive. "Though proscribed by my adoptive country, I will never let slip any occasion of serving her, or of proving she has never ceased to be dear to me," he wrote to a contact in the city before the Battle of New Orleans. This was self-serving. The Laffites may have had some loyalty to France, the place of their birth, but as for the United States or Spanish America,

Jean and Pierre showed no interest. They changed their loyalties as circumstances required. Privateer owners, investors, and agents all stood to make money from Spanish American privateering, and thus it is natural to wonder if perhaps they were generally like the Laffites: out to profit from the independence movement. Certainly money exerted a strong allure. But at the same time, nonmaterial factors were also involved.[17]

Given the difference in scale and scope of their enterprises, Baltimore privateer investors came from significantly different backgrounds than their Gulf Coast counterparts. Yet, men in both groups showed a similar complexity in their motivations. Baltimore privateer investors David De Forest and Robert M. Goodwin provide examples of the attitudes prevalent among backers of vessels arming in the Chesapeake. De Forest, a Connecticut Yankee who had moved to Buenos Aires, was proud of his adopted homeland and invested in privateers to advance the cause of independence. He observed the *Día de la Revolución de Mayo*, a celebration held in Buenos Aires each May 25 to commemorate the day in 1810 when Buenos Aires formed its own junta. De Forest continued the tradition even after he returned to Connecticut, and he expected it to continue after he died. He installed a tablet in his home engraved with a message for future owners: "I demand that you assemble your friends together on every 25th day of May in honor of the Independence of South America." At the same time, De Forest also hoped to leverage his position in Buenos Aires into a diplomatic post in the United States, adding luster to his golden years. He besieged Secretary of State John Quincy Adams with letters, urging the United States to accept his credentials. Adams refused. Officially receiving De Forest would have been tantamount to official recognition of the independence of the United Provinces, a step Adams could not take on his own. De Forest's desire for importance would have to wait.[18]

Robert M. Goodwin also appears to have held an affinity for Spanish America, but it was closely bound up with other motivations. Connected to the Ridgely family and the brother of a U.S. naval captain, Goodwin could have lived a lifestyle more gentlemanly than revolutionary. Yet, he had a touch of the wanderlust (De Forest described him as belonging to "the vagabond society"), which led him to go aboard the privateer *Independencia del Sud* as a marine. Later, Goodwin invested in the *Republicana* and ran the privateers' prize-goods laundering operation from St. Bart's. In 1819, the Portuguese consul, Thomas Stoughton, libeled Goodwin in New York City, seeking the return of the *Republicana*'s prizes. Goodwin took offense at some comments made by Stoughton's son,

James, who was a lawyer representing the Portuguese merchants. One day Goodwin and James Stoughton crossed paths on Broadway. Harsh words passed, a scuffle ensued, and Goodwin, armed with a sword cane, stabbed Stoughton, inflicting a mortal wound. Goodwin was tried for manslaughter and reviled in the press, though the trial resulted in a hung jury.[19]

One incident brings together the strands of self-interest, ideology, and an indifference to U.S. law prevalent among privateers: an 1818 celebration of George Washington's birthday held in Buenos Aires and organized by Baltimore privateer captains and investors. John Zimmerman chaired the preparations committee, and he was assisted by investors John R. Mifflin and William P. Ford, Captain John Chase, and Job Wheeden, a ship's surgeon. As the night wore on, the celebrants offered many toasts praising the love of freedom found in both North and South America. Mifflin hailed "the Forces who have fallen in the defense of the liberty of North America and South America." Privateer captain John Dieter lauded "the Patriots of North and South America." Wheeden raised a glass to "the heroes who have fought, bled, and died in their country's cause." Here, then, was a group of men, many of them Americans, who honored the memory of the president who signed the Neutrality Acts—a president who warned his countrymen against involvement in foreign wars—while they violated those Neutrality Acts and became directly involved in foreign wars. These men wanted to make money, and they were breaking the law to do it. But they also wanted South America to be free, like the United States.[20]

Jean and Pierre Laffite dominated Gulf Coast privateering, and they smuggled and owned privateers to make money. Both men had arrived in New Orleans with little property and few prospects, but given their entrepreneurial talents, it is unlikely they were part of the lowest class of the truly poor. Still, before turning to smuggling, neither Jean nor Pierre had made much of himself, and Pierre's struggles prior to smuggling slaves from West Florida showed how hard the legitimate world could be. The Laffites kept smuggling and privateering because, in spite of the tens of thousands of dollars in illegal goods and slaves that passed through their hands, they had constant cash-flow problems. They borrowed money to outfit their vessels. They did not pay it back on time. Lawsuits and indictments meant lawyers' bills, bonds, and, if a judgment went against them, settlements as well. The federal court ordered Pierre to pay some $9,500 to make restitution to the owners of the goods he had been caught smuggling. Then there were the old debts that lingered. In

1812, the owner of the slave Pierre had rented and sold during his 1806 trip to Pensacola resurfaced and filed suit. Pierre petitioned for bankruptcy protection in 1814, listing debts of $21,454.62 (the only credits he listed: "Mon Industrie").[21]

In the midst of these concerns, the men had growing families. Pierre arrived in New Orleans with a son, and before long he took up with a woman named Marie Louise Villard, a free mulatto or quadroon. The two never married, but marriage-like arrangements between European men and free women of color were common in New Orleans. Villard was Pierre's companion throughout his time there, and together they had at least six children. Marie's sister Catherine lived with her, Pierre, and the family. In 1815 she began a relationship with Jean, and their son, Jean Pierre, was born the next year. The Laffites may have made a lot of money, but between their highly leveraged business, their legal problems, and their expensive personal lives, they spent a lot, too.[22]

Other owners of Gulf Coast privateers were, like the Laffites, generally sea captains and small-scale merchants. They were marginal commercial men, such as Bernard Boudin, a merchant-tailor, and sea captains such as Rene Beluche, Ange-Michel Brouard, Pierre Lameson, and Dominique Youx. Since gulf privateer vessels were small, financial barriers to entering the business were easily overcome, and these men of lesser means could own their own privateers. Great merchants were not the prime movers of the business, although there were exceptions. The Baron Henri de Ste-Gême invested in privateers such as the Cartagenan-flagged *Cassadore*. A native of France, Ste-Gême had fled the revolution's antinoble mobs and lived in Saint-Domingue until the Haitian Revolution forced him to Louisiana, where he cultivated sugar and served with the Americans at the Battle of New Orleans—Jackson called him a "salty little rooster"—before returning to France in 1818, to enjoy the life of an absentee sugar planter. Another prominent investor, Jacob Hart, a ship owner and commission merchant, traded in the gulf to Pensacola, Havana, and Campeche as well as to Charleston, Baltimore, and New York. A member of the New Orleans Chamber of Commerce, he organized the city's Tuesday gala balls in the winter of 1806–7. He owned one privateer. Other men of distinction included Cartegenan merchants Juan de Dios Amador and Francisco Garcia del Fierro. Amador was the revolutionary governor of Cartagena, and del Fierro was his nephew. However, since they lived abroad, they were not typical of Louisiana privateer owners. In fact, both men had their vessels robbed by Louisiana captains.[23]

Like privateering, filibuster operations required investors, and the Mexican agents who operated out of Galveston enjoyed significant support in the United States. Or at least they thought they did. Oftentimes, the business backers of filibuster expeditions to liberate Mexico seemed more interested in liberating Mexican gold from its government. In Laffite mythology, they are known as the New Orleans Association, a term some diplomatic histories also employ, even though no contemporary evidence exists that any group used this name for themselves. (The name "New Orleans Association" apparently comes from a misunderstanding of the word "association" as it was used in the nineteenth century.) The group's ranks allegedly included prominent merchants, lawyers, and public officials such as John K. West, a merchant and ship owner; Abner L. Duncan, a lawyer and West's business partner; Benjamin Morgan, a merchant, banker, and insurance company executive; John B. Gilly, a merchant and politician; Edward Livingston, a lawyer and former mayor of New York City driven from office by scandal and now rebuilding his career in Louisiana; John R. Grymes, a former U.S. district attorney for Louisiana and Livingston's junior partner; Auguste Davezac, another attorney, who had read law under Livingston; Thomas Harman, a merchant; Vincent Nolte, a merchant; Bartholomé Lafon, an engineer, surveyor, and architect; Henry D. Peire, a former U.S. Customs agent and army major; Henry Perry, also formerly of the army; and merchant-planter Francois Dupuis. Daniel Todd Patterson, commander of the New Orleans Naval Station, and Customs Collector Pierre L. B. Duplessis are also frequently named as participants, as are two men about whom nothing can be found beyond their names: Chevalier Dows and someone called Smith.[24]

For these men, selling arms in support of a foreign war was a business—and a lawful one. The foreign arms trade was legal, although if a shipment were seized by the Spanish, they would have no legal recourse to recover their property. Consequently, they not only avoided censure but instead enjoyed long, distinguished careers, frequently becoming noted public servants. Davezac was U.S. ambassador to the Netherlands in the 1830s; Morgan held the presidency of the New Orleans branch of the Second Bank of the United States; Duncan ran for governor of Louisiana and had his name forwarded by Andrew Jackson for a federal judgeship; and Edward Livingston became Jackson's secretary of state. In light of their personal benefit as the Mexican patriots struggled, it is tempting to see these munitions-dealing merchants as guided mostly by profit. That is certainly possible. At the same time, there is scant direct evidence for any motive, and it is also possible that these men took the general enthusiasm for Spanish American independence felt across the country a step further into actually participating in aiding the Mexicans. It is also possible that they hoped to do both at the same time, advancing the cause of liberty as they advanced their own pecuniary interests as well.[25]

Sailors

Jonathan Falconar, a young Baltimorean, sought money and independence aboard the privateer *Buenos Ayres*, joining the crew in the fall of 1816 as the captain's clerk. As he left home, he wrote his older brother a note of defiance: "I have made up my mind as to my future Life, the first step into which is to leave this place. This would have been my aim long since had not poverty prevented me." At first, Falconar prospered. Sharing in the prize money, he lavished his sisters with a gift of one hundred dollars apiece and dreamed of buying land in Alabama, where he would "settle myself down in the dull pursuits of quiet life." But the good times did not last. The prizes dried up, the money grew scarce, and his brother tired of taking care of their mother on his own. If he did not come home, his brother wrote, "I do most *solemnly aver* that every tie of affection shall be broken and you no longer a Brother—I will treat you as one determined to destroy my plan and that of our mother & sisters and *cut you off forever.*" Landing in New Orleans, Falconar enjoyed the high life for a while longer, but by 1819 he was broken and begging to come home "almost as the prodigal son," he told his brother. In his plight, "neglected because I am poor avoided because unfortunate," Falconar could think of only one option. He sought out his old captain and attempted to sign up for another cruise.[26]

Early-nineteenth-century sailors lived a contradictory life of freedom and constraint. Subjected to harsh discipline aboard ship, they enjoyed liberty on shore, carousing themselves into a stupor that compelled a return to sea to leave their problems behind. The men before the mast of a Spanish American privateer were similarly caught between volition and necessity. Many privateersmen joined their vessels voluntarily. E. Williams, for example, happily went to work for Captain Vincent Gambi. "Being a sailor by profession & having intended to join the privateersmen," he testified, he "was engaged in N.O. by Vincent [Gambi] to work on board vessels fitting out [at] Barataria." Similarly, sailor Peter Franks said that when he joined a Venezuelan privateer at New Orleans, "he knew that she was going on a cruise." Joseph Smith, captain's clerk of the *Republicana*, affirmed that "all hands on board were aprized and informed of the operation subsequently intended." Nicholas Lusk was certainly one of them. He chose the *Republicana* in search of a "South American adventure." John Fitch also joined a privateer at New Orleans willingly. "After I went on Board & while she was laying in the river," he testified, "I signed the articles for cruising against Ferdinand the Seventh, & his Spanish subjects." During a trial, John Davis, a self-described "sea faring man," was asked if "any force or seduction" induced him to sign aboard a privateer. He gave a direct answer: "I joined her voluntarily." In a different case, sailor Thomas Hall also gave a direct answer. Asked, "Did you expect her to cruise or capture vessels after sailing from the United States?," he replied: "I did."[27]

Other sailors did not cast themselves with a privateer so eagerly. Some men had fallen in debt. Of the fourteen men deposed in the prosecution of innkeeper and shipping agent William Bush, five were in debt upon signing the shipping articles. Similarly, Henry Ford picked up a few U.S. Navy officers for his cruise in the schooner *General Artigas* because the vessel's owner, John Gooding, had paid their debts for them. Other men had fallen into a bottle. Three sailors of the *Congresso de Venezuela* testified that they signed the shipping articles "in a state of intoxication," not knowing even the name of the vessel. Samuel Scott admitted that he had joined the *Succesor* in Baltimore but could not recall the details. "I was groggy," he said. Edward Foley was more intentional in his drunkenness. He was searching for a ship in Baltimore in January, a time when few vessels ventured from port. The only one he could find was a privateer. Foley did not want a privateer, he later testified, but it was his only chance to avoid months in port running up debts. Faced with the inevitable, Foley did the only thing a man in his situation could do: "[I] got drunk and did ship on board the armed Brig."[28]

Sailors also chose a berth on a privateer to make the best of a bad situation. When John Oliver's vessel, a British merchantman, was captured by a French privateer, he joined its crew, eventually coming into Barataria, where he observed the Laffites' operation. Later, he threw in with a Spanish American privateer as well. The Cartagenan privateer *Nuestra Senora de la Popa* likewise added several reluctant seamen during its cruise, such as Felippe Brioner, who came aboard when his Spanish merchantman was captured. Later the *Popa* picked up five more men in Kingston, Jamaica, who were American prisoners of war just released with the end of the War of 1812. Brioner and the Americans all signed the ship's articles and put in for their share of the prize money at the end of the cruise.²⁹

Regardless of how sailors joined a privateer, they expected payment for their efforts. Some received advances before leaving port and prize shares when returning, as was standard practice for privateers. If shares were not forthcoming, it was time to leave. Others took their piece of the smuggled booty. Aboard the prize ship *Cleopatra* the intention to smuggle, one sailor said, "was as public as a gazette." When the ship was caught landing in Barataria by the navy, the crew grabbed "as many hats as they could carry, & some articles in sacks" and made for the swamps.³⁰

The sources of contention behind mutinies and other disturbances aboard ship illustrate the range of crews' motives. Mutinies originated in anger with a captain, but crews were angry for many reasons: at being forced into privateering, a lack of ideological zeal, an inability to find rich prizes, or flat-out dishonesty. The crew of Captain Stafford's *Patriota* became upset upon learning that their leader intended a privateering cruise instead of a merchant voyage. Robert Richards felt "betrayed" and estimated that at least two-thirds of the crew had "no idea, nor intention of going upon a Cruize." "Finding themselves thus entrapped," he later said, "much commotion was produced on board." After forty days at sea, that commotion erupted into full-scale mutiny. The crew seized the two bow guns, pointed them aft at the officers' quarterdeck, and demanded to go home. Stafford and his officers sprang to action, armed themselves, and ordered the men back to work. They refused. A standoff followed in which the captain "threatened & promised by turns"—threatening to blow up the ship himself and promising that he would still "make all their fortunes." After eighteen hours Stafford had won over enough men that the holdouts had no choice but to submit.³¹

John Chase aggravated his men by altering their mission from sailing for the United Provinces to sailing for General Artigas and the Oriental Provinces, a change he announced only once at sea, which upset some of the men, who "declared that they were for the Liberty & Independence of Buenos Ayres," and "being shipped for Buenos Ayres they would not declare for Artigas." Attempting to mollify them, "*Chase* made a speech and told the officers and crew if they would stick to him he would make their fortunes," as an innkeeper later heard.³²

Other crews found fault with a commander who did not make their fortunes fast enough. The men of the *Caroné*, frustrated by a lack of prizes, turned on their captain, William Saunders, declaring him "no Privateersman," because he was "too *mild* and *honest*." The ship's people elected David Ewing captain and deposited Saunders on a passing merchant vessel soon after. They began taking prizes within a few days. Ewing, evidently, was a Privateersman.[33]

Suspicion that payment would not be delivered as promised distressed other sailors. Captain Stafford had another run-in with his crew, this time over money. With his *Patriota* renamed *General San Martin*, Stafford put into Port-au-Prince, Haiti, to inquire after several of his prizes that the Haitian government had seized. While Stafford pressed his claim, the crew, fearing that he planned to defraud them, set sail, leaving Stafford alone on the docks. The vessel's owner made things right for the crew, offering them eighteen thousand dollars and thanking them for rescuing the ship from Stafford, "whose conduct," the owner admitted, "is not that of a gentleman."[34]

Early-nineteenth-century sailors also lived a life of racial and ethnic diversity aboard ship, which likewise worked out in contradictory ways for Spanish American privateers, who recruited men of many different nations to serve a distinctly national purpose. Spanish American privateers described their fellows as "mostly Italians, French, and Americans"; "mostly Spaniards, Italians, and French"; or "mostly Spanish, American, and French." One sailor, B. Bragden, disclaimed any national affiliation, testifying "that [as] he was born at sea [he] considers himself as not belonging to any particular nation." Ships resounded with the native languages of their polyglot crews. A prize crew steering the *Virgin del Mar* for shore included two men from Margarita who spoke French and Spanish; two mulattoes who spoke French, Spanish, and English; and one American who spoke English, a little French, and *un poquito* of Spanish. Jean Monier addressed his crew in French, Spanish, and English. Sailor Peter Franks claimed to know Italian, Spanish, and some French and English, though he admitted his knowledge of English was limited to "marine expressions." Meanwhile, black sailors were not only present aboard privateers but formed a substantial portion of some crews. The Venezuelan brig *Wilson* sailed with twenty-seven blacks among its crew of between eighty and ninety men—nearly one-third of its force, and the Venezuelan privateer *La Guerriere* reported its crew as "49 men—12 black, & most of the rest yellow," with yellow indicating a person of African descent. In one case, a man of African descent commanded a vessel, the *Little Pelican*, and its crew of fifty, "about 40 of whom were negroes," although it appears the vessel was not a regular privateer at the time but rather a privateer whose crew had mutinied and aimed, according to reports, to plunder "everything they fell in with and then to proceed to St. Domingo."[35]

This diversity played out in complex ways aboard ship, where freedom and slavery coexisted. Louis Crispin, who described himself as a "black man," subject of "the Empire of Haiti," and a "free man," sailed aboard the privateer *Guillaume*, a French vessel commanded by Louis-Michel Aury that had captured a Portuguese slaver. Crispin entered the privateer near Jacquemel, Haiti, while he was running a shallop to Aux Cayes. Later he was assigned to the *Massavito*'s prize crew, and at the end of the cruise, he received his share of the slaves' sale—$120—just like the others. In a similar way, the black sailors of the *Wilson* helped established their freedom and equality to other sailors by demonstrating that they participated in the prize-money system like everyone else. As their shipmates testified, they had "shipped with the rest of the crew on shares of prize money without wage," and on docking at Norfolk "the people of colour received their prize tickets and went on shore."[36]

The *Felix* shows the degrees of freedom aboard a single vessel. Two free men of color, a cook named Manuel and a carpenter named Charles Bernier, were present aboard the ship as it was fitting out in the Mississippi. So, too, were several runaway slaves, as well as seven or eight slaves apprehended as prizes. The vessel also employed a musician, suggesting that the privateer hoped to capture slaves since music was thought to help slaves exercise and stay in good shape while on the Middle Passage. Thus, for some, the *Felix*, like ships generally in the early nineteenth century, was a source of economic livelihood, freedom, and even acceptance by their fellow sailors. Or at least it had the potential to be since Bernier, who lacked protection papers, left before the ship sailed, and at least two runaways were reclaimed by their owners. For others, however, the very same ship was the means of their enslavement. When the musician Bon Herbert described the vessel's prizes in his deposition, he included the slaves in with the goods. Besides "several trunks of calicoes, a great quantity of rum, muslins, silk, &c.," he said, "there were also 7 or 8 negroes." Privateers may have been diverse, but they were no more just than the society ashore.[37]

Filibusters

Gregor MacGregor had a dream. He would liberate the Floridas from Spain. Raising a small army in the United States, he would attack the Spanish garrison at Amelia Island, in East Florida, just across the Georgia border. With the enemy vanquished, he would establish a prize court, commission privateers, and, once properly resupplied, he would push onto the mainland to take another colony from the tyrant Fernando. Steps one and two—recruit an army and seize Amelia Island—proceeded according to plan, but MacGregor ran into trouble implementing step three. He never could turn Amelia Island into an effective privateering center. Reinforcements never arrived, his men grew sick and surly, Louis-Michel Aury arrived and challenged his rule. After two months, MacGregor gave up. Leaving Amelia Island, he had another dream: he would raise an army in the Bahamas and land them near Tampa Bay, where he would link up with a group of Indians recruited by a former British officer and launch an invasion of East Florida, taking another colony away from the tyrant Fernando. And if that plan did not work out, he was sure to find another.[38]

At Amelia Island and Galveston, privateering merged with filibustering, and the two activities were often part of the same larger projects, projects spread by men such as MacGregor and Aury. As private military adventurers who aimed to take land away from Spain, it would seem that the filibusters were mostly land-grabbers out for themselves. A closer look, however, reveals that the filibuster leaders who sponsored privateering in the 1810s were cosmopolitan figures for whom attacking the Spanish borderlands from the United States was but one episode in a larger experience of warfare and revolution in Europe and North and South America. Their grievances against Spain were often ideological.[39]

For some Mexicans and Spaniards who passed through Galveston, privateering and invading Texas were part of a long-running project of colonial emancipation. For example, José Alvarez de Toledo y Dubois launched one of the first Mexican armed vessels from Louisiana directly following the Battle of New Orleans. He arranged weapons sales to the Mexican Congress and plotted filibuster expeditions. Born in Cuba and educated in Spain, Toledo was a veteran of the Peninsular War and had served in the Spanish Cortes, where his outspoken advocacy of Spanish American independence won the admiration of the body's American delegation and the disapproval of the peninsular representatives, who ultimately forced his dismissal. Coming to America in 1811, Toledo had gathered men, money, and munitions along the east coast; promoted the independence of Spanish America in the press; and lobbied the U.S. government for diplomatic recognition.[40]

José Bernardo Maximiliano Gutierrez de Lara, a Mexican merchant, deplored the Spaniards, who "for almost three hundred years" had been "owners of our soil, owners of our daughters, owners of our immense treasures, and, what is more, of our liberty." He entered the Mexican army within months of Father Hidalgo's cry for rebellion. In 1811, Hidalgo sent Gutierrez to the United States to lobby the government for support. Over the next eight years, he invaded Texas six times. Likewise, Juan Pablo Anaya was named an agent to the United States, and traveled to New Orleans in 1814, hoping to open diplomatic relations. On the way, he stopped at Barataria and recruited men to become privateers, although the commissions he promised never arrived, and later he bought munitions and involved himself in plans to attack Tampico and to invade Texas. Anaya, also inspired by Hidalgo, had joined the Mexican army in 1811, at the age of eighteen. After Anaya left New Orleans in 1815, he returned to the Mexican army.[41]

Meanwhile, despite their different backgrounds, Father José Manuel de Herrera, Colonel Joseph Savary, and Henry Perry seemed to have been attracted to Galveston by the prospect of promoting independence. De Herrera, the Mexican minister to the United States, was a priest, editor of a revolutionary newspaper, deputy to the Mexican Congress, and signer of the Mexican constitution. Accompanying him to Galveston was Savary, a free man of color who had served in the French republican army in Haiti fighting against rebelling slaves. Savary came to Louisiana in the 1809 migration of French-Haitian refugees and led a unit of free blacks at the Battle of New Orleans. He brought thirty or forty other free men of color to Galveston. He also brought his slave. Perry was a Connecticut native who had served in the U.S. Army in Louisiana and participated in previous filibuster expeditions into Texas. In 1815, he commanded his own filibuster army, which he had recruited with patriotism. "The favorable moment has at length arrived for making a successful attempt in favour of the patriots of New Spain," he wrote to a Louisiana newspaper. "Our cause embraces the best interest of humanity—the general enlargement of an oppressed people." Perry led his men from Louisiana to a position overlooking Galveston Bay, which he named Point Bolivar, and waited for reinforcements before pushing farther into Texas. Reinforcements never came, and the invasion failed, but Perry persevered and returned to Galveston for a new attempt. He would later die in Texas fighting the Spanish.[42]

Though not part of the original plans for Galveston, Francisco Xavier Mina arrived there in November 1816 with his own filibusters, and he would play an important role in the settlement. A Basque seminarian turned guerilla fighter in the Peninsular War, Mina reacted violently when King Fernando nullified the liberal reforms made in his absence. In 1814, Mina attempted to organize a new guerilla movement, but he failed and fled the country for London. There he met José Servando Teresa de Mier Noriega y Guerea, a Mexican priest banished to Europe for preaching a sermon in which he claimed that Mexico had been Christianized not by Spain but by the Apostle Thomas in the first century. Pledging themselves to "give liberty to all Spanish dominions," they traveled to the United States, secured followers, funds, and firearms, and then headed for Texas. After a protracted wait at Galveston, Mina landed in Mexico and issued a proclamation: "Mexicans, permit me to participate in your glorious struggles," it read. "Count me among your compatriots."[43]

These men were not angelic republicans, purely dedicated to the cause of liberty. Toledo, for example, was dishonest. When he dispatched the privateer *Aquilla* from New Orleans in February 1815, he lied to Andrew Jackson, who needed to approve all ship clearances while the city remained under martial law. Toledo promised that the vessel was not a privateer and that he intended to carry reports and a few passengers to Mexico. Jackson assented. The *Aquilla* went privateering. Toledo bragged that if he encountered any legal difficulty, "he would be able to convince his friends that he had nothing to do with it." Later, when the *Aquilla*'s captain was tried for piracy, Toledo paid two sailors to perjure themselves, winning the captain's acquittal.[44]

In addition, several filibuster and privateer leaders gave up on the revolution, sought a pardon from Spain, and renewed their loyalty to King Fernando. Toledo, de Herrera, and Anaya each did so, as did Juan Mariano Bautista de Picornell y Gomilla, another filibuster leader. This may indicate a poverty of commitment to independence. Other leaders persisted, even dying in the attempt to free Mexico. Yet, two other factors may explain their decision. One, the Spanish American Wars of Independence always provoked divided loyalties, since they were civil wars fought between Spaniards for the reform of the Spanish Empire and in opposition to Napoleon's invasion. Toledo and Picornell struck this note in their petitions for pardon. Toledo claimed he joined the independence movements to protect Spain from the "Tyrant of Europe"; Picornell said he found the liberal reforms of Spain's 1812 constitution sufficient, though he said this before Fernando revoked the reforms. Two, Spain was winning the war in Mexico, especially after 1815. The seeming inevitability of Spain's victory appears to have shaped Anaya's thinking when he accepted the Spanish viceroy's amnesty offer. Yet, Anaya did not necessarily forsake the cause by doing so. When Mexico gained its independence, Anaya was elected to the Congress. Similarly, de Herrera became a minister in the independent government. They may have thought it better to accept a pardon and live than to be executed as a rebel.[45]

Despite their broadly similar backgrounds and common goal of opposing Spanish absolutism, the leaders of Mexican filibustering and privateering operations worked independently of each other, which muted their ability to accomplish their objectives. At best, they simply did not get along. At worst, they actively undermined each other, and the good they could have done for the cause of independence died in their rivalries. As a result, the Mexican filibusters and privateers are often seen as hapless bunglers who preferred fighting each other to fighting for freedom. Many of the leaders lacked the temperament for command, but their inability to cooperate and coordinate was more than a personality flaw. After all, filibuster expeditions were usually led by men with backgrounds in the military, navy, or religious life who presumably knew something about discipline and teamwork. These leaders ultimately failed not simply because they lacked strong personalities but because they lacked a clear military structure: a chain of command, a way to enforce orders, loyalty to the state rather than to an individual. With the Mexicans nearly defeated, no central national body, such as the Mexican Congress, existed to enforce such hallmarks of a professional military. The underlying geopolitical conditions made filibusters and their privateering associates disorganized.[46]

No analysis of Spanish American privateering and filibustering would be complete without investigating the motives of MacGregor and Aury, two of the most intriguing leaders of filibustering and privateering. MacGregor and Aury are compelling figures, men who traveled widely, serving multiple nations in multiple wars of the early nineteenth century. Like others involved in Spanish American privateering, they were complex men shaped by the larger context of war and revolution in the early nineteenth century and by the peculiarities of their own personalities.[47]

By all indications, MacGregor was warm for the Spanish American cause. He risked his life fighting in Venezuela and New Grenada. He suffused his proclamations with pro-independence sentiment—the "Holy Cause of Independence," he once called it—and his private letters betray no contradiction. MacGregor's Amelia invasion had the blessing of representatives of Venezuela, Cartagena, Mexico, and Buenos Aires. They issued him a commission, based on the transplanted Scotsman's "zeal and devotion to the republic," to liberate the Floridas.[48]

MacGregor certainly wanted support from the U.S. government, but there is no evidence that he obtained it. When planning the expedition,

MacGregor met frequently with John S. Skinner, the postmaster and privateer investor. MacGregor wanted Skinner to convince the government that the United States should "connive at the occupation of [the Floridas] by a patriot force," because it would advance the cause of liberty "without necessarily involving a positive violation of any of our strictly neutral or pacific obligations." MacGregor also approached William Thornton, head of the patent office and a Spanish American sympathizer, with a similar request; Thornton then met with Secretary of State Richard Rush on MacGregor's behalf. But these importunities missed their mark. Skinner may have invested some of his own money, but he informed the government of MacGregor's request a month after the invasion. Rush dismissed the Scotsman as a nuisance. Nevertheless, MacGregor told his followers that he enjoyed backing in the United States. Still, when one follower pressed for details, the general "equivocated, or rather, denied it." Given MacGregor's tenuous hold on power, he had reason to exaggerate his resources.[49]

Through his transatlantic travels championing republicanism, perhaps MacGregor aimed to become a *caudillo*, or Spanish American regional chieftain. MacGregor personally knew *caudillos* who may have provided a model he intended to follow. MacGregor received his generalship from Francisco de Miranda, a Venezuelan leader who had a similar international profile as MacGregor. Miranda served in the Spanish, French, and Russian armies during the Napoleonic Wars, besides living in London and organizing a filibuster in the United States for an attack on Venezuela. MacGregor also knew Juan Bautista Arismendi, the *caudillo* of Margarita Island, who had used his position to sponsor privateering, operate an admiralty court, and aid expeditions heading onto mainland South America. Arismendi had even encouraged MacGregor to attack Florida. Thus, Miranda and Arismendi were the kind of men MacGregor encountered in South America. Conceivably, he hoped to emulate them. MacGregor had the military skills, charisma, and enthusiasm for independence that *caudillos* possessed. Yet he lacked the intimate connection to a particular place that, because of the personal nature of their rule, *caudillos* needed. MacGregor had never been to Amelia before he conquered it. Nor had he formed lasting relationships with the men he commanded or the people he would govern. He recruited his warriors just months prior, and on his arrival, many of Amelia's inhabitants fled.[50]

MacGregor also displayed some troubling personal habits. Even by the standards of *caudillos* his vainglory was excessive. After conquering Amelia, MacGregor proclaimed that "the 29th of June will be forever memorable in the annals of the independence of South America," for "on that day, a body of brave men, animated by a noble zeal for the happiness of mankind, advanced within musket shot of the guns at Fernandina, and awed the enemy into immediate capitulation." He also designed mementos of his accomplishments. To commemorate their triumph, MacGregor created an armband for his men, bearing the inscription "Vencedores de Amelia, 29 de Junio de 1817. 7 y 1," which referred to the Victors of Amelia and the date of the conquest, which was accomplished in the seventh year of Venezuelan independence, and the first of Amelia Island's. On another occasion, MacGregor ordered a medallion struck. It contained the Green Cross of Florida and was inscribed "Amelia Veni Vidi Vici"—"Amelia, I Came, I Saw, I Conquered"—on one side and on the other "Duce Mac Gregorio Libertas Floriarium"—"Liberty for the Floridas under the leadership of MacGregor."[51]

More disturbingly, MacGregor was deceptive. To fund the expedition he sold shares of Florida land. Later he rigged up a printing press to produce his own currency. Neither the shares nor the money were worth anything. MacGregor also told grandiose stories about himself. He claimed to be a scholar, educated at the University of Edinburgh (the finest school in Scotland), and the proud owner of 1,500 books. He exaggerated his military accomplishments, bragging that he had been indispensable to the British victory in the Peninsular Campaign and that he had single-handedly led the defense of Cartagena. MacGregor also pretended to be a nobleman, and he usually presented himself as Sir Gregor MacGregor. The source of this nobility varied. On some occasions he claimed to be a Scottish baronet and chief of the clan MacGregor. On others, he was a Knight of the Order of Christ, an honor earned from his heroism defending Portugal. MacGregor wanted to make Spanish America free. Yet, he also wanted glory, and he was not above enhancing that glory at the expense of the truth.[52]

Aury's motives were also multifaceted. By all evidence Aury embraced the cause of Spanish American independence as his own. He had served one Spanish American country or other since 1813, and he would continue to do so until he died in 1821, at the age of thirty-five. Aury devoted his adult life to Spanish American independence. It seems plausible that Aury believed in a kind of Bolivarian republicanism, a desire to make himself the kind of strongman who gave his people liberty. In that way, he was similar to other revolutionary leaders. Certainly, he was respected in South America. Vincente Pazos praised Aury as a "worthy officer and distinguished patriot" and deplored that U.S. newspapers and officials had "confounded [him] with pirates and malefactors." Nevertheless, Aury also had a tendency to alienate the men who served with him. At Galveston he had suffered through a mutiny from his sailors and an armed standoff with filibuster rivals for command only to be shunted aside by the Laffites, who pounced on the discord among Aury's followers. His rule at Amelia was similarly tumultuous as he jostled for preeminence with Ruggles Hubbard and Jared Irwin. Finally, Aury was a slave trader who commanded majority black crews, often recruited in Haiti, the home of Atlantic slave rebellion. American newspaper editors feared the explosive potential of Aury's men, refusing even to use the word "black" when libeling them as "the ***** troops and sailors, characters of the worst description from St. Domingo and other of the West-India islands." Yet if there was any consistency in Aury's life, it was his comfort with—indeed commitment to—profiting from the sale of fellow human persons. Aury traded slaves wherever he went, from the *Guillaume* to Galveston to Amelia Island and beyond. After leaving Amelia, as he launched a new expedition against Central America, he captured two Spanish vessels with a combined 520 slaves, while continuing to command a multiracial crew. Aury appears to have sailed with blacks because they were useful. In the *Guillaume*, they helped capture a slaver and at Galveston he put them to work salvaging and building shelter. At Amelia, their presence helped intimidate opponents. In his power struggle, Aury had a strong incentive to aggravate Irwin's followers. The more dissatisfied they became, the more trouble they would cause for their commander, and the more likely they would be to desert. Having black men in positions of authority achieved that end. The presence of free blacks also frightened Americans. As a Georgia planter informed the treasury secretary, Aury's men "make their neighborhood extremely dangerous, to a population like ours," for "it is said, that they have declared that if they are in danger of being overpowered, they will call to their aid every negro within their reach." Georgia planters benefitted from Aury's slave smuggling, but they also feared slave rebellions. With some Georgians convinced that a race war would start if the United States should move against Amelia, the blacks surrounding Aury helped ensure his safety. Ultimately, Aury was comfortable with both liberty and slavery.[53]

Conclusion

No single path brought these men to Spanish American privateering. They were Americans as well as foreigners: Frenchmen, Englishmen,

Spaniards, and Spanish Americans. Some foreigners resided in the United States permanently, others, temporarily. Those involved in privateering were sailors, sea captains, and merchants. Some had strong ties to their communities. Some were most comfortable at sea far from shore. A few were bound to their families while also faring the sea a thousand miles from home. Some men were international fighters for freedom. They went privateering to advance the ideology of independence. Others were opportunists. They sailed to make money. Others did both at the same time. As a group, then, they were good and evil, noble and depraved, selfish and self-sacrificing, cosmopolitan and attached to one place. As individuals, they exhibited any number of these traits. A few men, over the course of a career, exhibited them all. With their intriguing personalities, wide travels, and improbable adventures, it would be easy to call Spanish American privateers colorful. But in their backgrounds and motives they defy any simple characterization. They were more than colorful. They were full, complex persons.

Conclusion: Captain Chaytor Comes Home

In 1828, Captain Chaytor came home from the sea. At first, he opened a business based on his sailing experience and knowledge of Spanish America. Taking out an advertisement in the *Baltimore Patriot*, he offered his services as agent in any and all commercial transactions. He would see to the building, purchase, sale, or furnishing of vessels. He would find vessels ready for charter. He would broker sales of goods—whether whole ships' cargoes or a captain's private adventures. He would be a friend to travelers, offering a fount of local intelligence, and he would look after a fellow Baltimorean's business while away. Chaytor also offered to help anyone going to South America. He promised "information essential to comfort and safety—all acquired from actual observation and experience." The business did not last, and, unable to retire, Chaytor went back aboard a boat, though rather than an ocean-going schooner, it was a steamboat shuttling between Baltimore and Philadelphia.[1]

The Spanish American Wars of Independence were the last major conflict in the Atlantic world for a generation, and with the nations of Europe and the Americas mostly at peace, the occasion for privateering declined. By the 1850s, when tensions between the European powers flared into the Crimean War, privateering was increasingly seen as an anachronism in a world of large, steamship navies. Before the war, the belligerents agreed not to use privateers, and as part of the peace negotiations at the war's end, privateering was abolished by the Declaration of Paris (1856).[2]

In the United States, opposition to privateering had long been present, despite its popularity among seamen, for both humanitarian and commercial reasons. Benjamin Franklin had inveighed against privateering in the 1780s, even though he had helped commission vessels during the Revolution, and his remarks were often reprinted as the case against the practice gathered support. Privateering, some said, was a vestige of a barbaric past. It made war into plunder, and it threatened the peaceful commerce that tied nations together. John Quincy Adams went a step further and proposed to abolish not only privateering but also attacks on private property by naval vessels. Once an advocate of privateering—in 1803 he had called privateers a "militia moving upon the water"—Adams had been chastened by his experience with the Spanish American "piratical privateers," as he called them. Nevertheless, the United States refused to give up privateering. In a nation with a large coast and a small navy, privateers made sense, and it did no good to forego privateering if the British navy, the preeminent sea power, continued to take prizes. Adams's proposal got no further than a cabinet meeting, and a generation later, the reasoning against abolishing privateering remained the same. Officials in Washington changed their minds when the first shots of the Civil War were fired and the Confederates commissioned privateers. In the North, privateering was condemned as sheer piracy, and the Union attempted to eliminate privateering after all. The memory of Spanish American privateering resurfaced as a shameful episode of buccaneering.[3]

None of the men who boarded a Spanish American privateer knew what would become of privateering in the future, and it has been a major contention of the preceding pages that U.S. foreign relations are best understood in the context of the geopolitics of the times in which they occurred. Spanish American privateers responded to the specific conditions of the 1810s and its web of wars in Europe, the United States, and Spanish America. Expanding U.S. borders in the name of national destiny would not have made sense to them. Even U.S. officials, who did want to gain more territory in the Spanish borderlands, acted to meet the specific threats they faced rather than to implement a preconceived plan of Manifest Destiny. Granted, the U.S. government rarely succeeded in imposing criminal penalties on Spanish American privateers, but the civil courts frequently returned Spanish and Portuguese property to its owners and condemned privateer vessels to the United States. Geopolitics hampered U.S. law enforcement more than a lack of will alone.

Spanish American privateers were keenly aware of the power and limitations of the nations whose borders they crossed. The Laffites would have remained obscure, small-time merchants and slave dealers if not for the government's commercial, neutrality, and slave trade laws. Privateers and filibusters would never have set themselves up at Galveston and Amelia Island if not for their realization that they could make their own laws there and that their claims to sovereignty could protect them from the United States. Privateering would never have flourished in Baltimore if not for the efforts of international businessmen who knew how to manipulate the policies regulating foreign trade. In short, these men knew how nations mediated their relationship to the Atlantic world at a time when imperial collapse led to the formation of many new sovereign states.

Spanish American privateering involved the full range of maritime actors—sailors, captains, investors, and the numerous tradesmen and merchants who serviced their ships and sold their captured goods— and they each had their own ideas about the business they had joined, ideas that were political (sometimes), pecuniary (oftentimes), practical (most times), and personal (always). The variety of their backgrounds and motivations defies easy categorization. Like Captain Chaytor when he faced his dilemma in Buenos Aires—Should he break the law and become a privateer?—each man read his circumstances and chose for himself.

As he navigated the Chesapeake, no longer shaping his course with the wind but plodding his way via steam, Captain Chaytor settled into a life far different from chasing Spanish prizes. There was occasional excitement. He was blamed for a crash on one occasion, witnessed an explosion on another. He once transported the famous Congressman David Crockett, who called Chaytor "a good fellow." Perhaps a celebrity endorsement was good for business. Chaytor also watched as others surpassed him. Captain John Danels, a former neighbor, prospered. Danels moved his family to the tony Albermarle Street; the Chaytors stayed behind in the Fell's Point sailor town. Danels retired and contributed his time and treasure to charity; Chaytor worked. Chaytor may not have won riches like Danels, but he did have the satisfaction of helping to liberate a continent, and he retained the old title of commodore, though its origins in the Spanish American service were overshadowed by his steamboat duties. In 1845, a correspondent to the *Baltimore Sun* reported the pleasure of receiving "a hearty shake of the hand from Commodore Chaytor, the Prince of steamboat captains, and one of the best natured, most thoughtful old gentlemen alive." His kindly disposition was "a revenue to the [steamboat] company and my word for it," the correspondent concluded, "whenever the old man goes to sleep, the company will find it difficult to wake another like him." True, but the *Sun*'s readers did not know the full reason why. The next year, when the old man did finally go to sleep, the *Sun*'s obituary called Chaytor "the oldest and most experienced steamboat commander that belonged to the port of Baltimore." It made no reference to his earlier life as Diego, a privateer of the Americas.[4]

Notes

Abbreviations

ANBO	*American National Biography Online*, www.anb.org.
CPD	Depositions Regarding Baltimore Privateers in South American Waters. Records on Privateers and Pirates, 1813–1835. General Records of the Department of State, Record Group 59. National Archives at College Park, MD.
FHQ	*Florida Historical Quarterly*.
GA Adm.	Admiralty Case Files. United States District Court for Georgia (Savannah). Records of District Courts of the United States, Record Group 21. National Archives and Records Administration—Southeast Region (Atlanta).
HTO	*Handbook of Texas Online*, www.tshaonline.org/handbook/online.
JCPM	James Chaytor Papers. Maryland Historical Society, Baltimore.
JCPP	James Chaytor Papers. Princeton University Rare Books and Special Collections, Princeton, NJ.
LA Fed. Ct.	Federal Case Files. United States District Court for the Eastern District of Louisiana (New Orleans). Records of District Courts of the United States, Record Group 21. National Archives and Records Administration—Southwest Region (Ft. Worth, TX). Case numbers 1–769 have been microfilmed as *Case Files of the U.S. District Court for the Eastern District of Louisiana, 1806-1814*, National Archives Microfilm Publication M1082.
LH	*Louisiana History*.
LHQ	*Louisiana Historical Quarterly*.
MD Adm.	Admiralty Case Files. United States District Court for Maryland (Baltimore). Records of District Courts of the United States, Record

	Group 21. National Archives and Records Administration—Mid-Atlantic Region (Philadelphia).
MD Appel.	Appellate Case Files. United States Circuit Court for Maryland (Baltimore). Records of District Courts of the United States, Record Group 21. National Archives and Records Administration—Mid-Atlantic Region (Philadelphia).
MD Crim.	Criminal Case Files. United States Circuit Court for Maryland (Baltimore). Records of District Courts of the United States, Record Group 21. National Archives and Records Administration—Mid-Atlantic Region (Philadelphia).
NY Adm.	Admiralty Case Files. United States District Court for the Southern District of New York (New York). Records of District Courts of the United States, Record Group 21. National Archives Microfilm Publication M919, *Admiralty Case Files of the U.S. District Court for the Southern District of New York, 1790–1842.*
SCOTUS, Appel.	Appellate Case Files of the U.S. Supreme Court, 1792–1831. Records of the Supreme Court of the United States, Record Group 267. National Archives Microfilm Publication M214, *Appellate Case Files of the Supreme Court of the United States, 1792–1831.*
SWHQ	*Southwest Historical Quarterly.*
VA Adm.	Admiralty Case Files. United States District Court for the Eastern District of Virginia (Norfolk). Records of District Courts of the United States, Record Group 21. National Archives Microfilm Publication M130, *Admiralty Case Files of the U.S. District Court for the Eastern District of Virginia, 1801–1861.*

Introduction

1. Lyde Goodwin to James Chaytor, Jan. 11, 1816; Chaytor to Goodwin, Jan. 1816, JCPP.

2. For the background and military history of the Spanish American revolutions, see Jaime Rodriguez O., "The Emancipation of America," *American Historical Review* 105 (2000): 131–52; John Lynch, *The Spanish American Revolutions, 1808–1826,* 2nd ed. (New York: Norton, 1986); Jay Kinsbruner, *Independence in Spanish America: Civil Wars, Revolutions, and Underdevelopments* (Albuquerque: University of New Mexico Press, 1994); John Lynch, *Simón Bolívar: A Life* (New Haven: Yale University Press, 2006); and John Charles Chasteen, *Americanos: Latin America's Struggle for Independence* (New York: Oxford University Press, 2008).

3. Quotes: invoice, 1816; James Chaytor to R. M., April 18, 1816, JCPP.

4. Lewis Winkler Bealer, "The Privateers of Buenos Aires, 1815–1821: Their Activities in the Hispanic American Wars of Independence" (Ph.D. diss., University of California, Berkeley, 1935).

5. Donald Petrie, *The Prize Game: Lawful Looting on the High Seas in the Age of Fighting Sail* (New York: Berkley, 1999). For letter-of-marque versus commission, see Jerome Garitee, *The Republic's Private Navy: The American Privateering Business as Practiced by Baltimore during the War of 1812* (Middleton, CT: Wesleyan University Press, 1977), 90.

6. Charles G. Fenwick, *The Neutrality Laws of the United States* (Washington: Carnegie Endowment for International Peace, 1913).

7. Chaytor to J. A. Maston, May 8, 1816; portage bill, May 10, 1816, JCPP; *The Santissima Trinidad and the* St. Ander (1822), 20 U.S. 283. Chaytor claimed that the *Independencia* was not a privateer but a Buenos Aires naval vessel. However, the vessel was privately owned by Chaytor and others (see W. G. D. Worthington to John Quincy Adams, Mar. 7, 1819, in *Diplomatic Correspondence of the United States Concerning the Independence of the Latin-American Nations*, ed. William R. Manning, 3 vols. [New York: Oxford University Press, 1925-26], 1:523-25; and Anjel Justiniano Carranza, *Campañas Navales de la Republica Argentina*, 2nd ed., 4 vols. [Buenos Aires: Departmento de Estudios Historicos Navales, 1962], 2:203). For Buenos Aires's naturalization of foreigners, see Hans Vogel, "New Citizens for a New Nation: Naturalization in Early Independent Argentina," *Hispanic American Historical Review* 71 (1991): 107-31. It is not certain whether Chaytor could legally expatriate himself. U.S. naturalization law required immigrants to renounce their former allegiances before gaining U.S. citizenship, but it made no provision for moving the other way. Establishing a right to expatriation gained some support in the years leading up to the War of 1812 as the U.S. government sought to pressure Great Britain into relaxing its own policy of perpetual allegiance that legitimized pressing British sailors who had become American citizens into the Royal Navy. After the war, however, when impressment was no longer an issue, the matter of expatriation disappeared for a generation (see Gerald C. Harvey, "Expatriation Law in the United States: The Confusing Legacy of *Afroyim* and *Bellei*," *Columbia Journal of Transnational Law* 13 [1974]: 406-35; and Rogers M. Smith, *Civic Ideals: Conflicting Visions of Citizenship in U.S. History* [New Haven: Yale University Press, 1997]).

8. Ship's articles, May 16, 1816, JCPP.

9. I have counted 103 Spanish American privateers sailing to or from Baltimore and New Orleans or to locations near the United States in Galveston, Texas, or Amelia Island, East Florida. An additional seventeen French privateers also sailed from New Orleans. The number of men directly involved in privateering was determined by assuming an average crew size of thirty—a conservative estimate. For a full list and sources, see David Head, "Sailing for Spanish America: The Atlantic Geopolitics of Foreign Privateering from the United States in the Early Republic" (Ph.D. diss., SUNY–Buffalo, 2009), appendix D.

10. For an attempt to quantify the scale of captures by Spanish American privateers, see Matthew McCarthy, *Privateering, Piracy and British Policy in Spanish America, 1810-1830* (Woodbridge, UK: Boydell, 2013) and his captures dataset at www.hull.ac.uk/mhsc/piracy-mccarthy. Comparing the relative value of money between one year and another is difficult, in part because there is no one way to measure the changes. For simplicity's sake, I have used the Consumer Price Index (CPI) to determine that one dollar between 1810 and 1820, the primary years of this study, would be worth about twenty dollars in 2013 dollars, the latest year for which data are available. For a discussion of these issues and a calculator, see Lawrence H. Officer and Samuel H. Williamson, "Measures of Worth," www.measuringworth.com/worthmeasures.php.

11. For overviews of the literature, see William Earl Weeks, "New Directions in the Study of American Foreign Relations," and Kinley Brauer, "The Great American

Desert Revisited: Recent Literature and Prospects for the Study of American Foreign Relations, 1815–1861," both in *Paths to Power: The Historiography of American Foreign Relations to 1941*, ed. Michael Hogan, 8–43 and 44–78 (Cambridge: Cambridge University Press, 2000); Kinley Brauer, "The Need for a Synthesis of American Foreign Relations, 1815–1861," *Journal of the Early Republic* 14 (1994): 467–76; Bradford Perkins, "Early American Foreign Relations: Opportunities and Challenges," *Diplomatic History* 22 (1998): 115–20; and Peter P. Hill, "The Early National Period, 1775–1815," in *A Companion to American Foreign Relations*, ed. Robert D. Schulzinger, 48–63 (Malden, MA: Blackwell, 2003).

12. Especially helpful in applying the concept of geopolitics to the Spanish American Revolutions is Rafe Blaufarb, "The Western Question: The Geopolitics of Latin American Independence," *American Historical Review* 112 (2007): 742–63. For sailors as diplomatic actors with minds of their own, see Brian Rouleau, "How Honolulu Almost Burned and Why Sailors Matter to Early American Foreign Relations," *Diplomatic History* 38 (2014): 501–25.

13. For examples of early republic Atlantic histories, see Rafe Blaufarb, *Bonapartists in the Borderlands: French Exiles and Refugees on the Gulf Coast, 1815–1835* (Tuscaloosa: University of Alabama Press, 2005); James G. Cusick, *The Other War of 1812: The Patriot War and the American Invasion of Spanish East Florida* (Gainesville: University Press of Florida, 2003); and Andrew McMichael, *Atlantic Loyalties: Americans in Spanish West Florida, 1785–1810* (Athens: University of Georgia Press, 2008). For surveys that explore the Atlantic world of the nineteenth century and the chronological limits of the paradigm, see Joyce E. Chaplin, "Expansion and Exceptionalism in Early American History," *Journal of American History* 89 (2003): 1431–55; Donna Gabaccia, "A Long Atlantic in a Wider World," *Atlantic Studies* 1 (2004): 1–27; Alison Games, "Atlantic History: Definitions, Challenges, and Opportunities," *American Historical Review* 111 (2006): 741–57; Philip D. Morgan and Jack P. Greene, "Introduction: The Present State of Atlantic History," in *Atlantic History: A Critical Appraisal*, ed. Greene and Morgan (Oxford: Oxford University Press, 2009), 3–33; Aaron Spencer Fogelman, "The Transformation of the Atlantic World, 1776–1867," *Atlantic Studies* 6 (2009): 5–28; and David Head, "New Nations, New Connections: Spanish American Privateering from the United States and the Development of Atlantic Relations," *Early American Studies* 11 (2013): 161–75.

14. My thinking on the levels of engagement between the local and the Atlantic has been shaped by David Armitage's concept of cis-Atlantic history. According to Armitage, a study that is cis-Atlantic (from the Greek for "on this side") examines the relationship between local parts (such as individuals, institutions, cities, or regions) and the Atlantic whole. Although Armitage also includes nations as a possible whole, he does not discuss the ways in which small parts would relate to a larger nation part as well as to the Atlantic whole (David Armitage, "Three Concepts of Atlantic History," in *The British Atlantic World, 1500–1800*, ed. Armitage and Michael J. Braddick [New York: Palgrave Macmillan, 2002], 11–27).

15. For a discussion of the limitations of the weak state characterization of the early republic, see Samuel J. Watson, *Jackson's Sword: The Army Officer Corps on the American Frontier, 1810–1821* (Lawrence: University Press of Kansas, 2012), 7–11.

16. Works in the older tradition include Rufus K. Wyllys, "The Filibusters of Amelia Island," *Georgia Historical Quarterly* 12 (1928): 297–325; and Alfred Hasbrouck,

Foreign Legionaries in the Liberation of Spanish South America (1928; repr., New York: Octagon, 1969). For privateers and filibusters as implicated in American expansionism, see Frank L. Owsley Jr. and Gene A. Smith, *Filibusters and Expansionists: Jeffersonian Manifest Destiny, 1800-1821* (Tuscaloosa: University of Alabama Press, 1997). For cosmopolitanism, see Matthew Brown, *Adventuring through Spanish Colonies: Simón Bolívar, Foreign Mercenaries, and the Birth of New Nations* (Liverpool: Liverpool University Press, 2006); Robin Blackburn, *The Overthrow of Colonial Slavery, 1776-1848* (New York: Verso, 1988), 290-91; Jennifer L. Heckard, "The Crossroads of Empire: The 1817 Liberation and Occupation of Amelia Island, East Florida" (Ph.D. diss., University of Connecticut, 2006); Caryn Coss Bell, *Revolution, Romanticism, and the Afro-Creole Protest Tradition in Louisiana, 1718-1868* (Baton Rouge: Louisiana State University Press, 1997), 62-63; and Jane Landers, *Atlantic Creoles in the Age of Revolutions* (Cambridge: Harvard University Press, 2010), 130-37.

17. My thanks to Rafe Blaufarb for sharing his extensive notes on privateering found in *Lloyd's List*. For the activities of Spanish consuls, see Sean T. Perrone, "John Stoughton and the *Divina Pastora* Prize Case, 1816-1819," *Journal of the Early Republic* 28 (2008): 215-41.

18. For a discussion of these issues, see Walter D. Mignolo, *The Idea of Latin America* (Malden, MA: Blackwell, 2005).

19. For a discussion of these issues, see Chasteen, *Americanos*, 1-5.

1 / Diplomacy with Spain and Spanish America

1. Quotes: John Quincy Adams, May 11, 1819, Mar. 29, 1819, *Memoirs of John Quincy Adams*, ed. Charles Francis Adams, 12 vols. (Philadelphia: Lippincott, 1874-77), 4:363, 4:318-19. For Adams's personality and the significance of his diary, see Paul C. Nagel, *John Quincy Adams: A Public Life, a Private Life* (New York: Knopf, 1997).

2. For Adams's foreign policy, see Samuel Flagg Bemis, *John Quincy Adams and the Foundations of American Foreign Policy* (New York: Knopf, 1949); and William Earl Weeks, *John Quincy Adams and American Global Empire* (Lexington: University Press of Kentucky, 1992). For the argument linking the Transcontinental Treaty to later expansion, see Weeks, *John Quincy Adams and American Global Empire*, 176-79.

3. Timothy E. Anna, *Spain and the Loss of America* (Lincoln: University of Nebraska Press, 1983), 24-25.

4. Jaime Rodriguez O., "The Emancipation of America," *American Historical Review* 105 (2000): 131-52; John Charles Chasteen, *Americanos: Latin America's Struggle for Independence* (New York: Oxford University Press, 2008), 35-65.

5. Rodriguez, "Emancipation of America," 142-46; Chasteen, *Americanos*, 44-50, 53-54, 56-58, 65.

6. Chasteen, *Americanos*, 66-71, 73-77; Lynch, *Spanish American Revolutions*, 306-13.

7. Chasteen, *Americanos*, 88-90, 93-94, 98-100, 104-5, 115-16, 121-22; Lynch, *Spanish American Revolutions*, 313-19.

8. Chasteen, *Americanos*, 61, 81-82, 92-93, 95-97, 100-102; Lynch, *Spanish American Revolutions*, 195-207; Lynch, *Bolívar*, 57-64, 68-88.

9. Chasteen, *Americanos*, 105-6, 108-9, 118-19; Lynch, *Spanish American Revolutions*, 207-9.

10. Lynch, *Spanish American Revolutions*, 242.

11. Chasteen, *Americanos*, 58–61, 77–81; Lynch, *Spanish American Revolutions*, 58–60, 89–93.

12. Chasteen, *Americanos*, 82–84, 87–88, 116–18, 135; Lynch, *Spanish American Revolutions*, 92–102.

13. Chasteen, *Americanos*, 97–98, 124; Lynch, *Spanish American Revolutions*, 60–71; Lewis Winkler Bealer, "The Privateers of Buenos Aires, 1815–1821: Their Activities in the Hispanic American Wars of Independence" (Ph.D. diss., University of California, Berkeley, 1935).

14. James Madison, Proclamation, Sept. 1, 1815, in *A Compilation of the Messages and Papers of the Presidents, 1789–1897*, ed. James D. Richardson, 10 vols. (Washington: Government Printing Office, 1896–1899), 1:561–62.

15. Quote: The text of the Louisiana Purchase treaty may be found at http://avalon.law.yale.edu/19th_century/louis1.asp. See also J. C. A. Stagg, *Borderlines in Borderlands: James Madison and the Spanish-American Frontier, 1776–1821* (New Haven: Yale University Press, 2009), 39–42; Philip C. Brooks, *Diplomacy and the Borderlands: The Adams-Onís Treaty of 1819* (1939; repr., New York: Octagon, 1970), 4–5, 38–43; and Bemis, *Pinckney's Treaty*, 1–6, 309–10.

16. Stagg, *Borderlines*, 43–44; Rembert W. Patrick, *Florida Fiasco: Rampant Rebels on the Georgia-Florida Border, 1810–1815* (Athens: University of Georgia Press, 1954), 20–21; Brooks, *Diplomacy and the Borderlands*, 3–4.

17. James L. Lewis Jr., *The American Union and the Problem of Neighborhood: The United States and the Collapse of the Spanish Empire, 1783–1829* (Chapel Hill: University of North Carolina Press, 1998), 35–38; John A. Logan, *No Transfer: An American Security Principle* (New Haven: Yale University Press, 1961), 111–22.

18. Arthur Preston Whitaker, *The United States and the Independence of Latin America, 1800–1830* (1941; repr., New York: Russell and Russell, 1962), 62–66; Charles C. Griffin, *The United States and the Disruption of the Spanish Empire, 1810–1822* (1937; repr., New York: Octagon, 1968), 50–55; Caitlyn Fitz, "Our Sister Republics: The United States in an Age of American Revolutions" (Ph.D. diss., Yale University, 2010), chap. 2; Charles G. Fenwick, *The Neutrality Laws of the United States* (Washington: Carnegie Endowment for International Peace, 1913), 25–41.

19. For American reactions to developments in Spanish America, see Fitz, "Our Sister Republics," chap. 1; and Griffin, *United States and the Disruption of the Spanish Empire*, chap. 2.

20. Quotes: *Norfolk (VA) Gazette and Publick Ledger*, Aug. 3, 1808; *New-York Evening Post*, Aug. 23, 1808.

21. Quotes: *Connecticut Journal* (New Haven), Aug. 4, 1808; *Weekly Aurora* (Philadelphia), Sept. 3, 1811; *Poulson's American Daily Advertiser* (Philadelphia), May 12, 1812.

22. Quotes: *Palladium of Liberty* (Morristown, NJ), July 24, 1810; *Democratic Press* (Philadelphia), July 19, 1810. For the importance of toasting, see Fitz, "Our Sister Republics," 42–47.

23. Lewis, *American Union*, 38–39.

24. Quotes: Madison to Monroe, Apr. 18, 1815, qtd. in Stagg, *Borderlines*, 178; Adams, Dec. 1, 1817, and Jan. 10, 1818, *Memoirs*, 4:26, 37. See also Stagg, *Borderlines*, 175–82, 192.

25. Lewis, *American Union*, 71–77.

26. Ibid., 85–90.

27. Lewis, *American Union*, 87; Stagg, *Borderlines*, 52–86, 130–31, 182–83; Andrew McMichael, *Atlantic Loyalties: Americans in Spanish West Florida, 1785–1810* (Athens: University of Georgia Press, 2008).

28. Lewis, *American Union*, 87–89; Stagg, *Borderlines*, 182–87; Peter J. Kastor, *The Nation's Crucible: The Louisiana Purchase and the Creation of America* (New Haven: Yale University Press, 2004), 1–2.

29. Quotes: Luis de Onís to James Monroe, Jan. 2, 1817, and Feb. 22, 1816, and to John Quincy Adams, Sept. 19, 1817, in *Diplomatic Correspondence of the United States Concerning the Independence of the Latin-American Nations*, ed. William R. Manning, 3 vols. (New York: Oxford University Press, 1925–26), 3:1910, 1899, 1950. Lewis, *American Union*, 90–91; Stagg, *Borderlines*, 192–93; Brooks, *Diplomacy and the Borderland*, 61–68.

30. Quote: James Monroe, Annual Message to Congress, Dec. 2, 1817, in *Compilation of the Messages and Papers of the Presidents*, 2:13. See also Lewis, *American Union*, 105–11; and Chasteen, *Americanos*, 123–26, 128.

31. For Jackson's expedition into Florida, see Robert V. Remini, *Andrew Jackson and His Indian Wars* (New York: Penguin, 2001), 130–62. For a discussion of the controversy over whether the Monroe administration approved Jackson's attacks, see Daniel Feller, "The Seminole Controversy Revisited: A New Look at Andrew Jackson's 1818 Florida Campaign," *Florida Historical Quarterly* 88 (2010): 309–25.

32. Remini, *Andrew Jackson and His Indian Wars*, 163–68; Lewis, *American Union*, 121–22; Stagg, *Borderlines*, 198–200.

33. Lewis, *American Union*, 122–23; Bemis, *John Quincy Adams and the Foundations of American Foreign Policy*, 311–12. The importance of Jackson's invasion to bringing about the treaty is a matter of contention. For the argument that that was the decisive factor, showing Spain that the United States could take Florida any time it chose, see Bemis, *John Quincy Adams and the Foundations of American Foreign Policy*, 313–16; and Daniel Walker Howe, *What Hath God Wrought: The Transformation of America, 1815-1848* (New York: Oxford University Press, 2009), 97–108. Bradford Perkins, *The Creation of a Republican Empire, 1776-1865* (Cambridge: Cambridge University Press, 1993), 152, and George C. Herring, *From Colony to Superpower: U.S. Foreign Relations since 1776* (New York: Oxford University Press, 2008), 148–49, also emphasize Jackson's role. However, this argument does not fully account for the importance of the larger geopolitical situation or the U.S. need to acquire the Floridas in a way that would withstand international scrutiny. For the importance of international and legal factors, see Lewis, *American Union*, 120–22; and Stagg, *Borderlines*, 198–200. In addition, Weeks contends that Jackson's invasion convinced Onís that, without support from Spain's allies, he had few options left (Weeks, *John Quincy Adams and American Global Empire*, chap. 5). Finally, Owsley and Smith argue that the annexation of Florida was inevitable, even without Jackson's invasion (*Filibusters and Expansionists*, 161–63).

34. Brooks, *Diplomacy and the Borderlands*, 158–70; Bemis, *John Quincy Adams and the Foundations of American Foreign Policy*, 334–38; Stagg, *Borderlines*, 203–5.

35. Brooks, *Diplomacy and the Borderlands*, 172–91; Bemis, *John Quincy Adams and the Foundations of American Foreign Policy*, 350–52. For the Spanish revolt, see Chasteen, *Americanos*, 136; and Anna, *Spain and the Loss of America*, 215–20.

36. Quote: *Annals of Congress*, 15th Cong., 1st sess., House, 403-4, 1478. For Clay's approach to Spanish American affairs, see Halford L. Hoskins, "The Hispanic American Policy of Henry Clay, 1816-1828," *Hispanic American Historical Review* 7 (1927): 460-78; Robert V. Remini, *Henry Clay: Statesman for the Union* (New York: Norton, 1991), 154-57; and Merrill D. Peterson, *The Great Triumvirate: Webster, Clay, Calhoun* (New York: Oxford University Press, 1987), 52-55.

37. Hoskins, "Hispanic American Policy of Henry Clay," 466; Lewis, *American Union*, 107-11.

38. Chasteen, *Americanos*, 123-26.

39. Ibid., 128-30, 132-35.

40. Ibid., 136; Anna, *Spain and the Loss of America*, 215-20.

41. Chasteen, *Americanos*, 136-38, 148-50, 155-58.

42. Ibid., 139-10; Lynch, *Spanish American Revolutions*, 319-26.

43. Griffin, *United States and the Disruption of the Spanish Empire*, 265-76; Lewis, *American Union*, 157-69.

44. Quote: *National Advocate* (New York), July 10, 1818. See also James Moran, *Printing Presses: History and Development from the Fifteenth Century to Modern Times* (Berkeley: University of California Press, 1978), 59-70; Fitz, "Our Sister Republics," 154-69.

45. Quotes: song titles qtd. in Fitz, "Our Sister Republics," 147-48; toast: *Franklin Gazette* (Philadelphia), July 7, 1818. See also Simon Bainbridge, "Politics and Poetry," in *The Cambridge Companion to British Literature of the French Revolution in the 1790s*, ed. Pamela Clemit (New York: Cambridge University Press, 2011), 195. For a full version of the "Millions be Free" poem, see *A Tribute to Liberty; or, New Collection of Patriotic Songs, Entirely Original, To which are Added the Most Select songs which Have Lately Appeared in Public; and Other Miscellaneous Pieces; Together with a Collection of Toasts and Sentiments*, ed. R. Thompson (London, 1793), 61-62.

46. Fitz, "Our Sister Republics," 169-79; Mark Jaede, "Brothers at a Distance: Race, Religion, Culture and U.S. Views of Spanish America, 1800-1830" (Ph.D. diss., SUNY-Buffalo, 2001), 41-51.

47. Quote: Monroe, Dec. 2, 1823, Seventh Annual Message to Congress, in *Compilation of the Messages and Papers of the Presidents*, 2:209, 218. For the Monroe Doctrine, see Dexter Perkins, *The Monroe Doctrine, 1823-1826* (Cambridge: Harvard University Press, 1927); Ernest May, *The Making of the Monroe Doctrine* (Cambridge: Harvard University Press, 1975); Lewis, *American Union*, 177-86; Howe, *What Hath God Wrought*, 111-16; Herring, *From Colony to Superpower*, 151-57; and Jay Sexton, *The Monroe Doctrine: Empire and Nation in Nineteenth Century America* (New York: Hill and Wang, 2011).

48. Quotes: *Annals of Congress*, 19th Cong., 1st sess., Senate, 237 (Van Buren), 330 (Benton). For the Panama Congress, see Andrew Cayton, "The Debate over the Panama Conference and the Origins of the Second Party System," *Historian* 47 (1985): 219-38; Bemis, *John Quincy Adams and the Foundations of American Foreign Policy*, 555-61; Fitz, "Our Sister Republics," 236-90; Lewis, *American Union*, 209-14; Peterson, *Great Triumvirate*, 136-41; Remini, *Henry Clay*, 276, 285, 290-301; and Whitaker, *The United States and the Independence of Latin America*, 578-81. For the Spanish American side of the congress, see Lynch, *Bolívar*, 212-17.

2 / New Orleans and Barataria

1. Quotes: Edward Nicolls to [Jean Laffite], Aug. 31, 1814, Edward Nicolls and William H. Percy Letters, Historic New Orleans Collection, New Orleans, LA; Edward Nicolls to Alexander Cochrane, July 28, 1814, Alexander Cochrane Papers, ibid.; Hugh Pigot to Alexander Cochrane, June 8, 1814, qtd. in John Sugden, "Jean Lafitte and the British Offer of 1814," *LH* 20 (1979): 160–61; William C. Davis, *The Pirates Laffite: The Treacherous World of the Corsairs of the Gulf* (Orlando, FL: Harcourt), 166.

2. Quote: *Louisiana Courier* (New Orleans), Sept. 7, 1814. Davis, *Pirates Laffite*, 1–7, 51, 492–95n. The Laffites' birthplace is subject to controversy, due to the elaborate mythology that has surrounded them. Davis sorts through the various claims with a careful eye, and I have followed his account.

3. Quote: Nicholas Lockyer to W. H. Percy, Sept. 11, 1814, Cochrane Papers. The exact transactions between Laffite and the officers are subject to conjecture. I have included the major promises here. The letters are reprinted in Arsène Lacarrière Latour, *Historical Memoir of the War in West Florida and Louisiana in 1814–15, with an Atlas* (1816; repr., Gainesville: University of Florida Press, 1964), appendix, vii–xi. The story of the $30,000 bribe originated on page 19 of this work. A military engineer who participated in the Battle of New Orleans, Latour later became friends with Jean, but this is an outrageously high sum (more than $400,000 in 2013 dollars), and there is no evidence that British authorities authorized any payment for the Laffites (see Davis, *Pirates Laffite*, 553n; and Sugden, "Jean Lafitte and the British Offer," 164–65).

4. Jean Laffite to Nicholas Lockyer, Sept. 4, 1814, and to William C. C. Claiborne, Sept. 10, 1814, in Latour, *Historical Memoir*, appendix xii. For Blanque's background, see Davis, *Pirates Laffite*, 174; and deposition of John Paul Poulty, Aug. 13, 1806, *James and David Young v. Jean Blanque*, LA Fed. Ct., case 24. When Louisiana became a territory, one federal court was established at New Orleans to hear all federal cases. Each case was numbered.

5. Claiborne, Proclamation, Nov. 24, 1813, in *Official Letter Books of W. C. C. Claiborne, 1801–1816*, ed. Dunbar Rowland (1917; repr., 6 vols. ,New York: AMS, 1972), 6:279–80; John Crawford May Windship to William Plumer Jr., Apr. 2, 1814, in "Letters from Louisiana, 1813–1814," ed. Everett S. Brown, *Mississippi Valley Historical Review* (1925): 576; Robert C. Vogel, "The Patterson and Ross Raid on Barataria, September 1815," *LH* 33 (1992): 157–70.

6. Quote: Andrew Jackson, Proclamation, Sept. 21, 1814, in *Correspondence of Andrew Jackson*, ed. John Spencer Bassett, 7 vols. (Washington: Carnegie Institute, 1926), 258, 60. See also Davis, *Pirates Laffite*, 206–9.

7. Quote: James Madison, "Proclamation," Feb. 6, 1815, in *A Compilation of the Messages and Papers of the Presidents, 1789–1908*, ed. James D. Richardson, 20 vols. (New York: Bureau of National Literature and Art, 1908), 1:559. For the Baratarians role at the battle, see Robert C. Vogel, "Jean Laffite, The Baratarians, and the Battle of New Orleans: A Reappraisal," *LH* 41 (2000): 261–76; and Davis, *Pirates Laffite*, 213–23. For the battle generally, see Robert V. Remini, *The Battle of New Orleans* (New York: Viking, 1999). His account of the Laffites' role should be approached carefully since it draws heavily on Jane Lucas De Grummond's *The Baratarians and the Battle of New Orleans* (Baton Rouge: Louisiana State University Press, 1961), which used the fraudulent Jean Laffite autobiography, *The Memoirs of Jean Laffite*, trans. Gene

Marshall (1958; repr., n.p.: Xlibris Corp., 2000). In the 1940s, a retired railroad worker named John A. Lafflin claimed to have discovered, among a trunk of family papers, a manuscript autobiography written in the 1850s by Laffite. Renaming himself John Lafitte and announcing himself a descendant of the smuggler, Lafflin traveled the South promoting his discovery. The authenticity of the *Memoirs* is much disputed among Laffite enthusiasts and biographers. However, the text's claims (including that Jean did not believe in slavery and that he donated money to Karl Marx and Friedrich Engels) strain credulity.

8. For the geopolitics of the Spanish American Revolutions and nonstate actors such as the Laffites, see Rafe Blaufarb, "The Western Question: The Geopolitics of Latin American Independence," *American Historical Review* 112 (2007): 742–63.

9. Davis, *Pirates Laffite*, 9–19, 37–39. In 1804, the federal government divided the Louisiana Purchase in two, with most of the future state of Louisiana at first called the Orleans Territory and everything else, confusingly, called Louisiana. Baton Rouge and the area between the Mississippi River and the Pearl River, which today are part of the state, were once in Spanish West Florida. They were annexed by the United States in 1810. For simplicity, I have used Louisiana to indicate the area of today's state, even when discussing events before it achieved statehood in 1812.

10. John G. Clark, *New Orleans, 1718–1812* (Baton Rouge: Louisiana State University Press, 1970), esp. chap. 15; Adam Rothman, *Slave Country: American Expansion and the Origins of the Deep South* (Cambridge: Harvard University Press, 2005), chaps. 1 and 3; Paul F. Lachance, "The Foreign French," in *Creole New Orleans: Race and Americanization*, ed. Arnold R. Hirsch and Joseph Logsdon (Baton Rouge: Louisiana State University Press, 1992), 103–11; Peter Andreas, *Smuggler Nation: How Illicit Trade Made America* (New York: Oxford University Press, 2013), 82–91.

11. Quote: Joseph Dubreuil to Thomas Jefferson, June 2, 1804, qtd. in Rothman, *Slave Country*, 31. The foreign slave trade was partially forbidden under the Spanish, wide open under the French, curtailed severely under the 1804 Orleans Territory organization law, opened partially in 1805 to allow the entry of slaves transported from other U.S. states (who, as it turned out, were typically foreign slaves transshipped through South Carolina, the only state to allow the foreign slave trade), to total restriction on January 1, 1808 (see Clark, *New Orleans*, 316–25; and W. E. B. Du Bois, *The Suppression of the African Slave Trade to the United States, 1638–1870* [1896; repr., New York: Oxford University Press, 1969], 87–90).

12. Liliane Crété, *Daily Life in Louisiana, 1815–1830*, trans. Patrick Gregory (Baton Rouge: Louisiana State University Press, 1981); Peirce Lewis, *New Orleans: The Making of an Urban Landscape*, 2nd ed. (Charlottesville: University Press of Virginia, 2003); Ari Kelman, *A River and Its City: The Nature of Landscape in New Orleans* (Berkeley: University of California Press, 2003).

13. Stanley Faye, "Privateers of Guadeloupe and Their Establishment in Barataria," *LHQ* 23 (1940): 431–33, 443–44; Davis, *Pirates Laffite*, 49, 56.

14. For the status of the slave trade in Latin America, see Lynch, *The Spanish American Revolutions*; James Ferguson King, "The Latin-American Republics and the Suppression of the Slave Trade," *Hispanic American Historical Review* 24 (1944): 387–411; David Murray, "Latin America, Antislavery and Abolition," in *Encyclopedia of Antislavery and Abolition*, ed. Peter Hinks, John McKivigan, and R. Owen Williams, 2 vols. (Westport, CT: Greenwood, 2007), 2:408–18.

15. Edgar Stanton Maclay, *History of American Privateering* (New York: Appleton, 1899); Jerome Garitee, *The Republic's Private Navy: The American Privateering Business as Practiced by Baltimore during the War of 1812* (Middletown, CT: Wesleyan University Press, 1977); Jane Lucas De Grummond, *Renato Beluche: Smuggler, Privateer, Patriot, 1780–1860* (Baton Rouge: Louisiana State University Press, 1983).

16. Today, many geographical features include the name Barataria: Barataria Bay, Little Lake Barataria, Big Lake Barataria, and Bayou Barataria. Nineteenth-century Louisianans used these designations, too, but at the time Barataria was used in a more expansive sense to indicate the entire area south of the Mississippi River and west to the Bayou Lafourche or even farther to Terrebonne Bay. Barataria was a region rather than a specific place. Arsène Latour gives a contemporary understanding of what Barataria meant in *Historical Memoir*, 13. For the smugglers' use of Barataria, see Robert Vogel, "Jean Laffite, the Baratarians, and the Historical Geography of Piracy in the Gulf of Mexico," *Gulf Coast Historical Review* 5 (1990): 63–65; and Davis, *Pirates Laffite*, 56–57.

17. Harnett Thomas Kane, *The Bayous of Louisiana* (New York: William Morrow, 1944), 33–34; Latour, *Historical Memoir*, 13.

18. Depositions of Manuel Ruiz and James J. Connel, July 1813, *U.S. v. Juan Juanilleo alias Sapia*, LA Fed. Ct., case 774; testimony of John Oliver, Dec. 8, 1814, *Daniel Patterson and Others v. The Schooner* General Bolívar, LA Fed. Ct., case 760. See also, in the same case, testimony of William Hoey, Dec. 5, 1814; Joseph Costa, Dec. 5, 1814; James Hoskins, Dec. 5, 1814; and E. Williams, Dec. 8, 1814. For other examples of privateers landing goods directly at Barataria, see libels of Diego Francisco Unzaga, Dec. 1, 1814, *Diego Francisco Unzaga v. The Schooner* Dorada, LA Fed. Ct., case 763; Miguel Gomez de las Barcenas, Dec. 1814, *Miguel Gomez de las Barcenas v. The Spanish Schooner* Amiable Maria, LA Fed. Ct., case 764; depositions of John Randolph, Oct. 11, 1814, *U.S. v. Manuel Joachim*, LA Fed. Ct., case 773; William Godfrey, n.d., *U.S. v. Dominique Youx*, LA Fed. Ct., case 779; deposition of Andrew Whiteman, Nov. 24, 1813, CPD. Several additional depositions in *U.S. v. Youx* provide similar details, but the bottom third of each page is missing, making it impossible to identify the deponent.

19. Deposition of Andrew Whiteman, Nov. 24, 1813, CPD; Vogel, "Historical Geography of Piracy," 63–65, 72n; Davis, *Pirates Laffite*, 117.

20. Deposition of Andrew Whiteman, Nov. 24, 1813, CPD; testimony of John Oliver, Dec. 8, 1814, *Patterson v. The* General Bolívar, LA Fed. Ct., case 760; Davis, *Pirates Laffite*, 50–51. Elsewhere Davis implies that the Laffites owned the goods they smuggled and hid them in warehouses in the city to sell later (86–87). Other authors have maintained this part of the Laffite legend as well (see John Smith Kendall, "The Huntsmen of Black Ivory," *LHQ* 24 [1941], 15–16, who spoke of the Laffites' "system of piratical chain stores").

21. Libel of Vincent Dorgoigoite, Aug. 28, 1810, *Vincent Dorgoigoite v. Michel Bruard*, LA Fed. Ct., case 390; libel of Pedro de Reano, Dec. 17, 1816, *Pedro de Reano and Others v. Pierre Liquet and Certain Negro Slaves*, LA Fed. Ct., case 949; Davis, *Pirates Laffite*, 75.

22. Indictment, Oct. 27, 1814, *U.S. v. Jacques Cannon*, LA Fed. Ct., case 777; Davis, *Pirates Laffite*, 58–59, 76, 87–88, 95, 135; Walter Johnson, *Soul by Soul: Life inside the Antebellum Slave Market* (Cambridge: Harvard University Press, 1999), chap. 2; David

Head, "Slave Smuggling by Foreign Privateers: Geopolitical Influences on the Illegal Slave Trade," *Journal of the Early Republic* 33 (2013): 433–62.

23. John Cravath May Windship to William Plumer Jr., Apr. 2, 1814, in "Letters from Louisiana, 1813–1814," ed. Everett S. Brown, *Mississippi Valley Historical Review* 11 (1925): 575–76; Walker Gilbert to Thomas Freeman, Feb. 18, 1814, and Aug. 1813, qtd. in Davis, *Pirates Laffite*, 129, 116; testimony of John Oliver, Dec. 8, 1814, and Daniel McMullin, Dec. 25, 1814, *Patterson v. The Schooner* General Bolívar, LA Fed. Ct., case 760; John Foley to Pierre Duborg, Sept. 28, 1813, qtd. in Davis, *Pirates Laffite*, 117.

24. Latour, *Historical Memoir*, 14–15.

25. Walker Gilbert to Thomas Freeman, Feb. 18, 1814, qtd. in Davis, *Pirates Laffite*, 130; Proclamation of Claiborne, Mar. 15, 1813, in Claiborne, *Official Letter Books*, 6:232–33.

26. For a discussion of maritime distress, see Anthony P. Morrison, *Places of Refuge for Ships in Distress: Problems and Methods of Resolution* (Boston: Martinus Nijhoff, 2012); and Henry Wheaton, *A Digest of the Law of Maritime Captures and Prizes* (New York: McDermut and Arden, 1815). Louisiana federal judge Dominick Hall also explained the requirements of a distress claim in his opinion in *Jose Almiral* v. *The Ship* Amistad de Rues *and Cargo*, LA Fed. Ct., case 1136.

27. Libel of U.S., Apr. 6, 1810; port wardens' report, May 3, 1810, *U.S.* v. La Petite-Chance, LA Fed. Ct., case 344; *Rhode-Island American and General Advertiser* (Providence), May 18, 1810. Out of the ten French privateers operating from Louisiana, seven claimed distress in order to enter New Orleans.

28. Etat General de Resultat de la croisiere du corsair Francais Le Pandoure, n.d.; list of arms, n.d., Dominique Youx Papers, Historic New Orleans Collection, New Orleans, LA; Davis, *Pirates Laffite*, 85–86.

29. Depositions of Joseph Mandage, July 2, 1810, Louis Crispin, July 9, 1810, Jean Baptiste Larrey, July 9, 1810, and affidavit of William Carter, July 9, 1810, *William Carter* (qui tam) v. *Louis Aury*, LA Fed. Ct., case 376.

30. Quote: libel of William Allen, July 17, 1810, *William Allen* v. *The Ship* Alerta *and Cargo of Slaves*, LA Fed. Ct., case 381. See also indictment, July 10, 1810, and affidavit of Francisco Martinez Antonio Bortoluci, July 9, 1810, *U.S.* v. *Francis Brosquet*, LA Fed. Ct., case 378; libel of U.S., July 11, 1810, and deposition of William Allen, July 26, 1810, *U.S.* v. *The Ship* Alerta, LA Fed. Ct., case 379; libel of Blas Moran, n.d., *Blas Moran* v. *The Schooner* Alerta, LA Fed. Ct., case 380; *The Brig* Alerta *and Cargo* v. *Blas Moran* (1815), 13 U.S. 359.

31. Petitions of P.N. Paillet, n.d., *P. N. Paillet* v. *Caudole*, LA Fed. Ct., case 392; *P. N. Paillet* v. *Bonal*, LA Fed. Ct., case 394; *P. N. Paillet* v. *Coulon*, LA Fed. Ct., case 395; and deposition of John Chauvenette, Sept. 1810, *P. N. Paillet* v. *Cadet Bayonne*, LA Fed. Ct., case 393; Davis, *Pirates Laffite*, 60–63.

32. This unnamed schooner and the *Diligent* may have been the same vessel. The Laffites evidently purchased both vessels sometime in the fall or winter of 1812; they may have then burned the first vessel after it captured the *Dorada* in January 1813. Three pieces of evidence support this view: (1) Diego Francisco Unzaga, owner of the *Dorada*, alleged in his libel that his vessel was captured in 1813; (2) Andrew Whiteman swore that "the Brig taken on the first cruise [the *Dorada*] was afterwards used as a privateer & the first vessel burnt"; and (3) James Connel observed that a French privateer at Barataria was burned since it was a "dull sailor" (although he does not specify its

name). On the other hand, the indictment of the supplier Pierre Laverne states that the *Diligent* captured the *Dorada*; a note on the back of the indictment of sailor Jacques Cannon says that the *Dorada* was captured on Nov. 28, 1812; and John B. Loubie and someone called Mathieu were indicted for fitting out the *Diligent* on July 1, 1812. The timeline of these various accounts cannot be resolved. I have concluded that the *Dorada*'s owner would have known when his vessel was captured, and so I lean toward accepting that there was an unnamed Laffite schooner that captured the *Dorada* (see depositions of Andrew Whiteman, Nov. 24, 1813, CPD; James J. Connel, July 1813, *U.S. v. Juan Juanilleo alias Sapia*, LA Fed. Ct., case 774; libel of Diego Francisco Unzaga, Dec. 1, 1814, *Diego Francisco Unzaga v. The Schooner Dorada*, LA Fed. Ct., case 763; indictment, Oct., 1814, *U.S. v. Pierre Laverne alias Antoine Laverne alias Cadet Patte Grasse*, LA Fed. Ct., case 784; indictment, Oct. 27, 1814, *U.S. v. Jacques Cannon*, LA Fed. Ct., case 777; Davis, *Pirates Laffite*, 94–106). Captain Gianni's identity is also subject to dispute. There is no indication whether this is his first or last name, and court papers refer to him as "Janny," "Jannety," "Joanni," or "Johanny," which would seem to be an English-speaking clerk's way of rendering the Italian name Gianni. He also sported the nickname Barbienfume—Redbeard. However, in the secondary literature he is sometimes called Jean Jannet, since this name appeared in a document ratifying the Laffites' later takeover of Galveston Island in 1817 that was reprinted for a report to the U.S. Congress. Furthermore, as if this is not confusing enough, "Jannet" is also sometimes seen as person distinct from Gianni, with Barbienfume said to be a third person still. The best evidence, however, indicates that Gianni, Jannet, and Barbienfume were the same person. Jean Laffite, for example, specifically referred to the presence of "Jonny called Barbe enfume" at Galveston (see Register of Proceedings at Galveston, Apr. 20, 1817, 66; and Jean Laffite's Diary of a Voyage to Galveston, Mar. 27, 1817). Davis concludes that "Jannet" and Barbienfume are different people (Davis, *Pirates Laffite*, 60, 89–90, 321). However, Stanley Faye indicates that Barbienfume was Gianni's nickname (Stanley Faye, "Privateersmen of the Gulf and their Prizes," *LHQ* 22 [1939]: 1061–63).

33. On neutrality law, see Charles G. Fenwick, *The Neutrality Laws of the United States* (Washington: Carnegie Endowment for International Peace, 1913). For the text of the relevant acts, see Act of June 5, 1794, ch. 50, 1 *United States Statutes at Large*, 381–84; Act of June 14, 1797, ch. 1, 1 *United States Statutes at Large*, 520. Judge Hall explained the exception for transient sailors in his opinion in *Jose Almiral v. The Ship Amistad de Rues and Cargo*, LA Fed. Ct., case 1136.

34. Depositions of Andrew Whiteman, Nov. 24, 1813, CPD; James J. Connel, July 1813, *U.S. v. Juan Juanilleo alias Sapia*, LA Fed. Ct., case 774; indictment, Oct. 1814, *U.S. v. Pierre Laverne alias Antoine Laverne alias Cadet Patte Grasse*, LA Fed. Ct., case 784; testimony of William Hoey, Dec. 5, 1814, *Patterson v. The Schooner* General Bolívar, LA Fed. Ct., case 760. See also the testimony of James Hoskins, Dec. 5, 1814, and E. Williams, Dec. 8, 1814, in the same case. Unfortunately, case files often indicate only that a vessel was fitted out at Barataria without giving additional details (see *U.S. v. Pierre Liquet*, LA Fed. Ct., case 495; *U.S. v. Bernard Boudin*, LA Fed. Ct., case 600; *U.S. v. Mathieu alias Jean Guilliuame Bate and Francis de Terraine*, LA Fed. Ct., case 619; *U.S. v. Dominique Youx*, LA Fed. Ct., case 779; *U.S. v. William Flemming*, LA Fed. Ct., case 780; *U.S. v. The Schooner* General Bolívar, LA Fed. Ct., case 837; *U.S. v. Vincent Gambi*, LA Fed. Ct., case 844).

35. Indictment, May 8, 1810, *U.S.* v. *Marcellin Battigne*, LA Fed. Ct., case 348; deposition of William Allen, July 26, 1810, *U.S.* v. *The Ship* Alerta, LA Fed. Ct., case 379; *The Brig* Alerta *and Cargo* v. *Blas Moran* (1815), 13 U.S. 359.

36. Auguste Levasseur, *Lafayette en Amérique, en 1824 et 1825*, 2 vols. (Paris, 1829), qtd. in Crété, *Daily Life in Louisiana*, 24. Beverly Chew explained the customs procedure in his testimony, Apr. 20, 1818, *Almiral* v. *The Ship* Amistad de Rues, LA Fed. Ct., case 1136.

37. Beverly Chew to William Crawford, Oct. 17, 1817, 66; testimony of Chew, Apr. 20, 1819, *Almiral* v. *The Ship* Amistad de Rues, LA Fed. Ct., case 1136; Crété, *Daily Life in Louisiana*, 24.

38. Protest of Jose Rastigue, June 24, 1817; libel of Jose Almiral, Jan. 19, 1818; deposition of Peter Franks, Feb. 9, 1818; testimony of Benito Gomez, Hieronymo Mari Covitz, and Abraham Miller, Mar. 23, 1818; inspector's report, n.d., *Almiral* v. *The Ship* Amistad de Rues, LA Fed. Ct., case 1136. The *Congress of Venezuela* provides a similar example (see testimony of Boeshell, June 11, 1817; claim and answer of J. F. Lamoreaux, May 27, 1817; testimony of Miguel Munez, June 2, 1817, and James Benson, n.d.; depositions of Jose Ferre, June 2, 1817; Juan Guzmana, June 11, 1817; and Victoriano Comacho, n.d., *Gasper Hernandez* v. *The Spanish Schooner* Estrella, *Her Tackle, Apparel, Furniture, and Cargo*, LA Fed. Ct., case 1035).

39. Deposition of James J. Connel, July 1813, *U.S.* v. *Juan Juanilleo alias Sapia*, LA Fed. Ct., case 774; Davis, *Pirates Laffite*, 98–101, 103–4. Davis's handling of this incident is confused. For example, he contends that Jean did not claim distress even though he sought permission to sell prize goods in the city, which he could have done only by claiming distress. Furthermore, Davis argues that Laporte was duped by Jean. Given Laporte's extensive dealings with privateers, this seems unlikely (see affidavit of J. B. Laporte, May 15, 1817, *U.S.* v. *The Schooner* Musquito, LA Fed. Ct., case 978; answer of J. B. Laporte, June 6, 1818, *Juan Clemente Castillo* v. *The Sloop* San Felipe, *Her Tackle, Apparel, Furniture, and Cargo*, LA Fed. Ct., case 1032; libel of Thomas Stoughton, Oct. 3, 1817, and claim and answer of John B. Laporte Jr., Dec. 8, 1817, *Thomas Stoughton* v. *415 Boxes, Forty-seven Half Boxes, and Four Barrels of Sugar, Thirty-four Seroons of Tobacco, Thirteen Seroons of Cocoa, Sixty-one Bags of Coffee, Two Packages of Sole Leather, Twelve Demijohns of Honey, One Barrel of Molasses, and Two Bags of Segars*, NY Adm.; Stanley Faye, "The Great Stroke of Pierre Laffite," *LHQ* 23 [1940]: 776; and De Grummond, *Renato Beluche*, 159, 164–65).

40. For this incident, see deposition of Andrew Whiteman, Nov. 24, 1813, CPD; and Davis, *Pirates Laffite*, 118–22. Quotes are from Whiteman's deposition.

41. For examples of this contention, see Lyle Saxon, *Lafitte the Pirate* (New Orleans: Robert L. Crager, 1930); De Grummond, *The Baratarians*; and Winston Groom, *Patriotic Fire: Andrew Jackson and Jean Laffite at the Battle of New Orleans* (New York: Vintage, 2006).

42. For the Customs Service, see Carl E. Prince and Mollie Keller, *The U.S. Customs Service: A Bicentennial History* (Washington: U.S. Customs Service, 1989); Irving H. King, *The Coast Guard under Sail: The U.S. Revenue Cutter Service, 1789–1865* (Annapolis: U.S. Naval Institute Press, 1989). On gunboats, see Spencer C. Tucker, *The Jeffersonian Gunboat Navy* (Columbia: University of South Carolina Press, 1993); Gene A. Smith, *"For the Purposes of Defense": The Politics of the Jeffersonian Gunboat Program* (Newark: University of Delaware Press, 1995). Case files which expressly

mention a capture by customs or the navy include *U.S.* v. *Francis Brosquet,* LA Fed. Ct., case 378; *U.S.* v. *The Schooner* Presidente, LA Fed. Ct., case 811; *U.S.* v. *The Schooner* Philanthrope, *alias* Eagle, *alias* Petit Milan, LA Fed. Ct., case 812; *U.S.* v. *Certain Goods, Wares, and Merchandise Seized Onboard the Schooner* Non Such, LA Fed. Ct., case 814; *Diego Morphy* v. *The Spanish Schooner* Santa Rita *and Cargo,* LA Fed. Ct., case 817; *Diego Morphy* v. *The Spanish Polacre Brig* Nuestra Senora de Regla, LA Fed. Ct., case 852; *Diego Morphy* v. *The Spanish Ship* Cleopatra *and Cargo,* LA Fed. Ct., case 857; *U.S.* v. *The Schooner* Cometa *and Cargo,* LA Fed. Ct., case 909; *Felipe Fatio* v. *The Schooner* Three Keels (St. Anthony), *and Thirty-Two Negroes,* LA Fed. Ct., case 1083. See also Davis, *Pirates Laffite,* 75, 77, 84, 115.

43. Quotes: William Claiborne to Richard Rush, Oct. 30, 1814, in Claiborne, *Official Letter Books,* 6:300–302; William Jones to Pierre F. Dubourg, Sept. 27, 1813, qtd. in Davis, *Pirates Laffite,* 87. See also Davis, *Pirates Laffite,* 75, 126, 135.

44. David Porter to James Madison, Sept. 21, 1810, Naval History Society Collection, New-York Historical Society. See also David Foster Long, *Nothing Too Daring: A Biography of Commodore David Porter, 1780–1843* (Annapolis: U.S. Naval Institute Press, 1970), 54.

45. Outcomes for both criminal and civil cases can be found, if they were recorded, in the Louisiana federal court's minute book. Entries through 1814 appears on roll one of *Case Files of the U.S. District Court for the Eastern District of Louisiana, 1806–1814,* National Archives Microfilm Publication M1082. The minute book is continued in *Minutes of the U.S. District Court at New Orleans,* National Archives Southwest Region Microfilm Publication 7RA-119.

46. For Brosquet and Battigne, see the Louisiana federal court's minute book entries for *U.S.* v. *Francis Brosquet,* LA Fed. Ct., case 378, and *U.S.* v. *Marceline Battigne,* LA Fed. Ct., case 388, in *Case Files of the U.S. District Court for the Eastern District of Louisiana, 1806–1814,* roll 1.

47. Determining the number of civil cases involving privateers or smugglers is a knotty problem. Hall's clerk assigned each case that came before the court a unique number. Fifty-eight cases involving privateers or smugglers were given their own number. However, it often happened that multiple parties filed separate suits contending for the same property (the *Epine*'s cruise alone produced eleven suits). Therefore, it makes sense to combine these instances into one case. Based on this criterion, there were twenty-eight cases, those in which different prizes or privateers were involved. Results compiled from the Louisiana federal court's minute book (*Case Files of the U.S. District Court for the Eastern District of Louisiana, 1806–1814,* roll 1; *Minutes of the U.S. District Courts at New Orleans,* rolls 1–3). There was also one case adjudicated in the federal court in New York, where some prize goods ended up. It was resolved when the parties agreed to split the property (see motion of Thomas Stoughton, Jan. 20, 1818, *Stoughton* v. *415 Boxes, Forty-seven Half Boxes, and Four Barrels of Sugar,* NYDC, Adm.).

48. Gene A. Smith, "U.S. Navy Gunboats and the Slave Trade in Louisiana Waters, 1808–1811," *Military History of the West* 23 (1993): 140–41; Long, *Nothing Too Daring,* 40; Davis, *Pirates Laffite,* 83, 85, 130–31.

49. Quotes: William Jones to Pierre F. Dubourg, Sept. 27, 1813, and Walker Gilbert to Dubourg, Oct. 29, 1813, both qtd. in Davis, *Pirates Laffite,* 126, 128.

50. Davis, *Pirates Laffite,* 122–23, 134–35. For other examples of violence between privateers, smugglers, and U.S. forces, see deposition of John Smith, Jan. 22, 1812,

Daniel Patterson and Others v. *The Spanish Polacre* La Divina Pastora, *Her Tackle, Furniture, Apparel, and Cargo,* LA Fed. Ct., case 452; and Davis, *Pirates Laffite,* 84–87.

51. Herbert Heaton, "Non-Importation, 1806–1812," *Journal of Economic History* 1 (1941): 180–81.

52. For unsuccessful prize claims, see *Daniel Patterson and George Ross* v. *Certain Gold Coin,* LA Fed. Ct., case 750; *Daniel Patterson and George Ross* v. *Sixteen Plates of Bullion and Eight Pieces of Cannon,* LA Fed. Ct., case 753; *Daniel Patterson and George Ross* v. *Certain Bank Notes,* LA Fed. Ct., case 754; *Daniel Patterson and Others* v. *The Schooner* General Bolívar, LA Fed. Ct., case 760; and *William Lawrence and Daniel Patterson* v. *Seventy-four Pipes and Thirty-one Half Pipes of Wine,* LA Fed. Ct., case 762. For gunboat performance, see Gene A. Smith, *Thomas ap Catesby Jones: Commodore of Manifest Destiny* (Annapolis: Naval Institute Press, 2000), chap. 2; Tucker, *Jeffersonian Gunboat Navy,* 65; Smith, "For the Purposes of Defense," 20; and Davis, *Pirates Laffite,* 83, 85, 130–31.

53. Quote: Daniel T. Patterson to William Jones, Nov. 30, 1813; Patterson to Paul Hamilton, Nov. 10, 1812, qtd. in Christopher McKee, *A Gentlemanly and Honorable Profession: The Creation of the U.S. Naval Officer Corps, 1794–1815* (Annapolis: Naval Institute Press, 1991), 306. McKee finds that officers who served at New Orleans really were less likely to be promoted—and for exactly the reason they feared: the secretary of the navy would not promote officers who had seen only gunboat duty (see chap. 25).

54. For Louisiana politics in this era, see Joseph G. Tregle Jr., *Louisiana in the Age of Jackson: A Clash of Cultures and Personalities* (Baton Rouge: Louisiana State University Press, 1999), chap. 5; and Kastor, *Nation's Crucible,* chap. 5. Tregle explores the Creole mythology in his book as well as at length in his chapter "Creoles and Americans," in *Creole New Orleans,* 131–55. For slave rebellions, see Rothman, *Slave Country,* 106–17.

55. Quote: Petition of Ange-Michel Brouard, Mar. 26, 1810, in Claiborne, *Official Letter Books,* 5:27. For Claiborne's political calculations, see Peter J. Kastor, "'Motives of Peculiar Urgency': Local Diplomacy in Louisiana, 1803–1821," *William and Mary Quarterly* 58 (2001): 829–30; and Long, *Nothing Too Daring,* 53. For Claiborne's background, see Junius P. Rodriguez, "Claiborne, William Charles Coles," ANBO, www.anb.org/articles/02/02-00064.html; and Joseph T. Hatfield, *William Claiborne: Jeffersonian Centurion in the American Southwest* (Lafayette: University of Southwestern Louisiana Press, 1976).

56. Quotes: William Claiborne to Desforgues, Mar. 30, 1810, in Claiborne, *Official Letter Books,* 5:28–29; David Porter to Samuel Hambleton, Jan. 11, 1811, Porter Papers.

57. Quote: Thomas ap Catesby Jones to Secretary of the Navy, Oct. 31, 1855, qtd. in Smith, *Thomas ap Catesby Jones,* 22. For the blockade and its effects, see the *Yankee* (Boston), May 14, 1813; and Donald Hickey, *The War of 1812: A Forgotten Conflict* (Urbana: University of Illinois Press, 1989), 152–53, 214–16. For American trade policy, see Donald Hickey, "Trade Restrictions during the War of 1812," *Journal of American History* 68 (1981): 517–38.

58. As a neutral, the United States technically had two other options: it could have closed its ports to all combatants, although that would have closed even more ports to American sailors; or it could have flung its ports wide open and allowed any and every privateer to do whatever they wanted in port, although that would have certainly created chaos, and drawn the nation into war (see *The Brig* Alerta, *and Cargo* v. *Blas Moran* [1815], 13 U.S. 359). For Youx, see unknown doctor to M. McRea, n.d., Youx

Papers. For the *Carimasi*, see libel of Diego Morphy, June 19, 1815; answer of Juan Diego Amador, July 7, 1815; Supreme Court notice, Feb. 12, 1817, *Diego Morphy v. The Indagadora*, LA Fed. Ct., case 833.

3 / Baltimore

1. For Taylor's background, see his affidavit, Sept. 3, 1818 in *Thomas Stoughton on behalf of Juan Juando and Others v. Thomas Taylor*, NY Adm., roll 23; *American Watchman* (Wilmington, DE), Sept. 26, 1818; *Baltimore Patriot*, Nov. 25, 1818; Lewis Winkler Bealer, "The Privateers of Buenos Aires, 1815-1821: Their Activities in the Hispanic American Wars of Independence" (Ph.D. diss., University of California, Berkeley, 1935), 14-16, 28; and Feliciano Duarte Gámez, "El desafío insurgente. Análisis del corso hispanoamericano desde una perspective peninsular: 1812-1828" (Ph.D. diss., University of Cadiz, 2004), 605. For Taylor's mission to the United States, see Samuel Flagg Bemis, *Early Diplomatic Missions from Buenos Aires to the United States, 1811-1824* (Worcester, MA: American Antiquarian Society, 1940), 29-30; and Benjamin Keen, *David Curtis De Forest and the Revolution of Buenos Aires* (New Haven: Yale University Press, 1947), 103-4. For smuggling on the River Plate, see Jerry W. Cooney, "'Doing Business in the Smuggling Way': Yankee Contraband in the Río de la Plata," *American Neptune* 47 (1987): 162-68. In court, Taylor claimed to have been born a British subject in Bermuda and to have gone to Buenos Aires in the British Navy. *Lloyd's List* (London), Apr. 1, 1817, also refers to Taylor as British. Taylor swore he was an American citizen when he cleared the *Santafecino*; the *American Watchmen* article cites information gleaned from Taylor's father, and the newspaperman Hezekiah Niles said that as a child he had attended school with Taylor, which would have been in Wilmington, Delaware (see Hezekiah Niles to William Darlington, Feb. 5, 1816, William Darlington Correspondence, Library of Congress, Washington, DC; and Stephen M. Zeigler, "Niles, Hezekiah," ANBO, www.anb.org/articles/16/16-01202.html).

2. Quote: *New York Daily Advertiser*, Aug. 27, 1819. See also deposition of John Sands, Jan. 8, 1819, CPD; *American Beacon* (Norfolk, VA), July 3, 1816; *Essex (MA) Register*, July 13, 1816; *National Register* (Washington, DC), May 24, 1817; *U.S. v. Hutchings* (1817), 26 F. Cas. 440; Elias Glenn to James Monroe, Sept. 7, 1816, in *Documents Accompanying a Bill to Prevent Citizens of the United States from Selling Vessels of War to the Citizens or Subjects of Any Foreign Power* (Washington: William A. Davis, 1817), 11-13; Bealer, "The Privateers of Buenos Aires," 95-97.

3. For Baltimore's political leanings and reputation, see Laura Bornholdt, *Baltimore and Early Pan-Americanism: A Study in the Background of the Monroe Doctrine* (Northampton, MA: Smith College Studies in History, 1949), 6-8; Gary Lawson Browne, *Baltimore in the Nation: 1789-1861* (Chapel Hill: University of North Carolina Press, 1980), 64-65.

4. For Baltimore's growth, see Pearle Blood, "Factors in the Economic Development of Baltimore, Maryland," *Economic Geography* 13 (1937): 187-208; Stuart Weems Bruchey, *Robert Oliver, Merchant of Baltimore, 1783-1819* (Baltimore: Johns Hopkins University Press, 1956); Jerome Garitee, *The Republic's Private Navy: The American Privateering Business as Practiced by Baltimore during the War of 1812* (Middleton, CT: Wesleyan University Press, 1977); Browne, *Baltimore in the Nation*; Sherry Olson, *Baltimore: The Building of an American City*, 2nd ed. (Baltimore: Johns Hopkins University Press, 1997); Christopher Phillips, *Freedom's Port: The African American*

Community of Baltimore, 1790–1860 (Urbana: University of Illinois Press, 1997); Seth Rockman, *Scraping By: Wage Labor, Slavery, and Survival in Early Baltimore* (Baltimore: Johns Hopkins University Press, 2009), 18–38; and Richard Chew, "The Measure of Independence" (Ph.D. diss., College of William and Mary, 2002). On the importance of clipper ships, see Griffin, "Privateering from Baltimore," 2; and Howard Irving Chapelle, *The Baltimore Clipper: Its Origin and Development* (Salem, MA: Marine Research Society, 1930).

5. Garitee, *The Republic's Private Navy*, chap. 3; Browne, *Baltimore in the Nation*, 70–71, 82, 90–91.

6. For Baltimore and the geopolitics of the Spanish American Revolutions, see Rafe Blaufarb, "The Western Question: The Geopolitics of Latin American Independence," *American Historical Review* 112 (2007): 753–54.

7. For the composition of the group and their meetings, see deposition of John Sands, Jan. 8, 1819, CPD; and *New York Daily Advertiser*, Aug. 27, 1819. Members' background compiled as follows: Sands: *Federal Republican and Commercial Gazette* (Baltimore), Feb. 10, 1810; *Baltimore Patriot*, Mar. 16, 1813, Nov. 30, 1813; *Baltimore Price Current*, Feb. 5, 1814; George W. McCreary, *The Ancient and Honorable Mechanical Company of Baltimore* (Baltimore: Kohn and Pollock, 1901), 137. Karrick: *Baltimore Patriot*, Dec. 16, 1813, Sept. 2, 1814, Sept. 16, 1815, Feb. 26, 1816, Nov. 18, 1816; *Baltimore Price Current*, Mar. 28, 1812, Apr. 18, 1812, Apr. 25, 1812, Aug. 11, 1812, Nov. 7, 1812, Aug. 26, 1816, Sept. 2, 1815, May 4, 1816. Snyder: *Baltimore Price Current*, July 21, 1810; *Baltimore Patriot*, June 16, 1816, Oct. 1, 1817, June 29, 1818, Feb. 10, 1819, July 5, 1819, Feb. 14, 1823, June 30, 1823; "Snyder, Joseph," Dielman-Hayward Genealogical File, Maryland Historical Society; Garitee, *The Republic's Private Navy*, 33–35. Patterson: Garitee, *Republic's Private Navy*, 200, 262; Charlene Boyer Lewis, *Elizabeth Patterson Bonaparte: An American Aristocrat in the Early Republic* (Philadelphia: University of Pennsylvania Press, 2012). Murray: *Baltimore Patriot*, Jan. 16, 1816, Jan. 24, 1816, Mar. 14, 1816, May 7, 1816, May 24, 1816, Dec. 21, 1818, Aug. 3, 1819. Skinner: Harold A. Bierck Jr., "Spoils, Soils, and Skinner," *Maryland Historical Magazine* 49 (1954): 21–40, 143–55. Johnston: *Baltimore Price Current*, Sept. 2, 1815; *U.S. v. Perthshire alias Arismendi alias Snap Dragon alias Mendozina*, transcript of proceedings in MD Appel. The district court case file for this suit no longer exists, leaving the transcript copied and sent up to the circuit court on appeal as the only record. B. K. Harrison: deposition of Matthew Murray, Oct. 21, 1818, *Joaquim José Vasques v. Sundry Bales of Cotton, a Quantity of Sugar, Hides, and Sides of Leather*, NY Adm. This Murray was an innkeeper, not the investor.

8. Garitee, *Republic's Private Navy*, 65–66, 111–12; *New York Daily Advertiser*, Aug. 27, 1819; deposition of John Sands, Jan. 8, 1819, CPD; deposition of Robert M. Goodwin, n.d., *Joaquim José Vasques v. Robert M. Goodwin*, NY Adm.

9. See, for example, De Forest to Thomas Tenant, Jan. 7, 1819; to Jesse Putnam, Sept. 5, 1818; to John Gooding, Mar. 25, 1819; and to John D'Arcy and Henry Didier, July 28, 1819, De Forest Family Papers, Yale University Library Manuscripts and Archives, New Haven, CT. All four neutrality laws (1794, 1797, 1817, and 1818) employed the same language (see, for example, Act of June 5, 1794, ch. 50, 1 *United States Statutes at Large*, 381–84).

10. *Baltimore Price Current*, July 19, 1817; *Baltimore Patriot*, Apr. 17, 1816, Apr. 24, 1818, Nov. 4, 1818, Feb. 10, 1819, Apr. 20, 1819, Oct. 26, 1819, May 1, 1820, Mar.

21, 1822, Apr. 1, 1824. For the motives for joining a fire company, see Amy S. Greenberg, *Cause for Alarm: The Volunteer Fire Department in the Nineteenth-Century City* (Princeton: Princeton University Press, 1998), 52–60. For Hibernian societies, see Rockman, *Scraping By*, 31–32.

11. Quote: *Baltimore Patriot*, Feb. 25, 1817. See also *Baltimore Price Current*, July 1, 1815; *Washington (D.C.) Gazette*, Jan. 28, 1819; *Baltimore Patriot*, Dec. 17, 1822; Garitee, *Republic's Private Navy*, 268.

12. Garitee, *Republic's Private Navy*, 42–43, 202, 207, 263–68.

13. *Baltimore Price Current*, May 25, 1816; *Baltimore Patriot*, Oct. 12, 1816, Nov. 25, 1816; *Franklin Gazette* (Philadelphia), Mar. 10, 1818; *Baltimore Price Current*, Aug. 15, 1818; *Baltimore Patriot*, Mar. 29, 1821, Sept. 16, 1823, Jan. 9, 1834; Garitee, *Republic's Private Navy*, 263, 266.

14. Craig: *Baltimore Price Current*, Apr. 18, 1812, Aug. 9, 1817; *Baltimore Patriot*, June 21, 1815, Nov. 28, 1815, Dec. 16, 1815, Apr. 12, 1816, Nov. 25, 1816, June 5, 1818; Garitee, *Republic's Private Navy*, 260. Barron: *Baltimore Patriot*, Nov. 25, 1816, Sept. 26, 1817, Nov. 15, 1822. Lovell: Garitee, *Republic's Private Navy*, 258.

15. Head, "Baltimore Seafarers," 271. In the United States, the agent was called a ship's husband, and in Britain and France, he was called an *armateur* (see Garitee, *Republic's Private Navy*, 103; David J. Starkey, *British Privateering Enterprise in the Eighteenth Century* [Exeter, U.K.: University of Exeter Press, 1990], 67; and Patrick Crowhurst, *The French War on Trade: Privateering 1793–1815*, [Aldershot, U.K.: Scolar Press, 1989], 84).

16. Head, "Baltimore Seafarers," 275–76.

17. Ibid., 276.

18. Depositions of Samuel Beaver, Nov. 27, 1819, and Laurence Maddeson, Nov. 29, 1819, U.S. v. Irresistable, MD Adm.; deposition of Lindborn, CPD; petition of David De Forest, Jan. 21, 1817, U.S. v. The Schooner *Swift* alias *Mangoré*, Md Adm. For neutrality law and the munitions trade, see Charles G. Fenwick, *The Neutrality Laws of the United States* (Washington: Carnegie Endowment for International Peace, 1913), 70; Freeman Snow, *Cases and Opinions on International Law, with Notes and a Syllabus* (Boston: Boston Book Company, 1893), pt. 2, chap. 3; and William C. Morey, "The Sale of Munitions of War," *American Journal of International Law* 10 (1916): 467–91.

19. Depositions of John Williams, July 8, 1818; Isaac Miller, July 9, 1818; John Barnard, July 9, 1818; claim and answer of William Saunders, July 22, 1818; commission of the *Carony*, June 14, 1818; Henry Taggart to William Saunders, March 10, 1818, U.S. v. The Schooner Felix, GA Adm.

20. De Forest to Halsey, Feb. 13, 1816, and Feb. 15, 1816, De Forest Papers.

21. De Forest to William P. Ford, May 15, 1819, De Forest Papers; Keen, *David Curtis De Forest*, 98. De Forest carried on a regular correspondence with these men too voluminous to cite here. It can be found in his papers. Also, Estanislao's partner, Henry Hill, regularly wrote the same group, making clear the interlocking relationship between them (see Hill to De Forest, Sept. 18, 1817, and Oct. 11, 1817; to Lynch, Zimmerman, and Co., Oct. 11, 1817, and Oct. 18, 1817; and to Ford, Aug. 5, 1817, Henry Hill Papers, Yale University Library Manuscripts and Archives, New Haven, CT).

22. Depositions of Joseph Delacour, Jan. 16, 1819, and John Sands, Jan. 8, 1819, CPD; Henry Allen Coward, Sept. 5, 1818, U.S. v. The Brig Fourth of July alias La Fortuna alias Fortuna, MD Adm.; William Thornton, Aug. 28, 1818, and bill of sale of the

Fourth of July, Jan. 5, 1817, *Juando v. Taylor*, NY Adm.; *New York Daily Advertiser*, Aug. 27, 1819. Privateer vessels often sported patriotic names, but it is uncertain who actually chose them. Commissions were often referred to as "issued in blank," which suggests that the privateers themselves chose the names. However, several sources refer to blank commissions that nevertheless had vessel names already filled in. This seems to have been the case with Taylor's commission. For examples of "blank" commissions with vessel names included, see De Forest's contract for arming the *Tupacamaru* and the *Mangoré*, Oct. 24, 1815, Jonathan D. Meredith Papers, Library of Congress, Washington, DC, as well as *U.S. v. Bass* (1819), 24 F. Cas. 1028.

23. Lewis Morling, Sept. 1, 1818, *Juando v. Taylor*, NY Adm.; Henry Alan Coward, Sept. 5, 1818, *U.S. v. The* Fourth of July; Joseph Delacour, Jan. 16, 1819, CPD; *Washington City Weekly Gazette*, Apr. 19, 1817; *New York Daily Advertiser*, June 2, 1817; *Baltimore Patriot*, Nov. 25, 1818; deposition of Henry Allen Coward, *U.S. v. The* Fourth of July; Morling, *Juando v. Taylor*; Delacour, CPD; *Washington City Weekly Gazette*, Apr. 19, 1817; *New York Daily Advertiser*, June 2, 1817.

24. Fitting out, arming, clearing a vessel, and shipping a crew were key issues in many cases. For examples, see the libels of Joaquim José Vasques, Feb. 5, 1819, *Joaquim José Vasques v. John Gooding for the Illegal Seizure of the Portuguese Ship* Sociedade Feliz *and a Portuguese Brig, Name Unknown, and their Cargoes*; Joao José and Manuel Laurence, May 19, 1819, *Joao José, Manuel Laurence and Others v. Clement Cathell, Robert M. Goodwin, and Others for the Illegal Taking of the Portuguese Ship* Don Pedro Alcantara *and her Cargo*, MD Adm. For the sealing voyages, see libel of William Hall, June 15, 1818, *William Hall and Others v. The Brig* Velos *alias* Republicana, MD Adm.; Henry Trigger, Mar 25, 1819, *John B. Bernabeau v. The Brig* Arrogante Barcelonas, MD Adm.

25. Deposition of Joshua Chambers, Mar. 22, 1820, *José, Laurence and Others v. Clement Cathell, Robert M. Goodwin, et al.*; deposition of Joseph Smith, Aug. 28, 1819, *Vasques v. The Cargo of the Brig* Fanny, MD Adm.

26. Deposition of Joseph Smith, Aug. 28, 1819, *Vasques v. The Cargo of the* Fanny, MD Adm.; Ernest Obadele-Starks, *Freebooters and Smugglers: The Foreign Slave Trade in the United States after 1808* (Fayetteville: University of Arkansas Press, 2007), 25.

27. Case files often include detailed lists of items taken. See libel of Jacques Marie Angelucci, Feb. 17, 1819, *Jacques Marie Angelucci v. Sundry Bales, Boxes, and Trunks, Part of the Cargo of Five French Vessels, and David Ewing*; deposition of Francis Navarre, Feb. 24, 1819, *U.S. v. Eight Cases of Dry Goods, Four Pieces of Cloth, Four Pieces of Silk, Four Papers of Silk Handkerchiefs*, MD Adm.; libel of Joao José and Manuel Laurence, May 19, 1819, *José and Laurence v. Cathell, Goodwin, and Others*. Republicana captures: deposition of Joseph Smith, Aug. 28, 1819, *Vasques v. The Cargo of the Brig* Fanny, MD Adm. Danels captures: libel of John B. Bernabeau, Apr. 21, 1819, *John B. Bernabeau v. The Brig* Nereyda; libel of William R. Swift, Apr. 15, 1819, *William R. Swift v. John D. Daniels for the Illegal Capture of the Portuguese Brig* Globo *and Cargo, and Other Vessels*; libel of Joaquim José Vasques, Sept. 12, 1818, *Joaquim José Vasques v. Sundry Boxes and Bags of Gold and Silver Specie*). Monson capture: Luis de Onís to John Quincy Adams, Nov. 2, 1817, and June 9, 1818, in *Diplomatic Correspondence of the United States Concerning the Independence of the Latin-American Nations*, ed. William R. Manning, 3 vols. (New York: Oxford University Press, 1925–26), 3:1951–52,

1967–69. The $1.5 million figure is an estimate; Onis changed his numbers from one letter to the next.

28. *Sundry African Slaves, the Governor of Georgia Claimant* (1828), 26 U.S. 110 and *Ex parte Juan Madrazzo* (1833), 32 U.S. 627; W. R. Maron to Thomas Lloyd Halsey, Feb. 24, 1821; Adam Pond to Halsey, Halsey Letters in the Meredith Papers; The *Antelope* (1825), 23 U.S. 66; depositions of Joseph Delacour, Jan. 16, 1819, CPD; Francis Davis, William Shaw, and Thomas Taxey, Dec. 9, 1819, *U.S.* v. *Samuel Franklin*, MD Crim.; *Lloyd's List* (London), July 11, 1817; Adam Rockman, *Slave Country: American Expansion and the Origins of the Deep South* (Cambridge: Harvard University Press, 2005), 199; Rockman, *Scraping By*, 36–38.

29. For the incentives prize courts created for privateers, see Donald Petrie, *The Prize Game: Lawful Looting on the High Seas in the Age of Fighting Sail* (New York: Berkely, 1999), 144–163. For examples of Spanish American privateers using prize courts, see plea and answer of Joseph Almeida, Dec. 23, 1819, *John B. Bernabeau* v. *The Brig* Wilson, MD Adm.; claim and answer of Henry Child, Apr. 29, 1819, and decree and opinion of Theodorick Bland, Jan. 3, 1820, *Bernabeau* v. *The Brig* Nereyda, MD Adm.; plea and answer of George Wilson and Joseph Almeida, Dec. 20, 1819, *John B. Bernabeau* v. *The Cargo of the Armed Schooner* Almeida, MD Adm.; *Baltimore Patriot*, Apr. 17, 1818; and Bealer, "Privateers of Buenos Aires," 16, 102.

30. Quote: libel of Jacques Marie Angelucci, Feb. 17, 1819, *Angelucci* v. *Sundry Bales, Boxes, and Trunks*. See also Andrew Coop, Feb. 24, 1819, U.S. v. *Eight Cases of Dry Goods*, MD Adm.; deposition of Dixon B. Watts, June 9, 1820, *John Carrere, Claimant of Sundry Goods, Wares, and Merchandise* v. *James McCulloch, et al.*, MD Appel.

31. Depositions of Joseph Smith, Aug. 28, 1819, *Vasques* v. *The Cargo of the Brig Fanny*; Joshua Chambers, Mar. 22, 1820, *José and Laurence.* v. *Cathell, Goodwin, and Others*, MD Adm.

32. Quote: deposition of John Riper, Apr. 29, 1819, *Charles Mulvey* v. *150 Boxes of Sugar*, GA Adm. See also, in the same case, deposition of James Allen Robinson, July 2, 1821; and claim and answer of Richard Dennis, Apr. 16, 1819.

33. Taylor: depositions of Joseph Delacour, Jan. 16, 1819, and John Sands, Jan. 8, 1819, CPD; Henry Allen Coward, Sept. 5, 1818, *U.S.* v. *The Brig* Fourth of July, MD Adm. Stafford and Burke: libel of Joaquim Zamorano, June 27, 1817, *Joaquim Zamorano* v. *John La Borde and 500 Boxes of Sugar*, MD Adm.; deposition of Timothy Reagan, June 25, 1817, *Zamorano* v. *Sundry Goods*, MD Adm. See also the libel of Joaquim Zamorano, Oct. 13, 1817, *Joaquim Zamorano* v. *117 Boxes of Sugar*, and libel of John B. Bernabeau, Dec. 19, 1818, *John B. Bernabeau* v. *William J. Stafford, Henry Thompson, and the Proceeds of the Cargo of the Brig* St. Joseph, MD Adm.; *Baltimore Price Current*, July, 19, 1817. On the copy of this article I found in *Early American Newspapers*, New Orleans is crossed out and "Galveston Harriot S.A." has been written in by hand.

For a later cruise, Karrick purchased two schooners to meet the *Patriota* in the Caribbean and transport prize goods to Baltimore. See deposition of John G. Johnston, Nov. 20, 1819, *Juando* v. *Taylor*, NY Adm.; libel of John M. Gass, Oct. 26, 1818, *John M. Gass* v. *William Foster and Others*, MD Adm.; *New York Daily Advertiser*, Aug. 27, 1819.

34. Richard H. and William D. Douglass to W. S. Cooper, Nov. 23 and Dec. 5, 1816, R. H. Douglass and Company Letterbook, Maryland Historical Society, Baltimore.

35. Danels: libel of Vasques, Sept. 12, 1818, *Joaquim José Vasques v. Sundry Boxes and Bags of Gold and Silver Specie* (Asia Grande); libel of John B. Bernabeau, Apr. 2, 1819, *John B. Bernabeau v. The Ship* Nereyda; plea and answer of the Marine Bank of Baltimore, Dec. 18, 1818, *Vasques v. Sundry Quantities of Gold and Silver Coin or Bullion in Bags Boxes or Otherwise and the President and Directors of the Marine Bank of Baltimore* (hereafter Danels, Sundry Quantities, Gran Para), MD Adm. *Cora*: claim of David Thompson, May 24, 1819, *Joaquim José Vasques v. 113 Barrels and Sixteen Hogsheads of Sugar, 500 Hides, etc. of the Schooner* Cora, NY Adm., roll 24.

36. Quotes: deposition of Matthew Stewart, Mar. 2, 1819, *Vasques v. 127 Boxes of Sugar*; protest of Daniel Utley and Joshua K. Harrison, Dec. 13, 1816. See also plea of Daniel Utley, Dec. 19, 1816; and inspector's report, Dec. 16, 1816, *The Divina Pastora*, Appellate Case Files, SCOTUS, case no. 895.

37. *Boston Daily Advertiser*, Sept. 11, 1817; *Newburyport (MA) Herald*, Sept. 16, 1817; plea and answer of George Wilson and Joseph Almeida, Dec. 20, 1819, *John B. Bernabeau v. The Cargo of the Armed Schooner* Almeida, MD Adm.; *The Trial of William Holmes, Thomas Warrington, and Edward Rosewain, on an Indictment for Murder on the High Seas* (Boston: Joseph C. Spear, 1820).

38. John Kirvant & Sons to John Devereux, Dec. 19, 1816, and Samuel Starbuck to John Kirvant, Dec. 14, 1816, JCPM; libel of Joaquim José Vasques, Nov. 23, 1818, *Joaquim José Vasques v. The Brig* Paqueta de Oporto *and Cargo*, Civil Case Files, United States District Court for Maine (Boston, MA), Records of District Courts of the United States, Record Group 21; National Archives and Records Administration—Northeast Region (Waltham, MA); *Baltimore Patriot*, Apr. 15, 1819; deposition of Joseph Smith, Aug. 28, 1819, *Joaquim José Vasques v. The Cargo of the Brig* Fanny, MD Adm.

39. Deposition of John G. Johnston, Nov. 20, 1819, *Juando v. Taylor*, NY Adm.; *New York Daily Advertiser*, Aug. 27, 1819. Johnston's deposition, though filmed with this case file, was taken for another case, most likely *Vasques v. Sundry Bales of Cotton*, NY Adm.; *Boston Daily Advertiser*, Sept. 3, 1819.

40. Libel of the U.S., Mar 31, 1818; warrant, July 31, 1818; petition of John Clarke, Aug. 3, 1818; surety of Joseph Karrick and John Gooding on behalf of John Clarke, Aug. 10, 1818, *U.S. v. The Brig* Fourth of July, MD Adm.; *New York Daily Advertiser*, Aug. 27, 1819.

41. James Monroe to John Forsyth, Jan. 6 and Jan. 10, 1817, in *Documents Accompanying a Bill to Prevent Citizens of the United States from Selling Vessels of War to the Citizens or Subjects of Any Foreign Power* (Washington: William A. Davis, 1817), 3–5; James McCulloch to Bisco Dorsey, June 25, 1816, and to Monroe, July 23, 1816, in *Papers Relating to the Foreign Relations of the United States*, pt. 2 (Washington: Government Printing Office, 1872), 453–55. As part of the negotiations with Great Britain over the Civil War *Alabama* claims in 1872, the United States submitted documentation of its own actions as a neutral power restraining foreign warships during previous wars, including the Spanish American revolutions, which are included in the *FRUS* collection.

42. Act of March 3, 1817, ch. 58, 3 *United States Statutes at Large*, 370–71; Act of April 20, 1818, ch. 88, 3 *United States Statutes at Large*, 447–50; Act of May 15, 1820, ch. 110, 3 *United States Statutes at Large*, 597–98; John Quincy Adams, Jan. 21 and 22, 1820, *Memoirs of John Quincy Adams*, ed. Charles Francis Adams, 12 vols. (Philadelphia: Lippincott, 1874–77), 4:509–10; Maury Davidson Baker, "The United States

and Piracy during the Spanish-American Wars of Independence" (Ph.D. diss., Duke University, 1946), 127–28.

43. James McCulloch to William Lowry, Nov. 15, 1819; Alexander Beard, Oct. 29, 1818, and June 27, 1819; Lt. Marshall, Mar. 26, 1819, and Apr. 22, 1819; John Webster, Dec. 3, 1819; William Jackson, Dec. 3, 1819; and William Crawford, May 14, 1819, *FRUS*, 498, 485, 473, 491–92, 499–500, 499, 495; John Quincy Adams, Mar. 29, 1819, *Memoirs*, 4:318. This was not the same James McCulloch as in the landmark Supreme Court case *McCulloch v. Maryland*.

44. See David Head, "Sailing for Spanish America: The Atlantic Geopolitics of Foreign Privateering from the United States in the Early Republic" (Ph.D. diss., SUNY-Buffalo, 2009), 235–39.

45. The court's minute book does not record a verdict for each man indicted, but no notice of their conviction can be found in the newspapers, either. Given the notoriety of the charges and the high profile of some defendants, a guilty verdict would have been newsworthy. Initially, Karrick was convicted, and though the conviction was quickly set aside, when first announced, it was noticed in the papers (see *Alexandria [VA] Gazette and Daily Advertiser*, Dec. 18, 1818, and *Easton [MD] Gazette and Eastern Shore Intelligencer*, Dec. 21, 1818).

46. David De Forest to John Quincy Adams, Jan. 8, 1819, De Forest Papers.

47. Head, "Sailing for Spanish America," 228–30 Between 1816 and 1819, thirty-eight suits were initiated in the Maryland district court against privateers. I have counted as one suit instances in which the court joined the libels of multiple parties contesting the same property early on in the proceedings and which produced one case file that can now be found at the National Archives (see The *Sereno* and The *Perthshire* alias *Arismendi* alias *Snap Dragon* alias *Mendozina*). On the other hand, I have counted separately those libels which initially produced separate case files but were joined later on (for example, *Joaquim Zamorano v. Sundry Goods, Wares, and Merchandise*, *Joaquim Zamorano v. 117 Boxes of Sugar*, and *Joaquim Zamorano v. John LaBorde and 500 Boxes of Sugar* all involved cargo from the *Santa Maria* and were bundled together only as the cases were appealed). This method reflects how cases actually proceeded without changing the overall results. In four instances, no outcome could be found. In two cases, proceedings were discontinued, once because the Maryland court ceded jurisdiction to the federal court in Savannah, Georgia, and once because the libel was defective. I have counted this instance as a victory for the privateers because it left the contested vessel in their hands.

48. In Georgia, libels against privateers were dismissed in the cases of *U.S. v. The Schooner* Hornet (1817), *U.S. v. The Brig* General San Martin (1818), *U.S. v. The Schooner* Viper (1818). In *John H. Elton, Esq., Commander of the* Sarnac *v. The Schooner* Iris (1817), the libel was dismissed following an appeal to the Supreme Court. The cases of *Paul P. Thomason v. Sugars and Coffee, Part of the Cargo of the* Jean and Charles (1817) and *U.S. v. The Commodore Champlin and Her Prize the* Syrena (1818) yielded partial victories: a settlement was reached between privateers and the owners of the *Jean and Charles* and the *Commodore Champlin*, but the *Syrena* was returned to privateers (see decree, June 8, 1819, *U.S. v. General San Martin*, which also mentions the *Hornet* dismissal; order of the court, Feb. 9, 1820, *U.S. v. Viper*; C.M. Conrad to Clerk of the Court, May 6, 1850, *Elton v. Iris*; settlement, May 9, 1820, *Thomason v. Jean and Charles*; and order of the court, June 10, 1819, *U.S. v. Commodore Champlin*).

49. For a version of this argument, see Charles Griffin, *The United States and the Disruption of the Spanish Empire, 1810–1822* (New York: Columbia University Press, 1937), 116–19; and Fred Hopkins, "For Freedom and Profit: Baltimore Privateers in the Wars of South American Independence," *Northern Mariner/le marin de nord*, 18 (2008): 103.

50. For the challenge of defining piracy, see G. Edward White, "The Marshall Court and International Law: The Piracy Cases," *American Journal of International Law* 83 (1989): 727–35; and Alfred P. Rubin, *The Law of Piracy* (Newport, RI: Naval War College Press, 1988), chap. 3. For the case law, see *U.S.* v. *Palmer* (1818), 16 U.S. 610; *U.S.* v. *Klintock* (1820), 18 U.S. 144; *U.S.* v. *Smith* (1820), 18 U.S. 153; *U.S.* v. *Furlong, alias Hobson, U.S.* v. *Griffen and Brailsford, U.S.* v. *Bowers and Matthews* (1820), 18 U.S. 184 (also known as *U.S.* v. *Pirates*). For the revised law, see Act of March 3, 1819, ch. 77, 3 *United States Statutes at Large*, 510–14, and its renewal, Act of May 15, 1820, ch. 113, 3 *United States Statutes at Large*, 600–601.

51. Quotes: opinion of Joseph Story, *U.S.* v. *Smith* (1820), 18 U.S. 153; John Marshall to Bushrod Washington, Oct. 31, 1819, in *The Papers of John Marshall*, ed. James Hobson, 12 vols. (Chapel Hill: University of North Carolina Press, 1974–2006), 7:374.

52. Quote: Charles K. Mallory to Antonio Argote Villalobos, Apr. 1817; James Monroe to Luis de Onís, Jan. 19, 1816, in *Diplomatic Correspondence of the United States Concerning the Independence of the Latin-American Nations*, ed. William R. Manning, 3 vols. (New York: Oxford University Press, 1925–26), 3:1939n, 1:20. For letters from Spanish and Portuguese officials to American officials, see U.S. Department of State, "Spain, Illegal Armaments, and Occupation of Amelia Island," Mar. 14, 1818, ASP04 For.rel. 300, 183–202, *United States Serial Set Digital Collection*; and House Committee on Foreign Affairs, "Message from the President of the United States, Transmitting a Report in Reference to Claims of Citizens of the United States on the Government of Portugal," Feb. 4, 1852, 641 H.exdoc. 53, 161–75, *United States Serial Set Digital Collection*, which reprints correspondence from the 1810s. For Spanish consuls' opposition to privateering, see Sean T. Perrone, "John Stoughton and the *Divina Pastora* Prize Case, 1816–1819," *Journal of the Early Republic* 28 (2008): 215–41. For the U.S. government's inability to restrain its citizens, see James E. Lewis Jr., *The American Union and the Problem of Neighborhood: The United States and the Collapse of the Spanish Empire, 1783–1829* (Chapel Hill: University of North Carolina Press, 1998), 82–84.

53. *U.S.* v. *Thomas Taylor*; *U.S.* v. *Joseph Karrick*; *U.S.* v. *John Skinner*; *U.S.* v. *James Holmes*; *U.S.* v. *James Watkins*; *U.S.* v. *John Sands*, MD Crim. For Vasques's libels, see Apr. 15, 1818, *Vasques v. Joseph Karrick, Matthew Murray, John Snyder, Joseph Patterson, John S. Skinner, and John Chase for the Seizure of the Ship* Rainha dos Anjos *and Her Cargo*; Sept. 2, 1818, *Vasques v. Sundry Boxes of Gold and Silver Coin or Bullion and the President and Directors of the Marine Bank of Baltimore and the President and Directors of the Union Bank of Maryland*; Sept. 14, 1818, *Vasques v. John Chase, Joseph Karrik, Joseph Patterson, Matthew Murray, John Snyder, and John S. Skinner for the Illegal Seizure of the* Monte Allegre; Sept. 15, 1818, *Vasques v. The Ship* Monte Allegre, *Her Tackle, Apparel, Boats, Armament, and Appurtenances and the Cargo Thereof*; Sept. 15, 1818, *Vasques v. John Chase, Joseph Karrik, Joseph Patterson, Matthew Murray, John Snyder, and John S. Skinner for the Illegal Seizure of the Brig* Don Joao Sexto *and Her Cargo*; Sept. 15, 1818, *Vasques v. John Chase, Joseph Karrick, and Others for Trespass on the* Vasco de Gama *and Her Cargo*, MD Adm.; Sept . 24, 1818, *Vasques v.*

Sundry Bales of Cotton, A Quantity of Sugar, Hides, and Sides of Leather; and Mar. 1, 1819, *Vasques v. 127 Bags of Sugar, A Quantity of Rigging, Cables, Sails, and Other Articles*, NY Adm. Washington *(DC), Review and Examiner*, Jan. 4, 1819.

54. De Forest to Lynch, Zimmerman and Co. July 2, 1820, and Nov. 9, 1820, and to William Crawford, Aug. 1, 1820, De Forest Papers; Keen, *David Curtis De Forest*, 126–28, 158.

55. *Baltimore Patriot*, June 18, 1819, Mar. 29, 1821, and Sept. 16, 1823. For the impact of the Panic on Baltimore, see Browne, *Baltimore in the Nation*, 70–82; and Garitee, *Republic's Private Navy*, 231–37.

56. De Forest to D'Arcy and Didier, Aug. 7, 1820, to John Higginbotham, Oct. 17, 1819, and to Lynch, Zimmerman and Co., May 11, 1821. See also De Forest to John Gooding, Apr. 5 and Apr. 11, 1819, De Forest Papers.

57. De Forest to William Winder, Dec. 23, 1823, De Forest Papers.

58. Deposition of John G. Johnston, Nov. 20, 1819, NY Adm.

4 / Galveston and Amelia Island

1. Beverly Chew to William Crawford, Aug. 1, 1817, in U.S. Department of State, "Message from the President of the United States, Communicating Information of the Proceeding of Certain Persons who Took Possession of Amelia Island and of Galvezton, during the Summer of the Present Year, and Made Establishments There," Dec. 15, 1817, 6 H.doc. 12, *United States Serial Set Digital Collection*, 8–9 (hereafter: "Message on Certain Persons at Amelia Island and Galvezton").

2. Thomas Wayne to Benjamin Homans, Sept. 27, 1817, ibid., 42–43.

3. Stanley Faye, "The Great Stroke of Pierre Laffite," *LHQ* 23 (1940): 733–826; "José Alvarez de Toledo's Reconciliation with Spain and Projects for Suppressing Rebellion in the Spanish Colonies," ed. and trans. Harris Gaylord Warren, *LHQ* 23 (1940): 827–63; Harold A. Bierck Jr., "Pedro Gual and the Patriot Effort to Capture a Mexican Port, 1816," *Hispanic American Historical Review* 27 (1947): 456–66. Aury's background: Lancaster E. Dabney, "Louis Aury: The First Governor of Texas under the Mexican Republic," *SWHQ* 42 (1938):108–16, www.tshaonline.org/shqonline/apager.php?vol=042&pag=114; Stanley Faye, "Commodore Aury," *LHQ* 24 (1941): 611–97. Vincente Pazos to John Quincy Adams, Feb. 7, 1818, in U.S. Department of State, "Message from the President of the United States Transmitting, in Pursuance of a Resolution of the House of Representatives, of the 20th Instant, Information Not Heretofore Communicated, on the Occupation of Amelia Island," Mar. 25, 1818, 11 H.doc. 175, 33–34, *United States Serial Set Digital Collection*, 37 (hereafter: "Message on the Occupation of Amelia Island").

4. Quote: deposition of Juan Domingo Lozano, May 9, 1817, in "Documents Relating to the Establishment of Privateers at Galveston, 1816–1817" (hereafter: "Documents Relating to Privateers at Galveston"), ed. and trans. Harris Gaylord Warren, *LHQ* 21 (1938): 1091–92. Galveston description: David G. McComb, *Galveston: A History* (Austin: University of Texas Press, 1986), 6, 11; William C. Davis, *The Pirates Laffite: The Treacherous World of the Corsairs of the Gulf* (Orlando, FL: Harcourt), 307–8. Aury's administration: *Daily National Intelligencer* (Washington, DC), Nov. 21, 1816.

5. Deposition of Lozano, May 9, 1817, in "Documents Relating to Privateers at Galveston," 1093. One Aury commission is labeled "No 95," suggesting it was the ninety-fifth Mexican commission issued (see commission of the *Brutus*, July 2, 1817,

John H. Elton, on Behalf of the United States v. *The* Tentativa *and Slaves*, GA Adm.). However, I have been able to substantiate eighteen vessels commissioned by Aury in Texas. Others may have also issued Mexican commissions, and not all commissions were used. Number of commissions used compiled from: Beverly Chew to William Crawford, Aug. 30, 1817; protests of William B. Cox, July 25, 1817; Louis Dequemenil, July 29, 1817; Jean Baptiste Revarde, July 28, 1817, "Message on Certain Persons at Amelia Island and Galvezton," 14, 25–30; *U.S.* v. *The Schooner* Mosquito, LA Fed. Ct., case 978; *U.S.* v. *The* Independence *alias* Hotspur, LA Fed. Ct., case 1026; *U.S. on Behalf of Certain Spanish Subjects* v. *Certain Merchandise on Board the* Mount Vernon, LA Fed. Ct., case 1069; *U.S. on Behalf of Certain Spanish Subjects* v. *Ninety Boxes of Sugar, Part of the Cargo of the* Mount Vernon, LA Fed. Ct., case 1070; *Felipe Fatio* v. *The Schooner* Lameson *alias* Panchita, LA Fed. Ct., case 1227; Deposition of Lozano, May 9, 1817; report of Jean Laffite, May 1817, in "Documents Relating to Privateers at Galveston," 1090–93, 1102–5; Davis, *Pirates Laffite*, esp. 297, 312–13.

6. For the importance of documents, see Donald A. Petrie, *The Prize Game: Lawful Looting on the High Seas in the Days of Fighting Sail* (New York: Berkley, 1999). Examples of Aury's commissions can be found in the case files of *U.S.* v. *The Schooner* Mosquito, LA Fed. Ct., case 978; *Felipe Fatio* v. *The Schooner* Lameson *alias* Panchita, LA Fed. Ct., case 1227; and in Luis Aury Papers, Library of Congress, Washington, DC. For other ships' papers, see crew list, Feb. 10, 1817, passenger list, Feb. 15, 1817, and manifest, n.d., for the *Mosquito*, *U.S.* v. *The Schooner* Mosquito, LA Fed. Ct., case 978; clearance and manifest for the *Alonzo*, Mar. 31, 1817, *Felip Fatio* v. *285 Pieces of Mock Madras Handkerchiefs, Ninety-six Pieces of Listadores, Ninety Pieces Guianas, and One Piece Red Cloth*, LA Fed. Ct., case 1033, and *Fatio* v. *Thirteen Packages of Merchandise, and Other Merchandise*, LA Fed. Ct., case 1034, in *The* Nueva Anna *and* Liebre, SCOTUS, Appel., cases 999 and 1000.

7. Quotes: testimonies of Pierre L. B. Duplessis and Beverly Chew, June 10, 1817, *The* Nueva Anna *and* Liebre; Alexander Dallas to Duplessis, July 3, 1815, in John Bassett Moore, *A Digest of International Law as Embodied in Diplomatic Discussions, Treaties and Other International Agreements, International Awards, the Decisions of Municipal Courts, and the Writings of Jurists, and Especially in Documents, Published and Unpublished, Issued by Presidents and Secretaries of States of the United States, the Opinions of the Attorneys-General, and the Decisions of the Courts Federal and State*, 8 vols. (Washington: Government Printing Office, 1906), 1:170. See also libel of Felipe Fatio, May 19, 1817; clearance and manifest for the Alonzo, both Mar. 31, 1817, *The* Nueva Anna *and* Liebre; libel of the U.S., May 2, 1817; appraisement, May 8, 1817; deposition of Anthony Roman and Jacques Roman, Dec. 9, 1817; petition of Jean Fabiani, Feb. 21, 1818, *U.S.* v. *The Schooner* Matagorda *and Cargo*, LA Fed. Ct., case 1029.

8. Commission, Feb. 10, 1817; crew list, Feb. 10, 1817, passenger list, Feb. 15, 1817; manifest, n.d., of the *Mosquito*; Beverly Chew to John Dick, Mar. 8, 1817; report of John Rollins, Mar. 1, 1817; testimony of Jean Maye, Henry Mathieu, Fourton, Durand, and Beranville, n.d., *U.S.* v. *The Schooner* Mosquito, LA Fed. Ct., case 978. If the men were free sailors, it is suspicious that they did not carry their protection certificates, since these were usually prized by African American seamen (see W. Jeffrey Bolster, *Black Jacks: African American Seamen in the Age of Sail* [Cambridge: Harvard University Press, 1997], 5). At the same time, these documents attested to the sailors' status as American citizens, which would have put them in danger of violating neutrality law by sailing aboard a Mexican privateer.

9. Quotes: deposition of Lozano, May 9, 1817, in "Documents Relating to Privateers at Galveston," 1093; testimony of Lopez, June 10, 1817, *The* Nueva Anna *and* Liebre.

10. Faye, "Commodore Aury," 632–34; Harris Gaylord Warren, *The Sword Was Their Passport: A History of American Filibustering in the Mexican Revolution* (Baton Rouge: Louisiana State University Press, 1943), 142, 165–66; Davis, *Pirates Laffite*, 306.

11. The scheme of filibuster identification mentioned is my own attempt to distinguish one expedition from another, a difficult task, given that the same men participated in multiple invasions, joining together on some occasions and going alone on others. For filibuster operations in this period, the best source is still Warren, *The Sword Was Their Passport*, although for the Gutierrez-Magee expedition, an important contribution is J. C. A. Stagg, "The Madison Administration and Mexico: Reinterpreting the Gutiérrez-Magee Raid of 1812–1813, *William and Mary Quarterly* 49 (2002), 449–80. Robinson: Harold A. Bierck Jr., "Dr. John Hamilton Robinson," *LHQ* 25 (1942): 644–69. Humbert: John C. Fredriksen, "Humbert, Jean Joseph Amable," *American National Biography Online*, www.anb.org/articles/03/03–00229.html; Lacroix: Irenée Amelot de Lacroix, *Military and Political Hints Humbly Submitted to the Hon. the Members of Congress, and the General Officers of the Militia of the United States*, trans. Samuel Mackay (Boston: Etheridge and Bliss, 1808); Thomas Jefferson to Lacroix, Dec. 31, 1811, in *The Papers of Thomas Jefferson: Retirement Series*, ed. J. Jefferson Looney, 6 vols. (Princeton: University of Princeton Press, 2005–), 4:375–76. Toledo: Kristin A. Dykstra, "On the Betrayal of Nations: Jose Alvarez de Toledo's Philadelphia *Manifesto* (1811) and *Justification* (1816)," *CR: The New Centennial Review* 4 (2004): 267–305; Timothy Palmer, "Toledo y Dubois, Jose Alvarez de," *HTO*, www.tshaonline.org/handbook/online/articles/TT/fto10.html. Perry: Margaret S. Henson, "Perry, Henry," *HTO*, www.tshaonline.org/handbook/online/articles/PP/fpe42.html.

12. De Herrera: William H. Timmons, *Morelos of Mexico: Priest, Soldier, Statesman* (El Paso: Texas Western College Press, 1963), 105, 116, 135. Mina: Harris Gaylord Warren, "Francisco Xavier Mina," *Handbook of Texas Online*, www.tshaonline.org/handbook/online/articles/MM/fmi46.html. For relations with Aury, see Faye, "Commodore Aury," 641; Davis, *Pirates Laffite*, 306; William F. Lewis, "Simon Bolivar and Xavier Mina: A Rendezvous in Haiti," *Journal of Inter-American Studies* 11 (1969): 458–65; Warren, *The Sword Was Their Passport*, 148–60; and Harris Gaylord Warren, "Xavier Mina's Invasion of Mexico," *Hispanic American Historical Review* 23 (1943): 52–76.

13. Laffite's entry into spying: "Documents Relating to Pierre Laffite's Entrance into the Service of Spain," ed. Harris Gaylord Warren, *Southwestern Historical Quarterly Online* 44 (1940): 76–87, www.tshaonline.org/shqonline/apager.php?vol=044&pag=082; Stanley Faye, "The Great Stroke of Pierre Laffite," *LHQ* 23 (1940): 737–44; Davis, *Pirates Laffite*, 271–75. Pierre's espionage: Davis, *Pirates Laffite*, 275–80, 291–305. Jean's explorations: "Latour's Report on Spanish-American Relations in the Southwest," ed. Edwin H. Carpenter, *LHQ* 30 (1947): 715–37; Davis, *Pirates Laffite*, 281–89. Latour had recruited Jean into the spy network in Philadelphia. He was also one of the first to build the Laffites' legend in his book, *Historical Memoir of the War in West Florida and Louisiana in 1814–15, with an Atlas* (1816; repr., Gainesville: University of Florida Press, 1964). For Latour's background, see Gene A. Smith, "Arsène Lacarrière Latour: Immigrant, Patriot-Historian, and Foreign Agent," in *The Human Tradition in Antebellum America*, ed. Michael A. Morrison (Wilmington,

DE: Scholarly Resources Books, 2000), 83–98. For Jean's eastern activities, see Davis, *Pirates Laffites*, 246–58.

14. Quote: William Davis Robinson, *Memoirs of the Mexican Revolution: Including a Narrative of the Expedition of General Xavier Mina, with Some Observations on the Practicability of Opening a Commerce Between the Pacific and Atlantic Oceans Through the Mexican Isthmus in the Province of Oaxaca, and at the Lake of Nicaragua; and on the Future Importance of Such Commerce to the Civilized World, and More Especially to the United States* (Philadelphia: Lydia R. Bailey, 1820), 76. For the Pensacola plot, see Harris Gaylord Warren, "Pensacola and the Filibusters, 1816–1817," *LHQ* 21 (1938): 806–22. For the Laffites' reactions, see Davis, *Pirates Laffite*, 315–16.

15. Davis, *Pirates Laffite*, 318–19.

16. Depositions of John Ducoing and Raymond Espagnol, Oct. 7, *U.S. on Behalf of Certain Spanish Subjects v. Ninety Boxes of Sugar, Part of the Cargo of the Mount Vernon*, LA Fed. Ct., case 1070; register of the Proceedings at Galveston, Apr. 15, 1817, and declaration, Apr. 20, 1817, "Message on Amelia and Galveston," 44; report of Jean Laffite, May 1817, in "Documents Relating to Privateers at Galveston," 1105. Traditionally, the coup is seen as Jean's handiwork, but the only evidence for this comes from Jean himself, and he may have been trying to impress the Spanish with his control over events (see Davis, *Pirates Laffite*, 323–25; and Warren, *The Sword Was Their Passport*, 174–77).

17. Quotes: plan of Jean and Pierre Laffite, May, 1817, and Felipe Fatio to José Cienfuegos, May 21, 1817, in "Documents Relating to Privateers at Galveston," 1108, 1102.

18. Quote: Pierre to Jean Laffite, July 23, 1817, qtd. in Davis, *Pirates Laffite*, 341. For these developments, see ibid., 337–41.

19. Quote: Felipe Fatio to Luis Noeli, June 27, 1818, qtd. ibid., 366.

20. James G. Cusick, *The Other War of 1812: The Patriot War and the American Invasion of Spanish East Florida* (Gainesville: University Press of Florida, 2003); J. C. A. Stagg, "James Madison and George Matthews: The East Florida Revolution of 1812 Reconsidered," *Diplomatic History* 30 (2006): 23–55.

21. David Sinclair, *Sir Gregor MacGregor and the Land That Never Was: The Extraordinary Story of the Most Audacious Fraud in History* (London: Headline, 2003); Matthew Brown, "Inca, Sailor, Soldier, King: Gregor MacGregor and the Early Nineteenth-Century Caribbean," *Bulletin of Latin American Research* 24 (2005): 44–70.

22. David Bushnell, "The Florida Republic: An Overview," in *La República de Las Floridas: Texts and Documents*, ed. Bushnell (Mexico City: Pan American Institute of Geography and History, 1986), 10; Cusick, *Other War of 1812*, 104–6; T. Frederick Davis, *MacGregor's Invasion of Florida, 1817: Together with an Account of His Successors Irwin, Hubbard and Aury on Amelia Island, East Florida* (Tallahassee: Florida Historical Society, 1928), 6–9.

23. Quote: Proclamation of the Liberating Army, June 30, 1817, in Davis, *MacGregor's Invasion of Florida*, 16. Accounts of MacGregor's invasion, based on conflicting newspaper reports, vary in their details. For firsthand reports, see the *American Star* (Petersburg, VA), Oct. 6, 1817, which reprints a widely circulated account by one of MacGregor's soldiers, and "The Taking of Fernandina, Seen by a Participant," in Bushnell, *La Republica de las Floridas*, 56–59. See also Davis, *MacGregor's Invasion of Florida*, 15–18.

24. *Daily National Intelligencer* (Washington, DC), Sept. 13, 1817; Letter of Naturalization, Aug. 30, 1817, "Message on the Occupation of Amelia Island," 14. See also Davis, *MacGregor's Invasion of Florida*, 20–21, 24.

25. For the *Challenger* incident, see Davis, *MacGregor's Invasion of Florida*, 22–23. For vessel commissions, see David Head, "Sailing for Spanish America: The Atlantic Geopolitics of Foreign Privateering from the United States in the Early Republic" (Ph.D. diss., SUNY–Buffalo, 2009), appendix D.

26. Deposition of David Gelston, Mar. 24, 1818, and John Hall, Mar. 24, 1818, *Charles Mulvey v. 109 Slaves, Cargo of the* Politina, GADC; *American Star* (Petersburg, VA), Oct. 11, 1817; *Daily National Intelligencer* (Washington, DC), Sept. 13, 1817; Marilyn Maple, "Ruggles Hubbard, Civil Governor of Fernandina," *FHQ* 58 (1980): 315–19; Davis, *MacGregor's Invasion of Florida*, 24–27.

27. Davis, *MacGregor's Invasion of Florida*, 25–27; Jennifer L. Heckard, "The Crossroads of Empire: The 1817 Liberation and Occupation of Amelia Island, East Florida" (Ph.D. diss., University of Connecticut, 2006), 88–91.

28. Davis, *MacGregor's Invasion of Florida*, 26–32; Heckard, "Crossroads of Empire," 107–11.

29. Quote: *City of Washington Gazette* (Washington, DC), Jan. 22, 1818. See also Faye, "Commodore Aury," 643–44; Davis, *MacGregor's Invasion of Florida*, 34–36.

30. Quote: *Vermont Intelligencer* (Bellows Falls), Dec. 29, 1817. See also *Columbian Centinel* (Boston), Oct. 8, 1817; *New-Hampshire Patriot* (Concord), Oct. 14, 1817; *Hallowell (ME) Gazette*, Oct. 22, 1817; *Daily National Intelligencer* (Washington, DC), Oct. 24, 1817; *National Advocate* (New York), Oct. 25, 1817; Heckard, "Crossroads of Empire," 133–34. For commissions, see Head, "Sailing for Spanish America," appendix D.

31. Quote: John H. Elton to Benjamin W. Crowninshield, Oct. 10, 1817, "Message on Certain Persons," 37.

32. Quotes: Elton to Crowninshield, Oct. 10, 1817, "Message on Certain Persons," 37; Elton to Crowninshield, Oct. 19, 1817; Elton to Ruggles Hubbard, Sept. 9, 1817, in *Letters Received by the Secretary of the Navy from Commanders, 1804–1886* (hereafter: *Commanders' Letters*), National Archives Microfilm M147. See also Belton A. Copp to John Quincy Adams, Apr. 1, 1818, "The Patriot War, A Contemporary Letter," *Florida Historical Quarterly* 5 (1927): 162–67; Davis, *MacGregor's Invasion of Florida*, 46–47; Elton to Crowninshield, Sept. 3, 1817, Sept. 13, 1817, and Oct. 10, 1817, *Commanders' Letters*.

33. Charles H. Bowman Jr., "Vicente Pazos and the Amelia Island Affair, 1817," *FHQ* 53 (1975): 273–95.

34. Quote: *Chillicothe (OH) Weekly Recorder* Nov. 12, 1817. See also *Narrative of a Voyage to the Spanish Main*, 96–100; Davis, *MacGregor's Invasion of Florida*, 36–40. Previous works have emphasized that the conflict also had a national or ethnic component, with Aury leading what was called the "French party" and Irwin and Hubbard leading the "American party." Contemporary accounts use the terms "French party" and "American party," but evidence that the Amelia Island men identified themselves this way is tenuous. The earliest instance I can find of such language comes from an Oct. 4, 1817, letter published in the *Essex (MA) Patriot*, Oct. 25, 1817, remarking that some difficulties had arisen "between the American and French parties at Fernandina." A similar article, circulated in a number of papers, also reported that "the

French party" was fighting "all the Americans" (*New York Commercial Advertiser*, Oct. 28, 1817). In both cases, the terms appear to be shorthand for "Aury's followers" and "Irwin and Hubbard's followers." The only indications that the men themselves chose these names come from two sources: (1) a Georgia planter who said that "the parties are designated as the Americans and the French," though who designated them as such is not revealed (see McIntosh to William Crawford, Oct. 30, 1817, "Message on Certain Persons at Amelia Island and Galvezton," 20); and (2) the anonymous author of *Narrative of a Voyage to the Spanish Main*, who spoke of "the French party of Aury" and the affinity some of his fellow Brits felt for the English-speaking Americans. The author, however, used the terms in the context of a Francophobic attack on Aury as a typically unscrupulous French revolutionary. Plus, he also spoke of a moderate party, neither French nor American (96–98). Meanwhile, Captain Elton described seeing "a French party and an English party" (John H. Elton to Benjamin W. Crowninshield, Nov. 15, 1817, "Message on Certain Persons at Amelia Island and Galvezton," 39). The existence of well-organized national parties seems unlikely, given that a portion of Aury's followers were not French (or even Franco-Haitian) but Irish, Scottish, English, Dutch, and German (see Thomas Wayne to Benjamin Homans, Sept. 27, 1817, in "Message on Certain Persons at Amelia Island and Galvezton," 42).

35. Quote: Proclamation of Aury, Nov. 5, 1817, qtd. in Bowman, "Vicente Pazos and the Amelia Island Affair," 284.

36. Quotes: J. D. Henley and James Bankhead to Aury, Dec. 23, 1817, in U.S. Department of War, "Message from the President of the United States, Communicating Information of the Troops of the United States Having Taken Possession of Amelia Island, in East Florida," Jan. 13, 1818, 7 H.doc. 47, *United States Serial Set Digital Collection*, 10 (hereafter: "Message on Troops Possessing Amelia Island"); John Quincy Adams, Oct. 30, 1817, *Memoirs of John Quincy Adams*, ed. Charles Francis Adams, 12 vols. (Philadelphia: Lippincott, 1874–77), 4:15. See also *New York Commercial Advertiser*, Jan. 12, 1818; Davis, *MacGregor's Invasion of Florida*, 51–57; and Samuel J. Watson, *Jackson's Sword: The Army Officer Corps on the American Frontier, 1810-1821* (Lawrence: University Press of Kansas, 2012), 131–35. Aury found a new Spanish island to conquer, Old Providence, located about 150 miles east of present-day Nicaragua. He again established an admiralty court and launched several attacks along the coast of Central America. He even crossed paths again with MacGregor, who was organizing his own invasions of Portobello and Rio de la Hacha (in modern Panama and Colombia, respectively). Aury died at Old Providence in 1821, after falling off a horse (see Faye, "Commodore Aury," 647–97).

37. Quotes: House Select Committee on Foreign Affairs, "Report of the Committee to Whom was Referred So Much of the President's Message as Relates to the Introduction of Slaves from Amelia Island" (hereafter: "Report on the Introduction of Slaves from Amelia Island"), Jan. 10, 1818, 7 H.doc. 46, *United States Serial Set Digital Collection*, 4; David Head, "Slave Smuggling by Foreign Privateers: The Illegal Slave Trade and the Geopolitics of the Early Republic," *Journal of the Early Republic* 33 (2013): 433–62.

38. Quotes: James Monroe, "First Annual Message," Dec. 2, 1817, in *A Compilation of the Messages and Papers of the Presidents*, 10 vols. (Washington: Bureau of National Literature and Art, 1897–1902), 2:583; Monroe, "First Annual Message," Dec. 2, 1817, 2:14. See W. E. B. Du Bois, *The Suppression of the African Slave-Trade to the United*

States of America, 1638–1870 (1896; repr., New York: Oxford University Press, 2007), chap. 7.

39. Monroe, "First Annual Message," 583; "Message to Congress," 3; "Report on the Introduction of Slaves from Amelia Island," 1–2; John Quincy Adams, Oct. 30, 1817, *Memoirs*, 4:15; Monroe to James Madison, Dec. 22, 1817; Monroe to Thomas Jefferson, Dec. 23, 1817, in *The Writings of James Monroe, Including a Collection of His Public and Private Papers and Correspondence Now for the First Time Printed*, ed. Stanislaus Murray Hamilton, 7 vols. (New York: Putnam and Sons, 1898–1903), 6:45, 47.

40. Quote: Commission of Gregor MacGregor, Mar. 31, 1817, in U.S. Department of State, "Message from the President of the United States Transmitting, in Pursuance of a Resolution of the House of Representatives, of the 20th Instant, Information Not Heretofore Communicated, on the Occupation of Amelia Island," Mar. 26, 1818, 11 H.doc. 175, 33–34, *United States Serial Set Digital Collection*, 33–34. For a defense of MacGregor's legitimacy, see Pazos to Monroe, Feb. 7, 1818, in "Message on the Occupation of Amelia Island," 23.

41. Quote: Monroe, "Message to Congress," 4–5. The House Committee also cited the 1807 Slave Trade Abolition Act as grounds for intervention in that it provided for the navy to interdict the foreign slave trade (see House Select Committee, "Report on the Introduction of Slaves from Amelia Island," 46–47). For the No Transfer law, see John A. Logan, *No Transfer: An American Security Principle* (New Haven: Yale University Press, 1961), 119; William S. Belko, "The Origins of the Monroe Doctrine Revisited: The Madison Administration, the West Florida Revolt, and the No Transfer Policy," *Florida Historical Quarterly* 90 (2011): 157–92; and J. C. A. Stagg, *Borderlines in Borderlands: James Madison and the Spanish-American Frontier, 1776–1821* (New Haven: Yale University Press, 2009), 196, 286n.

42. Quote: see Frank L. Owsley Jr. and Gene A. Smith, *Filibusters and Expansionists: Jeffersonian Manifest Destiny, 1800–1821* (Tuscaloosa: University of Alabama Press, 1997), 139–40. See also Weeks, *John Quincy Adams*, 57, 63–64.

43. Weeks, *John Quincy Adams*, 57, 64. For Adams on "piratical privateers," see Adams, Mar. 26, 1818, July 18, 1818, Mar. 15, 1819, Mar. 29, 1819, Apr. 16, 1819, May 11, 1819, Aug. 17, 1819, *Memoirs*, 4:68, 112, 298, 317–18, 339, 362, 413. For Congress's request, see *Annals of Congress*, 15th Cong., 1st sess., 409. Adams's report is the "Message on Certain Persons at Amelia Island and Galvezton" cited above. Weeks erred by using a truncated version of the report that was published in the *Annals of Congress* (15th Cong., 1st sess., 1785–1814) and leaves out the documents Adams prepared on Amelia; it was also published as U.S. House, Select Committee on Foreign Affairs, "Suppression of Piratical Establishments," *United States Serial Set Digital Collection*, ASP04 For.rel.290.

44. Stagg, *Borderlines in Borderlands*, 121–22, 246–47n; Stagg, "James Madison and George Mathews," 23–55; Stagg, "The Madison Administration and Mexico: Reinterpreting the Gutierrez-Magee Raid of 1812–1813," *William and Mary Quarterly* 59 (2002): 449–80; Andrew McMichael, *Atlantic Loyalties: Americans in Spanish West Florida, 1785–1810* (Athens: University of Georgia Press, 2008), chap. 4; Lewis, *American Union*, 38, 82–84, 91–94, 246–47n.

45. Stagg, *Borderlines in Borderlands*, 4–5; Lewis, *John Quincy Adams: Policymaker for the Union* (Wilmington, DE: Scholarly Resources, 2001), xiii–xvii.

46. Monroe, "Message to Congress," Jan. 13, 1818, 3.

47. Quote: Charles Morris to Benjamin Crowninshield, June 10, 1817, "Message on Certain Persons at Amelia Island and Galvezton," 34–35. See also, in the same source, Beverly Chew to William Crawford, Aug. 1, 1817, Aug. 30, 1817, and Oct. 17, 1817, 8–15; and John Porter to Crowninshield, June 28, 1817, 35.

48. Owsley and Smith, *Filibusters and Expansionists*, 175; Weeks, *John Quincy Adams*, 64; Warren, *The Sword Was Their Passport*, 255–57; Griffin, *The United States and the Disruption of Spain's Empire*, 116.

49. Outcomes compiled from the Minute Book of the Louisiana District Court, *Minutes of the U.S. District Courts at New Orleans*, NARA Southwest Region microfilm 7RA-119, rolls 1–3. These figures do not include men indicted during these years who were accused of crimes committed aboard Cartagenan or Venezuelan vessels, which are included in the figures in chapter 3.

50. I have combined the following case numbers into one case: 812, 814, 816, and 817 (the *Eagle* cases); 852, 858, 864, 865, and 874 (the *Eliza* and *Alerta* cases); 1033 and 1034 (the Supreme Court case of *Nueva Anna* and *Liebre*); 1063, 1064, 1065, 1066, 1069, and 1070 (the *Mount Vernon* cases); 1223 and 1227 (the *Panchita* cases); and 1608 and 1609 (the *General Victoria* cases). Outcomes determined from the Minute Book of the Louisiana District Court.

51. William C. Davis, *Three Roads to the Alamo: The Lives and Fortunes of David Crockett, James Bowie, and William Barret Travis* (New York: HarperCollins, 1998), 55–61.

52. Harris Gaylord Warren, "The *Firebrand* Affair: A Forgotten Incident of the Mexican Revolution," *LHQ* 21 (1938): 203–12; Davis, *Pirates Laffite*, 261–63, 298–99, 310–12.

53. Lewis, *The American Union*, 91–94.

54. Beverly Chew to William Crawford, Aug. 1, 1817, Aug. 30, 1817, in "Message on Certain Persons at Amelia Island and Galvezton," 8–14. For U.S. territory priorities, see Lewis, *American Union*, 87–89. Like the explanations for failure of U.S. officials to enforce the law, previous accounts have stressed the personal characteristics of policy makers and the alleged existence of a program of pressuring Spain by proxy. Owsley and Smith "wonder why it [the U.S. government] did not take Galveston with the same rationale" as had been applied to Amelia. They speculate that Adams "lost interest" in acquiring Texas; that Adams did not want slavery to expand into Texas; or that Adams did not want more southwestern states in the union because it would dilute the power of New England (Owsley and Smith, *Filibusters and Expansionists*, 177–80). Weeks argues that the United States secretly wanted Jean Laffite in control of Galveston because Laffite led a gang of pirates "who preyed on Spanish shipping and who could be removed when necessary—as they were in March 1821" (Weeks, *John Quincy Adams*, 64).

55. Rafe Blaufarb, *Bonapartists in the Borderlands: French Exiles and Refugees on the Gulf Coast, 1815–1830* (Tuscaloosa: University of Alabama Press, 2005), chap. 4.

56. Ibid., 107–11, 115–16; Lewis, *The American Union and the Problem of Neighborhood*, 117.

57. Quote: José Cienfuegos to Juan Ruiz de Apodaca, July 17, 1818, qtd. in Davis, *Pirates Laffite*, 378. See also Davis, *Pirates Laffite*, 377–82; and Blaufarb, *Bonapartists in the Borderlands*, 111–14.

58. Quotes: George Graham to Jean Laffite, Aug. 26, 1818, in "Documents Relating to George Graham's Proposals to Jean Laffite for the Occupation of the Texas Coast,"

ed. and trans. Harris Gaylord Warren, *LHQ* 21 (1938): 217; John Quincy Adams, Nov. 20, 1818, *Memoirs*, 175–16. See also Davis, *Pirates Laffite*, 374–75.

59. Edward Austin Bradley, "Forgotten Filibusters: Private Hostile Expeditions from the United States into Spanish Texas, 1812–1821" (Ph.D. diss., University of Illinois, Urbana-Champaign, 1998), chaps. 5 and 6; Warren, *The Sword Was Their Passport*, chap. 11.

60. Indictment, Nov. 12, 1819; commission, n.d.; verdict, n.d.; James Monroe to John Nicholson, Apr. 3, 1820, *U.S. v. John Desfarges, Peter Morel, Robert Johnston, Charles Dickinson, Louis Pierre, Gervin Conchal, John McGee, Louis Phillip, John Trickhart, John Cousins, Ephraim Thompkins, Isaac Tillet, Thomas Thompson, Laurence Pagas, Joseph Vallert, Juan Raynor, Julien Seadoner, William McClure*, LA Fed. Ct., case 1440; *Rhode-Island American* (Providence), Oct. 29, 1819; *New-York Evening Post*, Dec. 23, 1819; *Eastern Argus* (Portland, ME), Nov. 12, 1819; Davis, *Pirates Laffite*, 404–8.

61. Davis, *Pirates Laffite*, 419–31, 445–65.

5 / Service and Toil in Spanish America

1. James Chaytor to W. G. D. Worthington, Dec. 14, 1826 ("mortification" and "toil"), JCPM; to Robert K. Lowry, Jan. 20, 1826 ("poco a poco"), JCPP

2. Chaytor to Sarah Chaytor, June 10, 1818; to Adam Guy, Apr. 17, 1817; to Charles K. Mallory, Apr. 17, 1817, JCPM; Chaytor to Worthington, Oct. 4, 1827, July 5, 1825, JCPP. Chaytor continued to sign letters "Diego Chaytor" or "DC" into the 1820s (see Chaytor to Myers, Dec. 20, 1825; to Lowry, Jan. 20, 1826; to Lowry and Myers, Mar. 1, 1826; to J. G. Scipe, Mar. 13, 1826; and to Williams, Nov. 8, 1828, JCPP).

3. Quotes: Joseph Almeida to Mallory, Nov. 6, 1819, *U.S. v. The Brig Wilson*, VAAdm. For Almeida's background, see David Head, "Independence on the Quarterdeck: Three Baltimore Seafarers, Spanish America, and the Lives of Captains in the Early American Republic," *Northern Mariner/Le marin du nord* 23 (2013): 1–20.

4. Deposition of William Thornton, Aug. 24, 1818, *Juando v. Taylor*, NY Adm.

5. Quote: Camilo Torres, 1814, qtd. in Daniel F. O'Leary, *The "Detached" Recollections of General D. F. O'Leary*, ed. R. A. Humphrey (New York: Oxford University Press, 1969), 38. For Monier and Lominé, see *Gasper Hernandez v. The Spanish Schooner* Estrella, LA Fed. Ct., case 1035; *Essex (MA) Register*, Dec. 14, 1811; Stanley Faye, "Privateersmen of the Gulf and Their Prizes," *LHQ* 22 (1939): 1049–50; and Jane Lucas De Grummond, *Renato Beluche: Smuggler, Privateer, Patriot, 1780–1860* (Baton Rouge: Louisiana State University Press, 1983), 73–74, 147, 148 154–55.

6. Quotes: [John Chase], *To the Public* (Baltimore: n.p., 1832), 18–20. Tatnall: *Georgian* (Savannah), Feb. 3, 1830, qtd. in [Chase], *To the Public*, 4; [George Law], *To the Citizens of Baltimore* (Baltimore: n.p., 1829), 19. See also *Baltimore Patriot*, Apr. 6, 1829.

7. Liquet: indictment, May 5, 1812, *U.S. v. Pierre Liquet*, LA Fed. Ct., case 495; commission, Dec. 20, 1813, *Patterson v. The Schooner* General Bolívar, LA Fed. Ct., case 760; libel of Pedro de Reano, Dec. 17, 1816, *Reano v. Pierre Liquet*, LA Fed. Ct., case 949; libel of Felipe Fatio, Aug. 11, 1817, *Fatio v. The Schooner* St. Anthony, LA Fed. Ct., case 1083; *United States Gazette* (Philadelphia), Dec. 17, 1805; *Connecticut Herald* (New Haven), Aug. 18, 1807; Beverly Chew to William Crawford, Aug. 30, 1817, in "Message on Certain Persons at Amelia Island and Galvezton, 6 H.doc. 12, 10, *Serial Set Digital*

Collection. Youx: *North American and Mercantile Daily Advertiser* (Baltimore), June 9, 1808; William C. Davis, *The Pirates Laffite: The Treacherous World of the Corsairs of the Gulf* (Orlando, FL: Harcourt, 2005), 30, 86; Faye, "Privateersmen of the Gulf," 1031–33. For the munitions trade to Haiti, see Peter P. Hill, *Napoleon's Troublesome Americans: Franco-American Relations, 1804-1815* (Washington: Potomac, 2005). According to Jane De Grummond, "Dominique *was* an American patriot" (De Grummond, *Baratarians and the Battle of New Orleans*, 158). See also Davis, *Pirates Laffite*, 216. Since the mid-nineteenth century, the story has circulated that Youx was an older brother of Jean and Pierre. However, there is no evidence that they were related. Davis sorts through the claims about Youx in *Pirates Laffite*, 493n.

8. Quote: testimony of José de la Rua, 1812, in Faye, "Privateersmen of the Gulf," 1017. See also libels of Juan de Dios Amador, Oct. 1, 1814, *Juan de Dios Amador v. The Polacre* Flora Americana, LA Fed. Ct., case 731; William Malus, n.d., *William Malus v. The* Flora Americana, LA Fed. Ct., case 741; Philip Lay and Augustus Lachataignerais, n.d., *Philip Lay and Augustus Lachataignerais v. The* Flora Americana, LA Fed. Ct., case 742; Pierre Seguin, n.d., *Pierre Seguin v. The* Flora Americana, 745; David Nagle, Nov. 7, 1814, *David Nagle v. Certain Goods of the* Flora Americana, case 751; indictment, Oct. 1814, *U.S. v. Bernard Laffone*, LA Fed. Ct., case 775. Amador's libel in LA Fed. Ct., case 731, has been mistakenly filmed with the documents in LA Fed. Ct., case 730.

9. Quote: libel of William R. Swift, Apr. 14, 1819, *Two Trunks of Merchandise, Two Saddles, Seven Muskets, etc., the Property of Portuguese Subjects, and Henry H. Ford*. See also depositions of William Landham, n.d., and George Williams, Feb. 2, 1819; protest of Carmen Coelho, Jan. 14, 1819, CPD; libel of Joaquim José Vasques, Feb. 5, 1819, *Joaquim José Vasques v. John Gooding for the Illegal Seizure of the Portuguese Ship Sociedade Feliz*; depositions of Christopher Dredge, Nov. 8, 1819; Stephen Barwell, Nov. 9, 1819; Landham, Nov. 9, 1819, *U.S. v. The Armed Schooner General Artigas, Her Guns, Stores, Rigging, Tackle, Apparel, and Furniture, Whereof Henry H. Ford Was Late Commander*, VA Adm. For Ford's military service, see "Officers of the Continental and U.S. Navy and Marine Corps, 1775–1900," Naval Historical Center, www.history.navy.mil/books/callahan/index.htm.

10. For Beluche, see De Grummond, *Renato Beluche*. The quote is from Bolívarto José Antonio Páez, Oct. 7, 1828, qtd. ibid. 246. De Grummond contends that Beluche was a relative of the Laffites, but there is no evidence of such a connection; the claim seems based on the similarity of their later pursuits.

11. Quote: Beluche, *Contesta a las falsas imputaciones con que ha intendo manchar su honor el Sr. General de la misma José Padilla en las notas que contiente el papel intitulado "Al Mundo Imparcial,"* qtd. in De Grummond, *Renato Beluche*, 224. For the *Josefa Segunda*, see deposition of James Houston, May 28, 1818, *U.S. v. The Brig* Josefa Segunda, *Her Tackle, Apparel, Furniture, and the Goods and Effects Found on Board*, LA Fed. Ct., case 1183; libel of U.S., Apr. 29, 1818; claim and answer of Carricabura, Arrieta, and Co., May 5, 1818; testimony of Francis Raymond, June 19, 1818; and testimony of William Whitney, June 19, 1818, *Carricabura, Arrieta, and Company v. The Brig* Josefa Segunda, *Her Tackle, Apparel, Furniture, and Cargo and 152 Negroe Slaves*, LA Fed. Ct., case 1221. For praise of Beluche for contributing to the end of slavery, see Robin Blackburn, *The Overthrow of Colonial Slavery, 1776-1848* (New York: Verso, 1988), 290–91.

12. Libel of John B. Bernabeau, Apr. 21, 1819, *John B. Bernabeau* v. *The Brig Nereyda and John Danels*, MD Adm.; libel of William R. Swift, Apr. 15, 1819, *William R. Swift v. John D. Daniels for the Illegal Capture of the Portuguese Brig Globo and Cargo, and Other Vessels*, MD Adm.; deposition of Andrew Lindborn, Apr. 20, 1819; Charles Staples and Joseph Atkinson, n.d., CPD; Poulson's *American Daily Advertiser* (Philadelphia), Sept. 28, 1818; *New York Commercial Advertiser*, Sept. 28, 1818; *Lloyd's List* (London), Sept. 29, 1818; Augustin Beraza, *Los Corsarios de Artigas* (Montevideo, 1949), appendix. For Danels's background, see Head, "Independence on the Quarterdeck," 1–20.

13. Decree and opinion of Bland, *Bernabeau* v. *Nereyda*, MD Adm.; depositions of Samuel Beaver, Nov. 27, 1819, and Laurence Maddeson, Nov. 29, 1819, *U.S.* v. *Irresistable*, MD Adm.; deposition of Andrew Lindborn, Apr. 20, 1819; Charles Staples and Joseph Atkinson, n.d., CPD; libel of William R. Swift, Apr. 15, 1819, *Swift* v. *Daniels*, MD Adm.; Thomas Lloyd Halsey to William H. Winder, Sept. 30, 1821 and Halsey to Henry Didier, Sept. 30, 1821, Halsey letters in the Jonathan Meredith Papers; "An Ordinance of the Government of Buenos Ayres, Regulating Privateers," 4 Wheaton, appendix 28; *American and General Advertiser* (Providence, R.I.), Feb. 5, 1819; Hopkins, "For Flag and Profit," 395.

14. Quotes: petition of John Ferguson, May 20, 1819, *U.S.* v. *John Ferguson*, MD Crim.; depositions of Lewis Gather and Samuel Purdy, Jan. 12, 1820, *U.S.* v. *William Bush*, MD Crim. See also *Extracts from the Life of Captain John F. Ferguson, who was Executed in the City of Baltimore, on the Thirteenth Day of April, 1820* (Baltimore, 1820), 14–15; plea and claim of Childs, Apr. 29, 1819, and opinion and decree of Bland, Jan. 3, 1820, *Bernabeau* v. *Nereyda*; *Alexandria (VA) Gazette and Daily Advertiser*, Apr. 19, 1819; *Niles Weekly Register*, Aug. 7, 1819, June 17, 1820; *National Register*, July 31, 1819.

15. William Dawkins to Danels, Apr. 4, 1823, Foreign Countries Miscellaneous Collection, 1572–1960, Central and South America Collection, New York Public Library; Hopkins, "For Flag and Profit," 399.

16. Finance Records, Mar. 1, 1826, St. Mary's College Collection, St. Mary's Seminary and University, Baltimore; *Four Generations of Commissions: The Peale Collection of the Maryland Historical Society*, comp. Eugenia Calvert Holland, Romaine Somerville, Stiles Tuttle Colwill, and K. Beverly Whiting Young (Baltimore: Maryland Historical Society, 1975), 104, 170–71. For Páez's background and American perceptions of his race, see Caitlyn Fitz, "Our Sister Republics: The United States in an Age of American Revolutions" (Ph.D. diss., Yale University, 2010), 124–28.

17. Jean Laffite to Jean Blanque, Sept. 4 and Sept. 7, 1814, in Arsène Lacarrière Latour, *Historical Memoir of the War in West Florida and Louisiana in 1814–1815, with an Atlas* (1816; repr., Gainesville: University Press of Florida, 1964), appendix, xii–xiii.

18. Keen, *David Curtis De Forest*, 135–46, 152–57.

19. Quote: De Forest to Lynch, Zimmerman, and Co., July 3, 1820, De Forest Papers. See also shipping articles, *Independencia del Sud*, JCPP; *The Trial of Robert M. Goodwin in the Court of Sessions, for the City and County of New-York, March Term, 1820, on an Indictment of Manslaughter for Killing James Stoughton, Esq. in Broadway in the City of New-York, December 21, 1819* (New York: John Low, 1820); Charles H. Haswell, *Reminiscences of New York By an Octogenarian* (New York: Harper and Brothers, 1896), 104.

20. *American Beacon* (Norfolk, VA), Oct. 5, 1818.

21. Quote: petition of Pierre Laffite, Feb. 28, 1814, Etat des affairs de Pierre Laffite, Historic New Orleans Collection–Williams Research Center, New Orleans. Davis, *Pirates Laffite*, 23–24, 88–89, 136–37.

22. According to Davis, Pierre had the following children: a son born in Haiti, Catherine Coralie (b. 1806), Martin (b. 1807), Jean Baptiste (b. 1808/1809), Rosa (b. 1812), Adele (b. 1819), Joseph (b. 1821); he also had a son named Pierre, who may have been the firstborn, a second son named Jean, and possibly a son named Eugene, though Eugene may have been invented by Laffite mythmakers (Davis, *Pirates Laffite*, 7, 23–24, 39, 87, 226, 251, 290, 410).

23. Boudin: indictment, Oct. 1815, *U.S. v. Bernard Boudin*, LA Fed. Ct., case 862; Davis, *Pirates Laffite*, 295. Beluche: De Grummond, *Renato Beluche*. Brouard: *American Citizen* (New York), Oct. 8, 1810; *Charleston (S.C.) City Gazette and Daily Advertiser*, Oct. 16, 1810. Lameson: Faye, "Privateersmen of the Gulf," 1084–88. Youx: Davis, *Pirates Laffite*, 30, 86; Faye, "Privateersmen of the Gulf," 1031–33. Ste-Gême: indictment, October 1814, *U.S. v. Henry St. Geme*, LA Fed. Ct., case 786; De Grummond, *Renato Beluche*, 95–96; Grace Elizabeth King, *Creole Families of New Orleans* (New York: Macmillan, 1921), 443–45; Andrew Jackson to Ste-Gême, Apr. 15, 1816, qtd. in Gerald Horne, *Negro Comrades of the Crown: African Americans and the British Empire Fight the U.S. before Emancipation* (New York: New York University Press, 2012), 67. Hart: *New-England Palladium* (Boston), Oct. 12, 1810; Bertram Wallace Korn, *Early Jews of New Orleans* (Waltham, MA: American Jewish History Society, 1969), 94–103. Amador and del Fierro: *Columbian Register* (New Haven, CT), Dec. 13, 1814; *Albany Advertiser*, May 8, 1816; Richard W. Slatta and Jane Lucas De Grummond, *Simón Bolívar's Quest for Glory* (College Station: Texas A&M University Press, 2003), 113.

24. The name "New Orleans Association" as well as the similar "Barataria Association" apparently gained currency with Stanley Faye (see Faye, "Commodore Aury," *LHQ* 24 [1941]: 631; Faye, "Privateers of Guadeloupe and their Establishment in Barataria," *LHQ* 23 [1940]: 443) and Jane Lucas De Grummond (*The Baratarians and the Battle of New Orleans*, 23), most likely as a misreading of the word "association" in nineteenth-century correspondence. Governor Claiborne, for example, denounced Vincent Gambi as "Formerly a Chief of the Barataria Association." By this he meant a group combined for a common purpose, in this case smuggling, not an organization with a formal structure (see Claiborne to Daniel Patterson, Apr. 5, 1815; Proclamation of William C. C. Claiborne, Apr. 14, 1813; Claiborne to James Wilkinson, Mar. 17, 1813, in *Official Letter Books of W. C. C. Claiborne, 1801–1816*, ed. Dunbar Rowland, 6 vols. [1917; repr., New York: AMS, 1972)], 6:233, 216, 355). Similarly, according to Harris Gaylord Warren, Spanish officials often described the New Orleans residents who supported Mexican activities with a Spanish term that can be translated as "association" (Warren, *The Sword Was Their Passport: A History of American Filibustering in the Mexican Revolution* [Baton Rouge: Louisiana State University Press, 1943], 119). Faye rendered this as "Association" and made it into a formal group. The composition of the group is revealed in two sources: The first is a list that Pierre Laffite drew up for Spanish officials soon after he had enlisted as a Spanish spy. In it, he named the men involved in selling munitions to the Mexicans (see Juan Ruiz de Apodaca to Francisco Vallesteros, Jan. 18, 1816, in Harris Gaylord Warren, ed., "Documents Relating

to Pierre Laffite's Entrance into the Service of Spain," *SWHQ Online* 44 [1940]: 76–87, www.tsha.utexas.edu/publications/journals/shq/online/v044/n1/contrib_DIVL1199.html). The second is Faye's reading of the correspondence of the Mexican minister to the United States, Manuel de Herrera, and the correspondence of Spanish officials in New Orleans (Consul Diego Morphy and Fr. Antonio de Sedella, who supervised intelligence gathering). The lists overlap but do not match. Moreover, while de Herrera is probably a reliable source in that he reported with whom he dealt, the conclusions of Spanish officials are more suspect, since they depended on the information gathered by their spies, and they filtered that information through their belief that New Spain was endangered by filibusters sponsored by the United States. In addition, it is important to note that Pierre reported only those men engaged in the munitions trade, which was legal (a fact previous works have overlooked). Pierre, then, may have composed his report to anger the Spanish, who deplored the munitions trade regardless of the law, while protecting the men he named from punishment in the United States. He thus confirmed his value as a spy by appearing to give the Spanish valuable intelligence, which Spanish officials could use in their protests to the United States but without making anyone vulnerable to sanction. The Spanish would have been especially pleased to have their anger with the customs collector and the naval commander validated. The evidence of Duplessis's involvement comes from Pierre (a G. Duplessis sailed a privateer to Galveston, but his identity is not known) (see *Fatio v. The Schooner* Lameson, LA Fed. Ct., case 1227). Patterson's possible connection is explored in chapter 4. Finally, it is worth noting that, as Davis speculates, Pierre may have settled scores against old enemies by placing their names on his list. Vincent Nolte, for example, had previously criticized the Laffites. That fact that he later signed a petition asking the navy for a convoy to protect his vessels from privateers suggests he was not involved (see Memorial of Merchants of New Orleans to Daniel Patterson, July 28, 1817, in "Message on Certain Persons at Amelia Island and Galvezton," 24–25; and Davis, *Pirates Laffite*, 276). Regardless of who was involved, to speak of a New Orleans Association confuses more than it explains. Backgrounds compiled from the following sources: West: *Daily National Intelligencer* (Washington, DC), Aug. 26, 1816; *City Gazette* (Charleston, SC), May 4, 1818; *Orleans Gazette* (New Orleans), Mar. 20, 1818; Mar. 23, 1818; June 15, 1818. Duncan: *Republican Watch Tower* (New York), Sept. 29, 1807; John G. Clark, *New Orleans, 1718–1812: An Economic History* (Baton Rouge: Louisiana State University Press, 1970), 340. Morgan: *Carolina Gazette* (Charleston, SC), May 3, 1804; Jared William Bradley, "Benjamin Morgan," in *Interim Appointment: W. C. C. Claiborne Letter Book, 1804–1805*, ed. Jared William Bradley (Baton Rouge: Louisiana State University Press, 2002), 282–98. Gilly: *Louisiana Advertiser* (New Orleans), Apr. 22, 1820; Davis, *Pirates Laffite*, 276. Livingston: Alexander De Conde, "Livingston, Edward," *ANBO*, www.anb.org/articles/03/03-00286.html. Grymes: *Independent Chronicle* (Boston), Jan. 13, 1817; *New York Times*, Dec. 18, 1854; "Grymes, John Randolph," *Dictionary of Louisiana Biography Online*, http://lahistory.org/site24.php. Davezac: Joseph G. Tregle, "Davezac, Auguste Genevieve Valentin," *ANBO*, www.anb.org/articles/03/03-00121.html. Harman: *Orleans Gazette* (New Orleans), July 2, 1819; Davis, *Pirates Laffite*, 276. Nolte: E. Clark Davis, "Nolte, Vincent Otto," *ANBO*, www.anb.org/articles/16/16-02166.html. Lafon: Stanley Faye, "Privateersmen of the Gulf and their Prizes," *LHQ* 22 (1939): 1068–70. Peire: Davis, *Pirates Laffite*, 262; William Henry Powell, *List of Officers of the Army of the United*

States from 1779–1900 (New York: L. R. Hamerly, 1900), 150. Dupuis: Davis, *Pirates Laffite*, 140. Patterson: John C. Fredriksen, "Patterson, Daniel Todd," *ANBO*, www.anb.org/articles/03/03-00373.html. Duplessis: John Wilds, *Collectors of Customs at the Port of New Orleans* (Washington: Department of the Treasury, 1991), 11.

25. Davezac: Tregle, "Davezac." Morgan: Clark, *New Orleans*, 290. Duncan: *The Papers of Thomas Jefferson: Retirement Series*, ed. J. Jefferson Looney, 23 vols. (Princeton: Princeton University Press, 2004–), 2:119n. Livingston: De Conde, "Livingston." For the munitions trade, see Fitz, "Our Sister Republics," 196–202.

26. Quotes: Jonathan Falconar to Abraham Falconar, Sept. 27, 1816, Oct. 17, 1817, and Mar. 23, 1819; Abraham to Jonathan, May 2, 1818, Abraham H. Falconar Papers, Maryland Historical Society, Baltimore. See also Jonathan to Abraham, n.d. [fall 1816?], Dec. 1816, Sept. 19, 1817, and Mar. 23, 1819.

27. Quotes: testimony of E. Williams, Dec. 8, 1814, *Daniel Patterson and Others v. The Schooner* General Bolívar, LA Fed. Ct., case 760; deposition of Peter Franks, Feb. 9, 1818, *José Almiral v. The Ship* Amistad de Rues *and Cargo*, LA Fed. Ct., case 1136; deposition of Joseph Smith, Aug. 28, 1819, *Vasques v. The Cargo of the Brig* Fanny, MD Adm.; Stephen Lusk to Nicholas Ridgely, June 24, 1818, Ridgely Papers, Maryland Historical Society, Baltimore; deposition of John Fitch, Nov. 5, 1818, *Antonio Argota Villalobos v. 100 Boxes of Sugar, Twenty Barrels of Coffee, and Some Hides Imported in the Sloop* James, GA Adm.; deposition of John Davis, July 27, 1819, *Pablo Chacon v. Eighty-nine Bales of Cochineal, Three Bales Jalap, and One Box Vanilla*, VA Adm.; answers to interrogatories of Thomas Hall, Oct. 14, 1817, *U.S. v. The Schooner* Hornet, GA Adm. For sailors' experience of freedom, see Paul A. Gilje, *Liberty on the Waterfront: American Maritime Culture in the Age of Revolution* (Philadelphia: University of Pennsylvania Press, 2004), chap. 1.

28. Indebted sailors: depositions of William Thompson, Prince P. Gifford, John Keyser, Samuel Jones, William Laborda, Jan. 12, 1820, *U.S. v. William Bush*, MD Crim. Navy officers: William Lendham, n.d., CPD. Drunken sailors: depositions of John Keyser, Lewis Gather, and Prince P. Gifford, Jan. 12, 1820, *U.S. v. Bush*, MD Crim.; deposition of Samuel Scott, Jan. 27, 1818, *John Madrazo v. Slaves, the Cargo of the* Isabelita, GA Adm.; deposition of Edward Foley, Jan. 12, 1820, *U.S. v. Bush*, MD Crim.

29. Deposition of John Oliver, June 20, 1810, *Carter v. Aury*, LA Fed. Ct., case 376; testimony of John Oliver, Dec. 8, 1814, *Daniel Patterson and Others v. The Schooner* General Bolivar, LA Fed. Ct., case 760; testimony of Felippe Brioner, n.d., and James Kelly, n.d., *Morphy v. The Spanish Ship* Cleopatra, LA Fed. Ct., case 857.

30. Quotes: Testimony of Mareo Pertosi, n.d., and Ambroise Cavas, n.d., *Diego Morphy v. The Spanish Ship* Cleopatra *and Cargo*, LA Fed. Ct., case 857. For sailors receiving advances or prize shares, see depositions of Philip Pachale, June 15, 1810, and Jean Baptiste Larrey, July 9, 1810, *William Carter (qui tam) v. Louis Aury*, LA Fed. Ct., case 376; deposition of Antonia Alticen, Sabastian Tun, Cayetano Mandana, Domingo Castro, and Francisco Acosta, July 28, 1817, *Felipe Fatio v. The Spanish Polacre* La Virgin del Mar, *Her Tackle, Apparel, Furniture, and Cargo*, LA Fed. Ct., case 1068; deposition of Andrew Whiteman, Nov. 24, 1813, CPD. For a sailor leaving, see deposition of James Davis, Jan. 9, 1818, *U.S. v. The Brig* General San Martin, GA Adm.

31. Depositions of Robert W. Richards, June 15, 1817, and Matthew Page Godfrey, Sept. 5, 1817, *Joaquim Zamorano v. Sundry Goods, Wares, and Merchandise*, MD Adm. See also deposition of Timothy Ragan, Oct. 10, 1817, in the same case.

32. Depositions of Joseph Delacour, n.d.; William Irving and Samuel B. Goodrich, Sept. 19, 1818; John Heviart, Oct. 20, 1818; John M. Gass, Oct. 18, 1818, CPD; Matthew Murray, Oct. 21, 1818, *Vasques v. Sundry Bales of Cotton*, NY Adm.

33. Deposition of Francis Navarre, Feb. 24, 1819, *U.S. v. Eight Cases of Dry Goods, Four Pieces of Cloth, Four Pieces of Silk, and Four Papers of Silk Handkerchiefs*, MD Adm.

34. Quote: Pierre Dupont to the officers and crew of the *San Martin*, Aug. 15, 1818, *U.S. v. The General San Martin* GA Adm. *New York Evening Post*, Aug. 28, 1818; *New York Daily Advertiser*, Aug. 29, 1818; *Argus* (Albany, NY), Sept. 1, 1818.

35. Quotes: depositions of John Randolph, Oct. 11, 1814, *U.S. v. Manuel Joachim*, LA Fed. Ct., case 773; unknown, n.d., *U.S. v. Dominique Youx*, LA Fed. Ct., case 779; Andrew Whiteman, Nov. 24, 1813, CPD; testimony of B. Bragden, July 9, 1818, *U.S. v. The Schooner* Felix, GA Adm.; Peter Franks, Feb. 9, 1818, and Inspector's Report, June 19, 1817, *José Almiral v. The Ship Amistad de Rues and Cargo*, LA Fed. Ct., case 1136; *Lloyd's List* (London), July 7, 1818. See also depositions of Miguel Munez, June 2, 1817; José Ferre, June 2, 1817; Juan Botel, n.d.; and Victoriano Camacho, n.d., *Hernandez v. The Spanish Schooner* Estrella, LA Fed. Ct., case 1035; Altonio Alticen, Sabastian Tun, Cayetano Mandana, Domingo Castro, Francisco José Acosta, all July 28, 1817, *Fatio v. The Spanish Polacre* La Virgin del Mar, LA Fed. Ct., case 1068. Crew lists were occasionally entered into evidence, and they reinforce these impressions. For example, of the thirty men aboard the Cartagenan privateer *Cometa*, there were ten Cartagenans, eight residents of Caracas, four Haitians, three men from Curacao, one Italian, one man from Malta, and one from Rio de la Hacha (in present-day Colombia). One sailor's place of residence is illegible, and although the captain, William Mitchell, had his space left blank, he was British (see *U.S. v. The Schooner* Cometa *and Cargo*, LA Fed. Ct., case 909; see also roll de equipage, n.d., *U.S. v. The Schooner* Presidente, LA Fed. Ct., case 811; and crew list, Mar. 1, 1815, *Diego Morphy v. The* Indagadora, LA Fed. Ct., case 833, although in this last case all the sailors were listed as residents of Cartagena, including men such as John Wyle and Charles Smith). For the racial descriptions of sailors, see W. Jeffrey Bolster, *Black Jacks: African American Seamen in the Age of Sail* (Cambridge: Harvard University Press, 1997), 234.

36. Deposition of Louis Crispin, July 9, 1810, *Carter v. Aury*, LA Fed. Ct., case 376; depositions of George Carthew and Andrew Johnson, Dec. 20, 1819, *U.S. v. The Brig Wilson*, VA Adm. Peter Linebaugh and Marcus Rediker have argued that the crews of age of sail ships were "motley," by which they mean that crews set aside their racial and ethnic differences to become politically motivated, class-conscious, and egalitarian. One angry Spaniard, the supercargo of the Cleopatra, used this term to describe the men who despoiled his ship. The privateers were "a motley set, of different colors," he said. Furthermore, some slaves ran away to privateers expecting to find liberty, if captains' declarations that they were not helping slaves run away are any indication. However, to link diversity to anticapitalist class-consciousness misunderstands what drove these sailors (see Peter Linebaugh and Marcus Rediker, *The Many-Headed Hydra: Sailors, Slaves, Commoners, and the Hidden History of the Revolutionary Atlantic* [Boston: Beacon, 2000], 27–28, 143–73, 212–14).

37. Quote: deposition of Bon Herbert, Jan. 7, 1813, *Graw v. The Spanish Polacre* San Francisco de Paula, LA Fed. Ct., case 505. See also, in the same case, depositions of Thomas Copping, Jan. 6, 1813, Alexis C. Bonami, Jan. 7, 1813; Paul Lanuse, Jan. 7, 1813;

Charles Bernier, Jan. 8, 1813; Angus Fraser, Jan.8, 1813; and Jean Marie Fourmis, n.d. A small but not insignificant number of black sailors served aboard slave ships during the age of sail (see Emma Christopher, *Slave Ship Sailors and Their Captive Cargoes, 1730–1807* [Cambridge: Cambridge University Press, 2006], esp. chap. 2). For ships as a source of livelihood, freedom, and acceptance for black sailors, see Bolster, *Black Jacks*. For shipboard musicians, see Robert Harms, *The Diligent: A Voyage through the Worlds of the Slave Trade* (New York: Basic, 2003), 295–98.

38. For MacGregor's background, see T. Frederick Davis, *MacGregor's Invasion of Florida, 1817: Together with an Account of His Successors Irwin, Hubbard and Aury on Amelia Island, East Florida* (Tallahassee: Florida Historical Society, 1928); David Sinclair, *Sir Gregor MacGregor and the Land That Never Was: The Extraordinary Story of the Most Audacious Fraud in History* (London: Headline, 2003); Matthew Brown, "Inca, Sailor, Soldier, King: Gregor MacGregor and the Early Nineteenth-Century Caribbean," *Bulletin of Latin American Research* 24 (2005): 44–70. For the Tampa plan, see [Charles Collins] to John Quincy Adams, Dec. 24, 1817, in U.S. Department of State, "Message from the President of the United States Transmitting, in Pursuance of a Resolution of the House of Representatives, of the 20th Instant, Information Not Heretofore Communicated, on the Occupation of Amelia Island," Mar. 26, 1818, 11 H.doc. 175, 33–34, *United States Serial Set Digital Collection*, 10–12.

39. For the view that filibusters of the 1810s simply took advantage of Spain's weakness to seize land and work out old grudges against Spain, see Robert E. May, *Manifest Destiny's Underworld: Filibustering in Antebellum America* (Chapel Hill: University of North Carolina Press, 2002), 4–5.

40. Kristin A. Dykstra, "On the Betrayal of Nations: José Alvarez de Toledo's Philadelphia *Manifesto* (1811) and *Justification* (1816)," *CR: The New Centennial Review* 4 (2004): 267–305; Timothy Palmer, "Toledo y Dubois, José Alvarez de," *HTO*, www.tshaonline.org/handbook/online/articles/TT/fto10.html; Warren, *The Sword Was Their Passport*, 10–15.

41. Quote: José Bernando Gutierrez de Lara to William Eustis, 1811, qtd. in David Narrett, "José Bernardo Gutierrez de Lara: Caudillo of the Mexican Republic in Texas," *SWHQ* 105 (2002): 202. See also Elizabeth Howard West, "Diary of José Bernardo Gutierrez de Lara, 1811–1812," *American Historical Review* 34 (1928): 55–77. Anaya: Horace Virgil Harrison, "Juan Pablo Anaya: Champion of Mexican Federalism" (Ph.D. diss., University of Texas-Austin, 1951), chap. 3. Unless indicated otherwise, the leaders' involvement with expeditions into Texas are taken from Warren, *The Sword Was Their Passport*.

42. De Herrera: William H. Timmons, *Morelos of Mexico: Priest, Soldier, Statesman* (El Paso: Texas Western College Press, 1963), 105, 116, 135. Savary: Marcus B. Christian, "Savary, Joseph," *Africana: The Encyclopedia of the African and African American Experience*, ed. Kwame Anthony Appiah and Henry Louis Gates Jr., 2nd ed. (New York: Oxford University Press, 2005), *Oxford African American Studies Center*, www.oxfordaasc.com.gate.lib.buffalo.edu/article/opr/t0002/e3480; Caryn Cossé Bell, *Revolution, Romanticism, and the Afro-Creole Protest Tradition in Louisiana, 1718–1868* (Baton Rouge: Louisiana State University Press, 1997), chap. 2. For Savary's slave owning (not previously noted), see deposition of Mariano Gonzales, Oct. 8, 1818, *Felipe Fatio v. The Schooner Lameson alias Panchita*, LA Fed. Ct., case 1227. Perry: *Washington (DC) Whig*, Sept. 18, 1815 (quote); Margaret S. Henson, "Perry, Henry,"

HTO, www.tshaonline.org/handbook/online/articles/PP/fpe42.html. Robinson: John Hamilton Robinson to Luis de Onís, 1812; Proclamation, Nov. 19, 1813, qtd. in Harold A. Bierck Jr., "Dr. John Hamilton Robinson," *LHQ* 25 (1942): 644–69 (quotes: 652, 660).

43. Quotes: José Servando Teresa de Mier Noriega y Guerea Mier, qtd. in Karen Racine, "Fray Servando Teresa de Mier: Anahuac's Angry Apostle," in *The Human Tradition in Mexico*, ed. Jeffrey M. Pilcher (Wilmington, DE: Scholarly Resources, 2003), 31; Proclamation of Martin Javier Mina y Larrea, Apr. 25, 1817, qtd. in Harris Gaylord Warren, "Xavier Mina's Invasion of Mexico," *Hispanic American Historical Review* 23 (1943): 58. For Mina's and Mier's backgrounds, see these articles. Some confusion surrounds Mina's first name since one of his relatives, Francisco Espoz y Mina, also led guerilla forces during the Peninsular War; it appears that later accounts have combined the two men's names. For Mina's role in the Peninsular War, see John Lawrence Tone, *The Fatal Knot: The Guerilla War in Navarre and the Defeat of Napoleon in Spain* (Chapel Hill: University of North Carolina Press, 1994), 74–78.

44. Quote: testimony of Abner L. Duncan, n.d., *Diego Morphy* v. *The Spanish Schooner* Santa Rita *and Cargo*, LA Fed. Ct., case 817. See also Davis, *Pirates Laffite*, 241.

45. Quote: petition of Juan Alvarez de Toledo, Dec. 12, 1816, in "Toledo's Reconciliation with Spain," 834. See also William Spence Robertson, *Iturbide of Mexico* (Durham, NC: Duke University Press, 1952), 159–60, 238–39; Warren, *The Sword Was Their Passport*, 88; Bierck, "Pedro Gual and the Patriot Effort to Capture a Mexican Port," 465; Harrison, "Juan Pablo Anaya," 167. Although Toledo and Picornell's pardon petitions are not transparent statements of their thinking, they suggest a possible alternative motive.

46. Owsley and Smith contend that "these leaders were unsuccessful simply because there were too many of them. Had all the groups united behind a single leader, they likely would have succeeded" (see Frank L. Owsley Jr. and Gene A. Smith, *Filibusters and Expansionists: Jeffersonian Manifest Destiny, 1800-1821* [Tuscaloosa: University of Alabama Press, 1997], 173). Griffin saw the expeditions as "fiascoes," Warren labeled them "futile," and Davis usually portrays them as hapless (Griffin, *The United States and the Disruption of Spain's Empire*, 107–15; Warren, *The Sword Was Their Passport*, 258; Davis, *Pirates Laffite*, 141–42, 232–33, 298).

47. Assessments of MacGregor and Aury vary widely, with MacGregor seen as everything from a romantic adventurer to a marauder and fraud; from a legitimate though ultimately unsuccessful revolutionary to a possible representative of America's expansionist agenda; from a man so committed to republicanism that no national boundaries could contain him to a transnational *caudillo* (see Davis, *MacGregor's Invasion of Florida*; Rufus K. Wyllys, "The Filibusters of Amelia Island," *Georgia Historical Quarterly* 12 [1928]: 297–325; Alfred Hasbrouck, *Foreign Legionaries in the Liberation of Spanish South America* [1928; repr., New York: Octagon, 1969], 154–57); Sinclair, *Sir Gregor MacGregor*; Bushnell, "The Florida Republic"; Owsley and Smith, *Filibusters and Expansionists*; Heckard, "Crossroads of Empire"; and Brown, "Inca, Sailor, Soldier, King"). Characterizations of Aury are no less contradictory. He was a pirate, an adventurer, a legitimate revolutionary, or an unusually enlightened racial egalitarian (see Charge to the Grand Jury [1859], 30 F.Cas. 1026; Willis Fletcher Johnson, *America's Foreign Relations*, 2 vols. [New York: Century, 1921], 1:307–8; Carlos Gilman Calkins, "The Repression of Piracy in the West Indies, 1824–1825," *United States Naval Institute Proceedings* 37 [1911]: 1205–18; Samuel Flagg Bemis, *John Quincy*

Adams and the Foundations of American Foreign Policy [New York: Knopf, 1949], 307; Owsley and Smith, *Filibusters and Expansionists*; Weeks, *John Quincy Adams and American Global Empire*; Bushnell, "The Florida Republic"; Heckerd, "Crossroads of Empire"; Caryn Coss Bell, *Revolution, Romanticism, and the Afro-Creole Protest Tradition in Louisiana, 1718–1868* [Baton Rouge: Louisiana State University Press, 1997], 62–63; and Jane Landers, *Atlantic Creoles in the Age of Revolutions* [Cambridge: Harvard University Press, 2010], 130–37).

48. Quotes: Gregor MacGregor, "Málaga Proclamation," Nov. 18, 1813, qtd. in Brown, "Inca, Sailor, Soldier, King," 52; "Gregor MacGregor's Commission," Mar. 31, 1817, in "Message on the Occupation of Amelia Island," 33–34. In an example of a private letter matching his public sentiments, MacGregor tried to interest James Chaytor in his Amelia project by asking for his "assistance in what is the desire of all the Independent governments of South America" (see MacGregor to James Chaytor, Apr. 20, 1817, JCPM).

49. Quotes: [John S. Skinner] to John Quincy Adams, July 30, 1817; [Charles Collins] to Adams, Jan. 19, 1818, in "Message on the Occupation of Amelia Island," 7–8, 15. Owsley and Smith adduce Skinner's letter as evidence that MacGregor "received what amounted to an unofficial blessing from the government of the United States" (Owsley and Smith, *Filibusters and Expansionists*, 125). But the letter's timing, if nothing else, precludes this interpretation. Similarly, Griffin indicates that Rush met MacGregor, and though he denied government support, he "allowed MacGregor to feel that he would not personally be sorry to see" Amelia fall (Griffin, *United States and the Disruption of the Spanish Empire*, 111). But Whitaker shows that Rush met with Thornton, not MacGregor, and that he dismissed the idea of supporting the invasion (Arthur Preston Whitaker, *The United States and the Independence of Latin America, 1800–1830* [1941; repr., New York: Russell and Russell, 1962], 237).

50. For MacGregor as *caudillo*, see Brown, "Inca, Sailor, Soldier, King," 48–57. For *caudillos* generally, see John Lynch, "Bolívar and the Caudillos," *Hispanic American Historical Review* 63 (1983): 3–35; Lynch, *Caudillos in Spanish America, 1800–1850* (Oxford: Oxford University Press, 1992). Miranda: Karen Racine, *Francisco de Miranda: A Transatlantic Life in the Age of Revolution* (Wilmington, DE: Scholarly Resources, 2003). Arismendi: Donna Keyse Rudolph and G. A. Rudolph, "Arismendi, Juan Bautista," *Historical Dictionary of Venezuela*, 2nd ed. (Lanham, MD: Scarecrow, 1996), 42; Robert L. Scheina, *Latin America's Wars: The Age of the Caudillo, 1791–1899*, 2 vols. (Washington: Potomac, 2003), 436–37n.

51. Quotes: Proclamation of MacGregor, July 1, 1817, qtd. in Davis, *MacGregor's Invasion of Florida*, 19–20; medallion inscription, qtd. in Sinclair, *Sir Gregor MacGregor*, 181–84.

52. For examples of MacGregor's currency and the commemorative medals he had struck, see Carling Gresham, *General Gregor MacGregor and the 1817 Amelia Island Medal* (self-published, 1992). MacGregor's claims are scattered throughout Sinclair's *Sir Gregor MacGregor* (see esp. 111–27, 178–82). A newspaper article about MacGregor's background, originally derived from British papers and widely reprinted in the United States, also contains many similar assertions, including that he was from "a respectable and ancient family"; that he had received a Spanish (not Portuguese) knighthood; that he was a Scottish general; and that he was "a man of considerable literary attainments, and took with him on his chivalrous expedition a noble library"

(see *National Register* [Washington, DC], Mar. 22, 1817; and *Camden [SC] Gazette*, Mar. 27, 1817). But these claims were inventions. MacGregor's father was a sea captain for the East India Company; his mother was a doctor's daughter. MacGregor's grandfather held a minor peerage, and he belonged to the clan MacGregor (a real coup once Sir Walter Scott published *Rob Roy*, the romance of that most famous MacGregor, in 1817). But any personal claim to the higher nobility or leadership of the clan was invented. Likewise, no record of his having attended the University of Edinburgh can be found. His pretensions to be a bibliophile usually surfaced in claims that he had lost his books in some misfortune. As for his military record, MacGregor's British unit saw combat only after he had resigned, and many others assisted at the defense of Cartagena (see Sinclair, *Sir Gregor MacGregor*, esp. 108–10; 117–21, 159). Brown rightly challenges the popular notion, produced in works such as Sinclair's, that MacGregor was simply a crook. Still, MacGregor need not have perpetrated the "most audacious fraud in history," as Sinclair puts it, to have practiced deception (Brown, "Inca, Sailor, Soldier, King," 45).

53. Quotes: Vincente Pazos to James Monroe, Feb. 7, 1818, in "Message on the Occupation of Amelia Island," 17–33; *Columbian* (New York), Nov. 1, 1817; McIntosh to William Crawford, Oct. 30, 1817, "Message from the President of the United States, Communicating Information of the Proceeding of Certain Persons Who Took Possession of Amelia Island and Galvezton," 20; *Lloyd's List* (London), June 8, 1821. See also Faye, "Commodore Aury, 612, 632–34, 678, 697; Warren, *The Sword Was Their Passport*, 142, 165–66; Davis, *Pirates Laffite*, 306; and John Lynch, *Simón Bolívar: A Life* (New Haven: Yale University Press, 2006), 92–95, 284–87.

Conclusion: Captain Chaytor Comes Home

1. *Baltimore Patriot*, July 9, 1829. See also *New York Evening Post*, Aug. 18, 1828; David Head, "Independence on the Quarterdeck: Three Baltimore Seafarers, Spanish America, and the Lives of Captains in the Early American Republic," *Northern Mariner/Le marin du nord* 23 (2013): 18.

2. Francis R. Stark, *The Abolition of Privateering and the Declaration of Paris* (New York: Columbia University Press, 1897), 139–52; Jan Lemnitzer, *Power, Law, and the End of Privateering* (New York: Palgrave Macmillan, 2014). Shifting trade patterns after 1815 also discouraged investment in privateers (see Henning Hillmann and Christina Gathmann, "Overseas Trade and the Decline of Privateering," *Journal of Economic History* 71 [2011]: 730–61).

3. For Adams's proposal, see Samuel Flagg Bemis, *John Quincy Adams and the Foundations of American Foreign Policy* (New York: Knopf, 1949), 436–47. For Franklin, see William Bell Clark, *Ben Franklin's Privateers: A Naval Epic of the American Revolution* (Baton Rouge: Louisiana State University Press, 1956). For a sample of antiprivateering statements, see *New York Evening Post*, Apr. 19 and Apr. 29, 1861; *New York Times*, June 9 and June 16, 1861; "Against Privateering," *American Museum, or, Universal Magazine, Containing Essays on Agriculture, Commerce, Manufacturers, Politics, Morals, and Manners; Sketches of National Characters, Natural and Civil History, and Biography; Law Information, Public Papers, Intelligence, Moral Tales, Ancient and Modern Poetry*, Feb. 1790, 102–3; "Privateering," *Moral Advocate, A Monthly Publication on War, Duelling, Capital Punishment, and Prison Discipline*, Mar. 1821, 13–15; "Piracy and Privateering," *Merchants' Magazine and Commercial Review*, Nov. 1845,

450–59; and House of Representatives, "Application to Abolish Privateering in Time of War," Jan. 11, 1820, ASP023 Nav.aff.178, *United States Serial Set Digital Collection*; *An Appeal to the Government and Congress of the United States Against the Depredations Committed by American Privateers on the Commerce of Nations at Peace with Us* (New York: n.p., 1819).

4. Quotes: *Easton (MD) Gazette*, January 31, 1835; *Baltimore Sun*, Aug. 6, 1845, Jan. 19, 1846. Head, "Independence on the Quarterdeck," 18–19.

Index

Adams, John Quincy: advocates abolition of privateering, 150; and Amelia Island, 108, 112; attitude toward Spanish American privateers, 13, 113; and David De Forest, 86, 132; defends Andrew Jackson's invasion of Florida, 29, 159n33; develops Monroe Doctrine, 35; and Galveston, 108, 119; historians evaluation of, 5, 13, 37; negotiations with Luis de Onís, 25-2, 29; and neutrality law enforcement, 86, 89; and Panama Conference, 35–36; and recognition of Spanish American independence, 31
Admiralty courts, 2, 9, 57, 59, 79, 87, 95, 104, 127, 145
Almeida, Joseph, 73, 79, 123–24
Amelia Island: geography, 102, 104; and Gregor MacGregor, 102, 104–5, 140–41, 144, 145–46; and Louis-Michel Aury, 106–8, 109–10, 111; patriot rivalries at, 105, 107–8, 147; privateering from, 92–3, 104–5, 106; and privateers' claims to legitimacy, 104, 107, 111, 114, 144, 151; slave smuggling at, 79, 104, 106–7, 109, 147; United States policy toward, 92, 108–9, 111–14
Anaya, Juan Pablo, 142, 143
Armadores, 73–74
Artigas, José Gervais, 19–20, 74, 138
Atlantic world, 6–7, 8, 43, 64, 66, 91, 93, 151
Aury, Louis-Michel: at Amelia Island, 106–13, 141; captain of the *Guillaume*, 49; and the Laffites, 100–1; later life and death, 182n36; Mexican governor at Galveston, 94–95, 97–99; motivations of, 144, 146–47; and slavery, 107–8, 147

Baltimore, 1, 8, 9, 85; attraction of Spanish American privateers to, 63, 64; federal court at, 86–87; growth of, 65–66; merchant community of, 63, 66–67, 68–73, 81, 83–84, 90, 132; slave smuggling at, 79; and War of 1812, 66, 67, 68, 73, 128
Barataria: and filibusters, 142; geography of, 38, 44, 104, 163n16; Laffites operations from, 38, 39, 44–45, 46, 48, 50, 51, 52, 53, 54, 136, 137; smuggling at, 44, 46, 47–48, 55, 126, 126, 138; slave smuggling at, 46–47, 49; U.S. Navy raid of, 41, 99, 125–26
Baratarians: in the Battle of New Orleans, 39, 41, 126; at Galveston, 92, 93
Barnes, James, 74
Battle of New Orleans, 25, 134, 142; Laffites' role in, 41–42, 131, 161n3
Beluche, Rene, 127–28, 134
Black sailors, 97, 107–8, 139–40, 147
Blanque, Jean, 39
Bolívar, Simon, 15, 18, 28, 32, 33, 34, 35, 94, 122, 124, 127; celebrated in the United States, 34
Bowie, James, 116

Brazil, 10, 19, 32, 33, 74, 78, 126, 128
Buenos Aires: junta of, 1, 18–19, 22, 28, 32, 63, 75, 128, 132; North American merchants in, 67, 74, 75, 132, 133; United States policy toward, 28–29, 31
Burke, David, 68, 81

Cartagena de Índias: junta of, 18, 44, 107, 134, 144; Spanish attacks against, 18, 20, 33, 102, 123–24, 146
Cartagenan privateers, 4, 43, 45, 46, 56, 57, 61, 124, 125, 126, 127, 134, 137, 191n35
Caudillos, 145–46
Champ d'Asile, 118
Chase, John, 84, 89, 125, 133, 138
Chase, Obadiah, 73, 77–78
Chaytor, James, 1–4, 11, 73, 83, 122–23, 149, 151–52
Chew, Beverly, 53, 92, 93, 96, 117
Citizenship, Spanish American republics and, 2, 63, 67, 73–74, 74–75, 76, 85, 104, 128, 129, 155n7
Civil court rulings, 57, 86–87, 88, 89, 115
Claiborne, William C. C., 39, 41, 48, 55, 60–61
Clay, Henry, 31, 36
Congress of Anáhuac, 16. See also Mexican Congress
Court records, as source, 9–10, 167n47, 175n47
Criminal court rulings, 56, 86, 115

Danels, John D., 73, 78, 82, 127, 128–30, 151
De Forest, David, 67–68, 74, 75, 86, 89–90, 132
Distress, entry to ports in, 7, 48–49, 52, 53, 56, 61–62, 81–82, 114
Donaldsonville, 45, 46, 48, 49, 50, 52, 54, 55
Duplessis, Pierre L. B., 96, 135, 189n24

East Florida, 8, 22, 27, 79, 92, 102, 111, 113, 140, 141
Elton, John H., 106, 107

Fernandina, East Florida, 92, 104, 105, 106, 146. See also Amelia Island
Fernando VII, 14–15, 18, 30, 32, 142
Filibusters, 6, 16, 27, 29, 99, 100, 112, 115, 116, 145, 151; and Amelia Island, 93, 104, 105, 109, 111; and Galveston, 93, 94, 98–99, 100, 101, 102, 114, 117, 118, 119, 120, 135, 141–44, 147; motivations of, 98, 140–47; number of expeditions, 98; organizational problems of, 144; and United States neutrality law, 20, 23, 28. See also Aury, Louis-Michel; Gutierrez de Lara, José Bernardo Maximiliano; Lallemand, Charles-Francois-Antoine; MacGregor, Gregor; Mina, Francisco Xavier; New Orleans "Association."
Firebrand incident, 116
Floridas: Andrew Jackson's invasion of, 29; and Gregor MacGregor, 102, 104, 105, 140, 144, 145, 146; and Louis-Michel Aury, 106, 107; and United States policy toward, 5, 13, 21, 22, 23, 25, 27, 30, 36, 112, 114, 117. See also East Florida; West Florida
Ford, Henry, 126
Fourth of July, 63, 66–67, 76, 84, 89, 91, 124
French consul, 53–54, 60–61
French privateers, 21, 38, 42, 45, 46, 48, 49–50, 51, 52, 53–54, 56, 60, 62, 93, 94, 124, 125, 126, 139, 140; in Guadeloupe, 43; ; motivations of, 127; preference for Louisiana, 43–44

Galveston: and filibusters, 97–99, 117–18, 119–20, 141, 142–43, 147; geography of, 94, 97; Laffites' evacuation of, 119–21; Laffites' operations at, 99–102, 114, 116, 118, 119–21; and Lallemand, Charles-Francois-Antoine, 118–19; legitimacy of, 94–97, 101; privateering from, 92–93, 94–95, 102, 141; Spanish designs against, 100–101, 119; United States policy toward, 113, 114, 117, 119
Gambi, Vincent, 51, 136, 188n24
Geopolitics: as diplomatic concept, 6; as influence on privateering, 37, 41, 42, 55, 61, 64, 79, 91, 93, 99, 105, 117, 118, 120–21, 126, 144, 150; as influence on United States foreign policy, 23, 26, 62, 114, 117, 121; and Spanish American revolutions, 1
Glenn, Elias, 86
Gooding, John, 73, 84, 90, 137
Goodwin, Lyde, 68–69, 73, 80, 90
Goodwin, Robert M., 77, 80, 83, 132–33
Graham, George, 119
Grand Colombia, 32, 33, 122, 127, 129
Gual, Pedro, 107

Guillaume, 94, 97, 140, 147
Gutierrez de Lara, Jose Bernardo Maximiliano, 98, 141–42; and Gutierrez-Magee expedition, 114

Haiti: and American fears of slave rebellion, 22, 147; French migration from, 42, 60, 107–8, 118, 125, 134, 142; and privateering, 74, 76, 81, 97–98, 106, 126, 139, 140, 147, 182n34; and Spanish American independence, 18, 32, 124
Haitian Revolution, 134, 142, 147
Hall, Dominick, 57, 164n26
Halsey, Thomas Lloyd, 74, 75
Herrera, José Manuel de, 94, 98, 142, 143–44, 188–89n24
Hidalgo, Miguel, 15, 16, 142
Hubbard, Ruggles, 105, 106, 107, 108, 147
Humbert, Jean Joseph Amable, 98, 120

Independencia del Sud, 2, 4, 11, 132, 155n7
Irwin, Jared, 105, 106, 107, 108, 147

Jackson, Andrew, 25, 29, 34, 36, 41, 114, 134, 135, 143

Karrick, Joseph, 66, 67, 83–84, 86, 89, 90, 175n45

Laffite, Jean: aided by French consul, 53–54; appearance of, 38; Battle of New Orleans, role in, 41; Britain's alleged attempt to bribe, 39, 161n3; and British invasion of gulf coast, 38; clashes with customs officers, 54; early life, 38, 43; exploration mission of, 100; later life, 120; offer to defend Barataria for the United States, 39; pardoned, 41; recruits sailors, 52; and William C. C. Claiborne, 39, 41
Laffite, Pierre: appearance, 38–39; Battle of New Orleans, role in, 41; clash with customs officers, 58; declares bankruptcy, 134; escape from jail, 39; sells rented slave, 42, 133–34; slave buying in West Florida, 42; works for sheriff, 50
Laffite brothers: business origins, 38, 43–44; business practices of, 45–46, 48, 52–53; evacuate Galveston, 120–21; family of, 134; exploits geopolitical tensions, 42, 62, 119, 121; and Galveston, 100–101, 102, 114, 118, 119–20; headquarters raided by U.S. Navy, 41;slave smuggling by, 46–47, 50; privateers owned by, 50–51, 120, 164n32; motivations of, 131–32, 133–34; Spanish espionage activities of, 99–101, 119
Lafon, Bartholomé, 135
Lafon, Bernard, 126
Lallemand, Charles-Francois-Antoine, 117–19
Latour, Arsène, 48, 100, 101
Liquet, Pierre, 125
Livingston, Edward, 135, 189n24
Louisiana: economy, 42, 47; federal court cases in, 115, 56; and filibusters, 98, 120, 135, 141, 142; geography, 43, 45, 53; politics in, 60–61; and slave trade, 43, 44, 46, 79, 116, 127; and smuggling, 42, 43, 45, 48, 55, 56, 95, 114; as territory, 162n9. *See also* Louisiana Purchase; Transcontinental Treaty
Louisiana Purchase, 21, 27, 36, 42, 60, 93, 127
Lominé, Charles, 124, 127
Long, James, 119–20

MacGregor, Gregor, 92, 93, 102–5, 109, 111, 123, 194n52; motivations of, 140, 141, 144–46; privateers commissioned by, 107
Madison, James: and expansionism, 113–14; Manifest Destiny, 6, 150; neutrality policy of, 20–21, 117; pardon of Laffites, 41, 62; Spanish American policy of, 22–23; Spanish policy of, 25; and Transcontinental Treaty, 25, 117; and War of 1812, 61
Marshall, John, 88
McCulloch, James, 85–86
Mexican Congress, 16, 94, 141, 142, 144
Mexico, 4, 6, 8, 44, 91, 94, 102; filibuster expeditions to, 93, 94, 98, 99, 100, 116, 118, 135, 141–44; independence movement in, 16, 32, 33, 93, 94, 111; munitions trade to, 100, 116; United States policy towards, 22, 33, 92, 96
Mexican privateers, 43, 56, 92, 95, 97, 115, 116
Mier Noriega y Guerea, José Servando Teresa de, 143

Mina, Francisco Xavier, 99, 100, 108, 142–43
Miranda, Francisco de, 145
Monier, Jean, 124, 127, 139
Monroe Doctrine, 5, 31, 34–35, 36
Monroe, James: and neutrality law, 84–85, 89; and occupation of Amelia Island, 108, 109, 111–14; Spanish American policy of, 28–29, 31; suppression of Galveston, 114–15, 117, 119
Morelos, Father Jose Maria, 16
Morillo, Juan Pablo, expedition of, 18, 20, 32, 33, 124
Munitions trade, 1, 23, 29, 75, 94, 100, 116, 126, 135, 142, 189n24
Mutiny, 83, 86, 88, 97, 124, 129, 138, 139, 147

Napoleonic Wars, 5, 19, 24, 37, 66, 118; and Spanish empire, 14–15, 18, 21
Neutrality, 21, 60, 65 , 86, 88, 116; influence on privateers, 6, 7, 42, 64, 76, 99, 107, 151; law of nations principles of, 23, 81; privateer violations of, 56, 62, 84, 86, 89, 109, 115, 127, 145; United States law of, 2, 23, 49, 51, 68, 75, 84–85, 133, 168n58; United States policy of, 4, 5, 7, 13, 20–21, 22, 23, 31, 61, 94, 107, 111; and United States relations with Spain, 28, 30; and United States relations with Spanish America, 6, 22–23, 31, 61–62, 107
New Grenada, Viceroyalty of, 18, 32, 102, 111, 144
New Orleans: Economy of, 21–22, 42, 47; and filibusters, 94, 98, 99, 100, 116, 119, 142, 143; French population of, 56, 60; geography of, 38, 43, 44, 53; geopolitical status of, 22, 42, 43, 61; Italian population of, 51; merchants in, 134, 135; naval station, 58, 59, 117; popular attitudes toward smuggling, 48, 55, 56; and privateers, 48–50, 52, 54, 81, 92, 95, 96–97, 126, 136, 137
New Orleans "Association," 135–36, 188n24
No Transfer Resolution, 112, 117
Nolte, Vincent, 135, 189n24

Onís, Luis de, 13, 14, 22, 25–26, 28, 29, 30, 88, 89
Oriental Provinces of the Río de la Plata, 4, 19, 32
Oriental Provinces privateers, 64, 74, 78, 79, 83, 91, 128, 138

Páez, José Antonio, 129
Panama Congress, 35–36
Panic of 1819, 90, 91
Patterson, Daniel Todd, 41, 59, 116–17, 135, 188n24
Pazos, Vincente, 107, 146
Picornell y Gomilla, Juan Mariano Bautista, 143
Piracy, 6, 13, 39, 52, 56, 63, 86, 87–88, 89, 115, 120, 143, 150
Porter, David, 56, 58, 60–61
Portugal, 14, 19, 77, 78, 102, 146, 150; vessels captured by privateers, 4, 49, 79, 126, 128, 140
Portuguese consul, 88–89, 126, 132–33
Privateer owners, 2, 46, 50–51, 57, 60, 66–73, 74, 76, 77, 80, 81, 86, 134; motivations of, 131–40
Privateer captains, 53, 77, 80, 81, 86, 94–95, 97, 120; motivations of, 123–36; as vessel owners, 66–67, 73, 74

Robinson, John Hamilton, 98

Sailors, 4, 5, 8, 59, 86, 128–29, 138–40; recruitment by privateers, 51, 52, 54, 77, 136–37. *See also* black sailors
San Martín, José, 28, 32, 33, 128
Sands, John, 63, 66, 76, 84, 89
Sauvinet, Joseph, 46, 51
Savary, Joseph, 142
Skinner, John S., 66, 67, 89, 145
Slave smuggling, 10, 27, 39, 43, 45, 46, 49–50, 52, 55, 92, 94, 95, 97, 104, 106–7, 109, 113, 116, 127, 147, 151; by Baltimore privateers, 78–79, 81; indictments for, 56, 86, 115; by Laffite brothers, 38, 42, 43, 45, 46–47, 102, 114, 133–34
Slavery, 22, 35–36, 58, 60, 102, 104, 140, 142; abolished in Spanish America, 16, 32, 35–36
Slave trade, 44; legal status of, 7, 42, 43, 44
Smuggling, 19, 22, 47, 57, 58, 63, 93, 101, 104, 127; economics of, 7, 10, 42, 43, 44, 61, 62, 99, 134; geography of, 42, 43, 44–45; and legal violations, 39, 41, 42, 54, 58, 92; popularity of 41, 47–48, 55–56, 61; strategies employed, 44–46, 77, 80–82, 84, 96, 106, 138. *See also* slave smuggling; United States Customs Service; United States Navy

Spain: and filibusters, 99–100, 102, 119, 140–41; and Napoleon, 1, 14–15, 18, 24; and Spanish America, 15–16, 18, 19, 20, 32, 33, 102, 143; United States deposit damage claims against, 22, 27, 30; United States relations with, 5, 20–22, 25, 26–28, 29, 30, 60, 61, 62, 88–89, 92, 96, 111, 112, 115, 116, 118; United States spoliation claims against, 21, 22, 27, 30; Vessels captured by privateers, 2, 4, 63, 67, 77, 78, 79, 91, 97, 126, 147. *See also* Fernando VII; Transcontinental Treaty

Spanish consul, 86, 88–89, 96, 101, 115, 124; as source for lawsuits, 9–10

Stafford, William Joseph, 138, 139

Stansbury, Nicholas, 68, 90

St. Bartholomew's, 77, 78, 80, 82, 83, 127, 132

Ste-Gême, Henri de, 134

Story, Joseph, 88

Taylor, Thomas, 63–64, 67, 73, 74, 76–77, 81, 83, 84, 89, 91, 124

Texas: borders of, 5, 21, 27, 28, 30; conflicting claims to, 92, 119; and filibusters, 94, 98, 100, 102, 114, 118, 141, 142, 143; and privateers, 95, 101, 106, 119, 120; United States expansion into, 112, 117

Toledo y Dubois, Jose Alvarez de, 98, 141, 143

Transcontinental Treaty (Adams-Onís Treaty), 5, 13, 25, 93, 119, 120, 121; approach of United States toward, 26–27, 33; approach of Spain toward, 27–28, 29; and Treaty of Aix-la-Chapelle, 30; and Andrew Jackson's invasion of Florida, 29; terms of, 30; ratification of, 30

United Provinces of the Río de la Plata, 1, 20, 31, 32, 33, 64, 67, 74, 132; privateers commissioned by, 4, 76, 91, 128, 138. *See also* Buenos Aires

United Provinces privateers, 2, 13, 20, 63, 74, 76, 111, 122, 124–25, 128, 129, 136, 138, 144

United States Customs Service, 5, 9, 42, 48, 49, 58–59, 76, 85–86, 88–89, 92, 109; and attempted interdiction of privateers, 48, 53, 54, 61–62, 76, 77, 81, 82, 84, 85, 95, 97, 99, 114, 117, 120; corruption of, 46, 58; procedures of, 48, 49, 53, 55, 80, 106

United States relations with Spain, 5, 20–22, 25, 26–28, 29, 30, 60, 61, 62, 88–89, 92, 96, 111, 112, 115, 116, 118; deposit damage claims, 22, 27, 30; spoliation claims, 21, 22, 27, 30. *See also* Transcontinental Treaty

United States relations with Spanish America, 61–62; popular attitudes toward, 23–25, 34; recognition of independence, 23, 28, 31, 33–34. *See also* Monroe Doctrine; neutrality; United States relations with Spain

United States Navy, 55, 57, 79, 84, 125, 137, 138, 150; prize claims of, 56, 59; officers' opinion of New Orleans station, 57–58, 59, 61; patrol off Amelia Island, 92, 106–7, 108, 109; patrol of gulf coast, 55–56, 58, 60, 114, 116, 120; raid of Barataria, 41, 99, 125–26

Upper Peru, 19, 20, 32, 33

Venezuela, 4, 16, 18, 20, 22, 24, 28, 32, 33, 44, 75, 79, 91, 102, 108, 111, 124, 128, 129, 144, 145, 146

Venezuelan privateers, 43, 53, 56, 64, 75, 127, 136, 137, 139

War of 1812, 5, 6, 25, 26, 27, 44, 61, 66, 67, 68, 73, 128; privateering in, 11, 44, 67, 91, 128, 150

West Florida, 21, 22, 27, 42, 113, 133

Worthington, W. G. D., 122–23

Youx, Dominique, 49, 61, 125–26, 134

Early American Places

On Slavery's Border: Missouri's Small Slaveholding Households, 1815–1865
by Diane Mutti Burke

Sounding America: Identity and the Music Culture of the Lower Mississippi River Valley, 1800–1860
by Ann Ostendorf

The Year of the Lash: Free People of Color in Cuba and the Nineteenth-Century Atlantic World
by Michele Reid-Vazquez

Ordinary Lives in the Early Caribbean: Religion, Colonial Competition, and the Politics Of Profit
by Kirsten Block

Creolization and Contraband: Curaçao in the Early Modern Atlantic World
by Linda M. Rupert

An Empire of Small Places: Mapping the Southeastern Anglo-Indian Trade, 1732–1795
by Robert Paulett

Everyday Life in the Early English Caribbean: Irish, Africans, and the Construction of Difference
by Jenny Shaw

Natchez Country: Indians, Colonists, and the Landscapes of Race in French Louisiana
by George Edward Milne

And a Child Shall Lead Them? Slavery, Childhood, and Abolition in Jamaica, 1788–1838
by Colleen A. Vasconcellos

Privateers of the Americas: Spanish American Privateering from the United States in the Early Republic
by David Head